EGYPTIAN CULTS ON THE BLACK SEA COAST

ЕГИПЕТСКИТЕ КУЛТОВЕ ПО КРАЙБРЕЖИЕТО НА ЧЕРНО МОРЕ

ÉCOLE FRANÇAISE D'ATHÈNES
ΓΑΛΛΙΚΗ ΣΧΟΛΗ ΑΘΗΝΩΝ

ИБ & ЦТ
БАН

BULGARIAN SCIENCE FUND

ИНСТИТУТ ЗА БАЛКАНИСТИКА С ЦЕНТЪР ПО ТРАКОЛОГИЯ
БЪЛГАРСКА АКАДЕМИЯ НА НАУКИТЕ
INSTITUTE OF BALKAN STUDIES WITH CENTER OF THRACOLOGY
BULGARIAN ACADEMY OF SCIENCES

ÉCOLE FRANÇAISE D'ATHÈNES
ΓΑΛΛΙΚΗ ΣΧΟΛΗ ΑΘΗΝΩΝ
ФРЕНСКО УЧИЛИЩЕ В АТИНА
FRENCH SCHOOL AT ATHENS

This volume is the sixth in the "Mediterranean Studies" series published by the French School at Athens [Études méditerranéennes, 6] - https://editions.efa.gr

Prepress: Cveti Pavlova / Предпечатна подготовка: Цвети Павлова
Print by Paradigma publishing House / Отпечатано от издателство „Парадигма"

ISBN Institute of Balkan Studies with Center of Thracology, Bulgarian Academy of Sciences 978-619-7179-45-3
ISBN École française d'Athènes 978-2-86958-630-7

EGYPTIAN CULTS ON THE BLACK SEA COAST

ЕГИПЕТСКИТЕ КУЛТОВЕ ПО КРАЙБРЕЖИЕТО НА ЧЕРНО МОРЕ

EDITORS:
VESSELA ATANASSOVA
LAURENT BRICAULT

СЪСТАВИТЕЛИ:
ВЕСЕЛА АТАНАСОВА
ЛОРАН БРИКО

Summary

Съдържание

Foreword:

Doing things in Egyptian Way

In the *Adventures of Wenamun* the King of Alashia (Cypros) stated that Amun created all lands, but the land of Egypt first of them all and the art and science were invented in Egypt and afterwards they reached him out. From the beginning of time till now in the minds of people Egypt is in the bottom of the intellectual development of the Eastern Mediterranean World. Egypt is the most ancient, monumental and powerful kingdom for the inhabitants of the Classical civilizations. The most ancient writing system was invented by Egyptians and when the first visitors from the Aegean land came to this Land of Mystery the Egyptian scribes could show them king lists stretching back thousands of years. The science and art of medicine, mathematics, astronomy, engineering, architecture and the development of agriculture were the fields of human activities in which the ancient Egyptians had no equal.

Предговор:

Защо и днес постъпваме като египтяни

В *Приключенията на Венамун*, царят на Алашия (Кипър) заявява, че Амун е създал всичките земи, но земята на Египет най-рано от всичките, и че изкуството и науката са били изобретени в Египет и след това са стигнали до него. От началото на времето до днес, в съзнанието на хората, Египет е в основата на интелектуалното развитие на източносредиземноморския свят. Египет е най-древното, монументално и могъщо царство, с което жителите на класическите цивилизации встъпват в контакт. Най-древната писмена система е изобретена от египтяните и когато първите посетители от егейския свят идват в тази земя на мистерии, египетските писари им показвали списъци на царете, простиращи се хиляди години назад. Науката, лечителското изкуство, медицината, математиката, астрономията, инженерните знания, архитектурата и развитието на селското стопанство били областите на човешката дейност, в които древните египтяни нямали равни.

Fig. 1.
Reconstruction of the Bull Fresco in Minoan style from Tell el-Dab'a (Egypt).

Фиг. 1. Реконструкция на фреското с бикове в Минойски стил от гробницата в Тел ел-Даба (Египет). (after Bietak et al. 2007, fig. 59).

Already by around 3000 BCE cultural and artistic exchanges between Egypt and Crete were taking place. Later with the arrival of Greek merchants, soldiers and artists these exchanges had expanded. Egypt is the first kingdom with which the Aegean people from the second millennium BCE can be shown to have traded. This cultural interaction went both ways. It has long been recognized that the Greek statues of *kouroi* have their origins in Egyptian art. The same could be said about the development of some aspects of architecture in Greece. Examples of Greek cultural influence could be found in Egyptian tomb paintings from Dynasty 18 showing Minoans (**Fig. 1**). It was sensational the discovery of Cretan frescoes of bull-leapers that decorated the walls of an Egyptian palace at Avaris (Tell el Daba) in the Nile Delta. This reminds us that the direction of influence does not always follow the dynamics of power.

Още около 3000 г. пр.Хр. се осъществява културен и художествен обмен между Египет и Крит. По-късно с пристигането на гръцки търговци, войници и художници този обмен се разширява. Египет е първото царство, с което може да се докаже, че хората от Егейско море от второто хилядолетие пр.Хр. са търгували. Това културно взаимодействие се разгръщало и в двете посоки. Отдавна е признато, че гръцките статуи *kouroi* водят началото си от египетското изкуство. Същото може да се каже и за развитието на някои аспекти на архитектурата в Гърция. Примери за гръцко културно влияние могат да бъдат намерени в египетски гробнични изображения на минойци от Династия 18 (**Фиг. 1**). Сензация предизвика откриването на критски фрески на „акробати" върху бикове, които украсявали стените на египетски дворец в Аварис (Тел ел-Даба) в делтата на Нил. Това ни напомня, че посоката на влияние не винаги следва динамиката на властта и силата.

The earliest evidence of Egyptian contact with Aegean dates from the mid-third millennium BCE when Egyptian stone vessels began reaching the Island of Crete. These vessels are from the Dynasty 5 (ca. 2498-2345 BCE) although it is quite possible they are imported exotics from later times. These connections strengthened in the first centuries of the second millennium BCE.

There is a little evidence for people from Aegean living in Egypt during the second millennium BCE but merchants must have been a common sight. New Kingdom Egyptian tomb paintings of the *fifteenth* century BCE depicting Minoans and Egyptian imitations in faience of Minoan vessels attest to the high regard in which they were held.

Intercultural connections suggest a level of both sides influence far greater than mere trade with luxury goods. The *sistrum*, a musical instrument used in Egyptian religious rituals was found at several sites on Crete as a part of images or made of bronze or terracotta (**Fig. 2**). In turn perfumed olive oil and aromatic plants were supplied in Egypt. The Cretan influence in medicine is shown by the London Medical Papyrus, where the medical recipe in the "language of Keftiu (Cretans)" has been preserved. After 1450 BCE when the Greeks from Greek mainland took power over Crete, they also maintained close ties with Egypt.

Най-ранните доказателства за египетски контакт с островите от Егейско море се датира от средата на третото хилядолетие пр.Хр., когато египетски каменни съдове започват да достигат до остров Крит. Съдовете са от Пета династия (ок. 2498 – 2345 г. пр.Хр.), въпреки че е напълно възможно да са внесена екзотика от по-късни времена. Тези връзки се засилват през първите векове на второто хилядолетие пр.Хр.

Има малко доказателства за хора от островите на Егейско море, живеещи в Египет през второто хилядолетие пр.Хр., но търговците трябва да са били обичайна гледка. Рисунките в египетските гробници от Новото царство от петнайсти век пр.Хр., изобразяващи минойци, както и египетските имитации на фаянсови минойски съдове, свидетелстват за високия интерес на египтяните към този регион.

Междукултурните връзки предполагат ниво на влияние и на двете страни, много по-голямо от обикновената търговия с луксозни стоки. *Систрумът*, музикален инструмент, използван в египетските религиозни ритуали, е намерен на няколко места на о-в Крит като част от изображения или изработен от бронз или теракота (**Фиг. 2**). От своя страна в Египет се доставят ароматизиран зехтин и ароматни растения. Критското влияние в медицината се вижда от Лондонския медицински папирус, където е запазена медицинската рецепта на „езика на Кефтиу (критяните)". След 1450 г. пр.Хр., когато гърците от континенталната част на Гърция поемат властта над Крит, те също поддържат близки връзки с Египет.

Fig. 2.

Clay imitation of Egypt.an *sistrum* from Crete, around 2000 BCE.

Фиг. 1. Глинено копие на египетския музикален инстримент *систрум* от Крит, около 2000 пр.Хр.

During the reign of Amenhotep III (ca. 1390-1352 BCE) a mission to the Greek world was sent. According to the inscription on a statue base of the King from his mortuary temple at Komel – Hetan in Thebes the mission traveled throughout the Aegean, including to Crete and Mycenae. Objects bearing royal Egyptian names which have been found in Mycenae are probably gifts from this mission. Also, around this time, a large number of jars with scented olive oil was sent to Egypt. There is a remarkable painted papyrus from the fourteenth century BCE found at Amarna where Mycenaean mercenaries fighting for the pharaoh against Libyan invaders are attested. A wooden model boat from a new Kingdom tomb at Gurob in the Fayum copies the Greek rather than the Egyptian design. All these suggests that there may have been close personal connections between these cultures.

At the end of the Bronze Age Egypt had to repulse the forces, whom the inscriptions call "Sea Peoples". Among these warriors and refugees from around the Mediterranean were Mycenaeans from mainland Greece. Remembrances of this troubled time could be found in book 14 of the Odyssey, in which Odysseus describes himself as a Cretan sailor who raided the Egyptian Coast and was captured. After the "Sea Peoples" wars no material evidence for trade survives until several centuries later.

По време на управлението на Аменхотеп III (ок. 1390 – 1352 г. пр.Хр.) е изпратена мисия до гръцкия свят. Според надписа върху основата на статуя на царя от неговия заупокоен храм в Комел – Хетан в Тива, мисията пътува из Егейско море, включително до Крит и Микена. Предмети, носещи египетски царски имена, които са открити в Микена, вероятно са подаръци от тази мисия. Също така по това време голям брой съдове с ароматизиран зехтин са изпратени в Египет. Разполагаме със забележителен папирус от четиринайсти век пр.Хр., намерен в Амарна, съдържащ изображения на микенските наемници, които се бият за фараона срещу либийските нашественици. Дървен модел на лодка от гробница от епохата на Новото Царство от Гураб във Фаюм копира по-скоро гръцки, отколкото египетски модел. Всичко това предполага, че може да е имало близки лични връзки между тези култури.

В края на бронзовата епоха Египет трябвало да отблъсне пълчищата, които надписите наричат „морски народи". Сред тези воини и бежанци от Средиземноморието имало микенци от континентална Гърция. Спомените за това смутно време могат да бъдат намерени в книга 14 на Одисея, в която Одисей описва себе си като критски моряк, който нападнал египетското крайбрежие и бил заловен. След войните с „морските народи" няма материални доказателства за търговски контакти между египтяни и представители на гръцкия свят в продължение на няколко столетия.

The Greeks arrived in significant numbers in Egypt in the time of Dynasty 26 (664-525 BCE). It was Psamtik I (ca. 664-610 BCE) who invited them. Herodotus (2.152) describes the story how Psamtik reclaimed the throne with the assistance of Ionian and Carian soldiers. Later he settled the mercenaries in camps along the Nile. The King Apries (589-570 BCE) is mentioned to have a bodyguard of 30.000 Greeks and Carians. After he was overthrown by Amasis (570-527 BCE) he retained the Greek mercenaries and relocated them to Memphis. The King dedicated offerings in Greek sanctuaries and married a Greek princess from Cyrene.

There is interesting evidence of the presence of Greeks from a hieroglyphic inscription on the sarcophagus of Wahibr(ee)mkhat (around 600 BCE) whose both parents bore Greek names – Aleksikles and Zenodote. On the base of the colossi of Ramses II at Abu Simbel graffiti could be seen left by Greek soldiers in 591 BCE including their names and hometowns in Ionia. They were part of Psamtik II army.

The words *obelisk* and *pyramid* are from Greek origin: the first one means literally "little skewer", the second one comes from "pyramis", which is the little wheat cake.

Greek merchants established a trading colony at Naukratis in the Delta in the time of Amasis. Herodotus hardly mentions Greeks living in Egypt, but archaeological evidences are more

Гърците пристигат в значителен брой в Египет по времето на Династия 26 (664 – 525 г. пр.Хр.). Поканил ги е Псаметик I (около 664 – 610 г. пр.Хр.). Херодот (2.152) описва историята как Псаметик си връща трона с помощта на йонийски и карийски войници. По-късно той заселва наемниците в лагери по поречието на Нил. Споменава се, че цар Априес (589 – 570 г. пр.Хр.) има охрана от 30 000 гърци и карийци. След като бил свален от Амасис (570 – 527 г. пр.Хр.), Амасис задържа гръцките наемници и ги премества в Мемфис. Царят посвещава дарове в гръцки светилища и се жени за гръцка принцеса от Кириния.

Има интересни доказателства за присъствието на гърци в Египет от йероглифен надпис върху саркофага на *Wahibr(ee)mkhat* (около 600 г. пр. Хр.), чийто родители са носели гръцки имена – *Aleksikles* и *Zenodote*. В основата на колосите на Рамзес II в Абу Симбел могат да се видят графити, оставени от гръцки войници през 591 г. пр.Хр., включително техните имена и родни градове в Йония. Те били част от армията на Псаметик II.

Думите обелиск и пирамида са от гръцки произход: първата буквално означава „малко шишче“, втората идва от „пирамис“, което е малко пшенично кексче.

Гръцки търговци основават търговска колония в Навкратис в Делтата на Нил по времето на Амасис. Херодот почти не споменава гърци, живеещи в Египет, но археологическите доказателства са informative. There is a number of bronze statuettes dedicated by Greeks to Egyptian gods. By around 600 BCE the influence of Egyptian art and architecture is attested in Greece. Before this time the Greeks had no tradition of carving stone sculpture but thanks to the trade development and the presence of Greek mercenaries in Egypt as well, the doors of Egypt for artist finally were opened. Since than the Greek own large–scale architecture and statues had appeared.

In 332 BCE Alexander the Great was welcomed in Egypt as a liberator and became an Egyptian pharaoh. His general Ptolemy founded a new Dynasty who ruled Egypt for three centuries and in 30 BCE the country was absorbed by Rome. The Ptolemies and the Roman emperors have themselves represented in Egypt as traditional pharaohs. The worship of Serapis, Isis and other Egyptian deities, promoted under the Ptolemies, continued to expand over the lands of the Classical World under the Romans. By the Ptolemies time we see the Egyptian boats sailing even the Black Sea. In exchange, foreign deities, such as the Thracian Heron appeared in Egypt in the early imperial period and grew in influence. During the reign of Octavian August (27 BCE–14 CE) a real Egyptomania started in Rome. Obelisks and monumental sculpture were brought to Rome. Egyptian deities were welcomed by the elite and occupied the everyday life and pyramidal

по-информативни. Запазени са редица бронзови статуетки, посветени от гърците на египетските богове. Около 600 г. пр.Хр. влиянието на египетското изкуство и архитектура вече трайно е засвидетелствано в Гърция. Преди това време гърците не са имали традиция да дялат каменни скулптури, но благодарение на развитието на търговията и присъствието на гръцки наемници в Египет, вратите на Египет за художника най-накрая са отворени. Оттогава се появява собствената гръцка мащабна архитектура и статуи.

През 332 г. пр.Хр. Александър Велики е посрещнат в Египет като освободител и става египетски фараон. След смъртта му неговият генерал Птолемей основава нова династия, която управлява Египет в продължение на три века и през 30 г. пр.Хр. страната е погълната от Рим. Самите Птолемеи и римските императори са били представени в Египет като традиционни фараони. Поклонението на Серапис, Изида и други египетски божества, насърчавано при Птолемеите, продължава да се разширява в земите на класическия свят при римляните. По времето на Птолемеите виждаме египетски кораби да плават дори в Черно море. В замяна чужди божества, като Тракийския Херос, се появяват в Египет в ранния имперски период и влиянието им бързо нараства. По време на управлението на Октавиан Август (27 – 14 г. пр.Хр.) в Рим започва истинска египтомания. В Рим са пренесени обелиски и монументална скулптура. Египетските божества са приветствани от елита и проникват в ежедневния живот на римляните. Започва строителството tombs began to be constructed. Egyptian deities and pictures of everyday life were displayed everywhere.

In the end, Egypt spiritually conquered the West, which defeated it by the force of its weapons! As a result, today in 21st century in our everyday life we are doing things in Egyptian way without knowing this fact. This is because "Amun created all lands, but the land of Egypt… first of them all. After all, art came from it to reach me (= us!), after all, science came from it to reach me (= us!)."

Prof. Sergei Ignatov,
New Bulgarian University

на пирамидални гробници. Египетски божества и картини от египетското ежедневие са изложени навсякъде.

В крайна сметка Египет завладява духовно, покорилия го със силата на оръжието си Запад! В резултат на това днес в 21 век в нашето ежедневие ние постъпваме като египтяни без дори да осъзнаваме този факт. Това е така, защото „Амун е създал всички земи, но земята на Египет… най-рано от всичките. Та нали изкуството е произлязло от Египет, за да стигне до мен (= нас!), та нали науката е произлязла от Египет, за да стигне до мен (= нас!)."

Проф. Сергей Игнатов,
Нов български университет

Introduction:
The Cults of Isis, from 'Oriental' to 'Global'

Laurent Bricault

Въведение:
Култът към Изида – от „източен" до „глобален"

Лоран Брико

Настоящият текст проследява развитието в изследванията на култа към Изида, които обхващат повече от един век и които прерастват днес в колективна дейност на редица учени, чиито усилия са насочени към това да представят сложното и разнообразно естество на тази богиня. Дисертацията на Ж. Лафай *История на култа към божествата от Александрия извън Египет* (G. Lafaye, *Histoire du culte des divinités d'Alexandrie hors de l'Égypte*), публикувана през 1884 г., разкрива ново поле на изследвания, посветено на взаимодействието между египетската цивилизация и класическата култура на гръко-римския свят, с особен акцент върху разпространението и почитането на няколко божества (Изида, Сарапис, Харпократ и Анубис). С невероятния синтез, направен от Франц Кюмон в *Източните религии в римското езичество* (Franz Cumont, *Les Religions orientales dans le paganisme romain*), публикуван за първи път през 1906 г. и преиздаван четири пъти оттогава насам, тази представа за разпространението на божествата започва да се приема като „свещена". Въведеното от Кюмон понятие „източни култове" има огромен успех и дори поставя началото на утвърдената днес поредица *Въведение в източните култове в римската империя* (*Études préliminaires aux religions orientales dans l'empire romain*). Основана от ученика на Кюмон Маартен Йозеф Вермазерен в Лайден половин век по-късно, през 1961 г. тази поредица се разраства значително благодарение на френския египтолог Жан Льоклан, който оглавява изследванията върху *Историята на разпространението на египетските култове* в Практическото училище за висши изследвания в Париж. В продължение на повече от двадесет и пет години представата за „източни религии" и „разпространението на култове" дава тласък на редица значими публикации, най-вече корпуси с надписи или с други паметници от даден регион или култ към дадено божество. Изключително богати и ценни, тези колекции рядко поставят под въпрос блестящото проучване на Кюмон. Чудесната книга на Робер Тюркан, озаглавена *Източните култове в римския свят* (Robert Turcan, *Les cultes orientaux dans le monde romain*), публикувана в Париж през 1989 г. (трето издание: 2004), свидетелства за дълготрайното влияние, оказано от Кюмон, макар че заглавието на английското ѝ издание *Култовете в римската империя* (*The Cults of the Roman Empire*), което е публикувано в Лондон през 1996 г., показва определено развитие и известно разграничаване от тези определения.

През 2001 г., когато под влияние на Льоклан в Париж излиза от печат *Атлас на разпространението на египетските култове* (*Atlas de la diffusion des cultes isiaques*), това виждане, според което вълна от религии връхлита от Изток, за да залее Рим, се оказва твърде опростено и монолитно – то започва да се пропуква. Новото поколение изследователи има подготовка в областта на интердисциплинарния подход и съчетава в работата си забележителните материали, събрани през изминалия век, с нови методи, което разгръща една вдъхновяваща област на проучвания. Тази дейност дава изцяло нов живот на изследователското поле, като подлага на размисъл представите от миналото и предлага изцяло нови възгледи. Създаването на няколко проекта (епиграфски, нумизматични, археологически, библиографски и т.н.) и тяхното детайлно изпълнение допълнително улесняват работата с извори и спомагат значително за преразглеждането на египетските култове, на тяхното естество и на отношенията между Египет и останалата част от гръко-римския свят.

Всичко това показва, че култовете далеч не са единствената движеща сила в тези отношения и че те са вплетени в мрежа от връзки – между култове, култури, икономически дейности и хора. Представата за разпръскването на култовете продължава да заема основно място, но тя е само етап от един цялостен процес. За да се осъществи устойчиво взаимодействие между божеството и тези, които го почитат, също толкова важни фактори са неговата рецепция, установяване и накрая неговото усвояване. Настоящият текст показва, че актуалните изследвания са посветени именно на този калейдоскоп от различни интерпретации, *interpretationes variae* – *graeca*, *romana*, *judaica*, *christiana* и дори *aegyptiana* (тъй като Изида се завръща по египетските земи след своето пътешествие из Средиземноморието и просъществува съвместно със своите изконни образи). Тяхно начинание е да го анализират и да определят мястото му в цялостния контекст на гръко-римската средиземноморска общност.

As an antipasto to the *Egyptian Cults of the Black Sea Coast* symposium, this paper will briefly trace the development of scholarship devoted to Isis for more than a century, culminating in the present-day collective effort among numerous scholars to recognize the complex and varied nature of this goddess.

Early days

The publication of the thesis of Georges Lafaye (**Fig. 1**), *Histoire du culte des divinités d'Alexandrie hors de l'Égypte*, in Paris in 1884 gave birth to a new field of research, one devoted to the interaction between Egyptian civilization and the classical Greco-Roman world, particularly the diffusion of the worship of several divine figures. This book es-

▲
Fig. 1.
Georges Lafaye

▼
Fig. 2.
Franz Cumont

tablishes a number of guidelines: these deities – four in number (Isis, Sarapis, Harpocrates, and Anubis) – were from Alexandria, and their worship outside Egypt could be studied as well, regardless of what happens on the land of the pharaohs.

Although it is logically often outdated today, it truly established the structure of a new field of research by calling upon archaeological documentation hitherto completely ignored, although from then on found to be of enormous value.

Indeed, it was through Phoenician trade that Egyptian images and themes, or, more often, egyptianizing, that is to say, not authentically Egyptian – a questionable and often debated discussed notion (see recently Pearson 2021, 8-14) – had initially spread in the Mediterranean and, via Carthage, to the Iberian and Italian peninsulas. Following Herodotus, who visited Egypt in the fifth century BCE, but perhaps already even before him, the Greeks engaged in an *interpretatio graeca* of the pharaonic pantheon, comparing Amon to Zeus, Neith to Athena, Osiris to Dionysos, Horus to Apollo, Isis to Demeter, to mention but a few.

With the advent of the Ptolemaic kingdom and the Hellenistic *oikoumene*, a new process came to light. Four deities, Isis, Sarapis, Anubis and Harpocrates, along with, to a much lesser extent, some others more or less directly linked to them (Osiris, Horus, Apis, Hermanubis, Nephthys, Bastet, Neilos, Hydreios), saw their worship spread, together or separately, out of the Nile Valley. This phenomenon is perfectly perceived by Lafaye, who writes, to qualify this object of study, of "Alexandrian divinities", with the capital of the Ptolemies appearing to him as the focus point from which this divine pantheon would have emerged.

Cumont and his legacy

Two decades after Lafaye's book, these divinities were integrated into what still remains today one of the major works in the history of religions. In 1905, the Belgian scholar Franz Cumont (**Fig. 2**) gave a series of lectures at the Collège de France in Paris that was quickly published under the title *Les Religions orientales dans le paganisme romain*. Reprinted several times, the book took its final form in the 4th edition of 1929. Numerous pages (Cumont 1929^{4}, 115-159) are dedicated to the gods and the "Egyptian cults" considered as a product of the Ptolemies' imperialism and whose success was such that like other religions from the East (those of Cybele, Mithras, Dionysus, Dolichenus to name but a few), they submerged the excessively emotionless and cold traditional and ancestral cults of imperial Rome, sacralising both the concept of "Oriental cults" and that of the "diffusion" of these cults. In his book, Cumont, however, appears more interested in the religious feeling of the Ancients and its external manifestations than in *realia*. But the success of the book is such that it killed in the bud any attempt to resume the *dossier* of these Egyptian and "traveling gods", even if the synthesis – as brilliant as it was for the time – really preceded a deep and critical analysis of these sources. For many decades, most scholars would only refer to Cumont, at best briefly pointing out some of the Egyptian or Egyptian-style objects uncovered from time to time throughout the Mediterranean world.

There were, however, some exceptions. A librarian in Vienna, Theodor Hopfner (**Fig. 3**), brought together in his *Fontes historiae religionis aegyptiacae* (Bonn 1922-1925) the ancient Greek and Latin literary texts relating to the religion of Ancient Egypt, without translating them into a modern language. This large collection, still useful, was however very poorly disseminated and remains mostly unknown.

In the USA, a professor at the University of Missouri, Thomas Allen Brady (**Fig. 4**), wrote a short essay, regularly reissued, for the Anglo-Saxon public, *The Reception of the Egyptian Cults by the Greeks (330-30 BC)* (Columbia 1935), followed by his *Repertory of Sculpture and Figured Monuments Relating to the Cult of the Egyptian Gods* (Columbia 1938), conceived as the counterpart of Cumont's work.

Last but not least, in 1937, the Hungarian historian and numismatist András Alföldi (**Fig. 5**) published in Leipzig a very dense volume untitled *A festival of Isis in Rome under the Christian Emperors of the IVth century*, which gathers and analyses with great expertise the coins with isiac types struck in Rome in the 4th century, to be distributed during the New Year's *Vota Publica*. The catalogue,

▲

Fig. 3.

Theodor Hopfner

◄◄

Fig. 4.

Thomas Allen Brady

◄

Fig. 5.

András Alföldi

▲
Fig. 6.
Jean Leclant

▼
Fig. 7.
Peter Marshall Fraser

rich with hundreds of fully illustrated specimens, now outdated, remained a reference for years. A new one will appear this year, due to Cristian Mondello and myself (Mondello & Bricault 2024-2026).

But, for the most part, the archaeological documentation would remain scattered in dozens of studies (journal articles, museum catalogues, excavation reports, short notices), or else, all too often, unpublished.

A new start from France

A new start came from France, in the fifties. In 1954, the French Egyptologist Jean Leclant (**Fig. 6**) started to publish in the Vatican's periodical *Orientalia* an annual chronicle indicating the scattered finds of small objects of Egyptian origin or style, the *aegyptiaca*. The discovery of a statuette of an Egyptian funeral servant (an *oushebti*) in Blendecques, in the North of France, provided this young scholar the opportunity to highlight, in a short but fundamental paper (Leclant 1956; see also Bricault 2023), the need for establishing regional corpuses listing all the *aegyptiaca* found outside Egypt.

This initiative was well received. Twelve years before his famous *Ptolemaic Alexandria*, Peter Marshall Fraser (**Fig. 7**) from Oxford University published in 1960 a double inquiry (Fraser 1960) in which he questioned Cumont's "imperialist" theory, which had dominated the field for half a century. According to him, this theory can no longer be supported if one uses a much broader documentation than the one used by the Belgian scholar. P. M. Fraser's "anti-imperialist" thesis was well received in the sixties. Such vocabulary, as always, is of importance, as a marker of an era and the ideologies that cross it. In the following years, the supporters of the two theses clashed, some claiming the attraction exerted on the Greeks, then on the Romans, by the fascinating religion of Ancient Egypt, while the others defend the idea of an *Isispropaganda* orchestrated by the Egyptian clergy (Harder 1943/1944), one or the other thesis being assumed to explain all the case studies. Anti-colonialism, marxism, structuralism seized on this affair to affix to the "History of the diffusion of Egyptian cults out of Egypt" – as Jean Leclant's chair at the École Pratique des Hautes Études in Paris was formally known – grids of global explanations. Both of these theses presuppose that one would be faced with coherent, homogeneous sets of people: on the one hand Greeks or Romans eager for exoticism, on the other a so-called Egyptian clergy anxious for proselytizing. The publication of thousands of documents in the following decades would undermine these intellectual and much too theoretical schemes.

The era of the EPRO

Cumont's concept of "Oriental religions" was so successful that it gave birth, half a century after its first publication, to the now classic series of the *Études préliminaires aux religions orientales dans l'empire romain*, founded in 1961 in Leiden by a former *discipulus* of Cumont, Maarten Jozef Vermaseren (**Fig. 8**). For more than twenty-five years, the concepts of "religions orientales" and "diffusion des cultes" gave rise to many important publications, mainly corpora of inscriptions or other objects from a particular territory or divinity's cult, like those of M. M. Kobilyna and Margarita Tacheva-Hitova (**Fig. 9**) focused respectively on the north bank of the Black Sea (Kobilyna 1976) and Moesia Inferior and Thracia (Tacheva-Hitova 1983).

These enormously rich and precious collections rarely, if ever, questioned Cumont's brilliant work and conclusions. Among the hundred or so volumes published between 1961 and 1985, a good fifth concern more or less directly the "études isiaques", providing researchers and students with thousands of unpublished or little-known documents. The publications followed each other at a steady pace, establishing a true archaeological map of the testimonies relating to the "Oriental religions" across the Roman Empire, where *isiaca* appear in very large numbers.

In parallel with the development of these valuable geographically focused collections, the creation of thematic and / or disciplinary collections would allow scholars to put in large series most of these documents and thus to engage in analyses on different scales, from the individual to the pan-mediterranean.

In 1969, the Czech epigraphist Ladislav Vidman (**Fig. 10**) published in Berlin a *Sylloge Inscriptionum Religionis Isiacae and Sarapiacae*, a convenient and rigorous collection of epigraphic texts relating to the cults of Isis, in which are presented and commented upon – in Latin – 851 inscriptions. At the same time, the Welsh scholar John Gwyn Griffiths (**Fig. 11**) and some of his students published in a few years (1970-1975) several fundamental works on four essential literary sources, Herodotus, Diodorus, Plutarch and Apuleius (Gwyn Griffiths 1970 & 1975; Burton 1972; Lloyd 1975-1993). It was also during the seventies that there appeared the monographs of Michel Malaise (Malaise 1972) (**Fig. 12**) and Françoise Dunand (Dunand 1973) on the diffusion of Egyptian cults in Italy and the Eastern Mediterranean, by Wilhelm Hornbostel on Sarapis (Hornbostel 1973), Vincent Tran tam Tinh on Isis (Tran tam Tinh 1973) and Jean-Claude Grenier on Anubis (Grenier 1977). During the following decade, several studies were published in the *Lexicon*

▲
Fig. 8.
Maarten Jozef Vermaseren

▼
Fig. 9.
Margarita Tacheva-Hitova

▲
Fig. 10.
Ladislav Vidman

▲▲
Fig. 11.
John Gwyn Griffiths

Iconographicum Mythologiae Classicae but also in the volume (II, 17.3 of 1984) of the series *Aufstieg und Niedergang des römischen Reiches*, culminating with Reinhold Merkelbach's magnum opus (Merkelbach 1995).

The abundance of these publications, the considerable quantity of sources now available make the idea of a synthesis more and more illusory each day, and gradually deconstruct that of Cumont. What we thought we knew needs to be nuanced, the theses and theories of the past, so firmly rooted in the beliefs and conceptions of the epochs that saw them flourish, seem no longer operative. New questions emerge, new approaches, new ways of thinking about history and especially the history of religious things. In many ways, Robert Turcan's fine book entitled *Les cultes orientaux dans le monde romain* (Paris 1989) may appear as a swan song. Three times reprinted, translated into several languages, it closes a chapter in the history of religions. The title of the English edition (*The Cults of the Roman Empire* [London 1996]) already showed some evolution away from Cumont's categorization.

Modern times

The time seems to have come to open a new chapter (Pailler 1989). The end of the 1980s and the following decade saw the publication of books as important as they were stimulating, reviving, renewing a great deal of questioning, in which the Isiac world appeared only marginally: for example that of Robin Lane Fox, *Pagans and Christians in the Mediterranean World from the Second Century AD to the Conversion of Constantine* (London 1988), or the *Religions of Rome* (Cambridge 1998) written by Mary Beard, John North and Simon Price.

Even as, under the influence of Leclant, there still appeared in 2001 an *Atlas de la diffusion des cultes isiaques* (Bricault 2001), the simplistic and monolithic vision of a religious outflow coming from the East and breaking upon Rome began to crack. A new generation of scholars, trained in interdisciplinarity and relying on both the exceptional documentation gathered from the past century, and new approaches in an effervescing area of scholarship, would radically revitalize this research field, challenging old concepts while presenting new ones. Furthermore, an ongoing reconsideration of the nature of the Isiac cults as well as relations between Egypt and the rest of the Greco-Roman world based on the sources continues to be greatly facilitated by the establishment of several new projects: the epigraphical corpus *Recueil des Inscriptions concernant les cultes isiaques* (Bricault 2005, now online at http://ricis.huma-num.fr), which replaced Vidman's *Sylloge*; the numismatic corpus *Sylloge Nummorum Religionis Isiacae et Sarapiacae* (Bricault 2008); the archaeological catalogue *Iseion* (Kleibl 2009) devoted to all known Isis sanctuaries; the repertoire of gems bearing the image of Serapis (Veymiers 2009) or the lychnological corpus devoted to Isis and her circle (Podvin 2011).

In 1999, Leclant and I organized the 1st international symposium on Isis studies, which offers the opportunity to draw up the assessment and the perspectives of that field of research (Bricault 2000). The impulse is launched and six other international symposiums devoted to Isis studies followed, most of them co-edited with the Dutch scholar Miguel John Versluys (see the survey by Bricault & Veymiers 2012). In addition to these triennial meetings, scientific events more or less directly focused on the Isiac world have multiplied for twenty years, revealing new documents and proposing a wide context of hundreds of objects of extremely varied natures. This symposium, thanks to Vessela Atanassova and our Bulgarian colleagues, is one of the last ones to date.

All these led us to create a regularly published collection of studies, the *Bibliotheca Isiaca* (2008–), and even a new series called the *Supplements to the Bibliotheca Isiaca*, which will be the place to publish the iconographical series *Thesaurus Iconographicus Cultuum Isiacorum* (*ThICIs*), a work in progress directed by Richard Veymiers. A first volume has been published, devoted to the *Serapeum of Carthage* (Laporte & Bricault 2020). Three more volumes are on press.

▲

Fig. 12.

Michel Malaise

New questions

The tremendous richness of this abundant material offers the opportunity to better understand not only the factors and the vectors of diffusion of the cults of Isis throughout the Greco-Roman world between the end of the 4th century BCE and the end of the 4th century CE, but also how, once integrated to varying degrees into a new religious system, they become integral elements of the religious offerings of the first centuries of our era. Hellenized, Romanized, they are undeniably capable of subsequent quasi-autonomous developments, which must be analysed with *finesse*, by questioning the reception of these cults, regarding what made their success in the Greek world, then in Roman Empire, including in their original lands. For a better understanding of the essence of what were the cults of Isis in the Greco-Roman world, it is essential to reflect on the appropriations and the reappropriations of which they were the object over time, on what could be called their "cultural biography". All the colleagues present at the Varna symposium *Egyptian Cults on the Black Sea Coast* are part of that *Grand Narrative*.

Among the new questions that arise, two theoretical ones are of particular interest:

> 1. How do we understand the relation between the often very local characteristics of something that was clearly a Mediterranean-wide phenomenon, at the same time?
>
> 2. How do we to understand the (shifting) meaning of "Egyptian" in a Hellenistic or Roman context over time?

A panel of young scholars tried to propose some first answers ten years ago, during a fruitful workshop in Leiden (Bricault & Versluys 2012).

The sanctuaries of these gods, from the gigantic Serapeum of Alexandria (Sabottka 2008) or the imposing Iseum of the Campus Martius in Rome (Versluys, Bülow-Clausen & Capriotti Vittozzi 2018) to the humblest rustic chapel, each provide a lot of information that makes it imperative to take into account the multitude of particular cases in order to avoid, as far as possible, reductive visions capable of transforming Rome and Delos, or even the eleventh book of Apuleius' *Metamorphoses* and the Augustan poets into a generality which they are absolutely not. The Orontes pouring into the Tiber, oriental religions submerging Rome participate in a vision of things that is mainly due to Juvenal and the Romans of the most traditional Republican or post-Republican Rome. But it is different for other people, at other times, in other places, in different contexts. Thessalonica and its Italians (Steimle 2008), Eretria and its Egyptians (Bruneau 1975), Petra and its nomadic caravans (Vaelske 2013), Ostia and its cosmopolitan harbour (Van Haeperen 2019), the road between Coptos and Berenice with all its *praesidia* in the eastern Egyptian desert (Cuvigny 2021; Bricault & Pantalacci 2024) show that there are different levels of reception, penetration and visibility for these cults, various strategies of appropriation as well, that it is important to distinguish with method and precision.

If it is necessary to question the multicultural contexts that may represent Athens, Delos or Rome, we must not neglect the local micro-contexts, whatever they are, revealing different kind of religiosity, anchored in ancestral and traditional identity, but also likely to evolve, though no doubt differently, from one territory to another, from one moment to another, from one individual to another. In this perspective, it is not only the gods or the thoughts of some so-called classical ancient writers that we must analyse, but also the world of the devotees, the divine servants, and the networks that have been woven at one end to the other side of the Mediterranean and sometimes far beyond (Nagel 2019; Mazurek 2022). The serialization of similar documents can sometimes reveal unexpected and fascinating networks.

In guise of conclusion

It thus appeared that the cults of Isis were not – far from it – the only vector of the complex and fruitful relations between Egypt and the Others, but that they were interwoven into a network of connections: cultic, cultural, political, economic and human. If the concept of cultic dissemination remained fundamental, it was only one stage of the process. For the relationship between divinity and worshippers to be established sustainably, reception, implantation, and finally appropriation were equally essential. As this paper shows, I hope, it is this kaleidoscope of *interpretationes variae* – *graeca*, *romana*, *judaica*, *christiana*, and even *aegyptiana*, since Isis returned to Egyptian soil after her peregrinations around the Mediterranean, subsequently co-existing with her ancestral forms – that current research endeavors to analyze and place in the global context of the Greco-Roman Mediterranean *koine* (Bricault, Müskens & Versluys 2015).

Hypanis
Olbia
Tyras
Borysthenes
Palus M
Panticapeum
Tyras
BOSPORUS
Hierasus
Kerkenitis
Nympha
Troesmis
Chersonesus
Istrus
Tomis
Danuvius
Callatis
Pontus Euxinus
MOESIA INFERIOR
Dionysopolis
Marcianopolis
Odessus
Mesembria
Sinop
Anchialus
Abonuteichus
Deultum
Amastris
PAPHLAGONIA
Cius
Tium
Pompeiopolis
THRACIA
Heracleia
Chrysorhoas
Bizye
Prusias
BITHYNIA
Phryxou L.
Perinthus
Byzantium
Nicomedia
Rhaedestum
Germanicopolis
Besbicos
Nicaea
Creteia
Sestus
Apameia
GALATIA
Cyzicus
Prusa
Parium
Iuliopolis
Abydus
Sebaste Trocmi
Hamamlu
Caesarea G.
Sangarius
Poemanenum
Midaeum

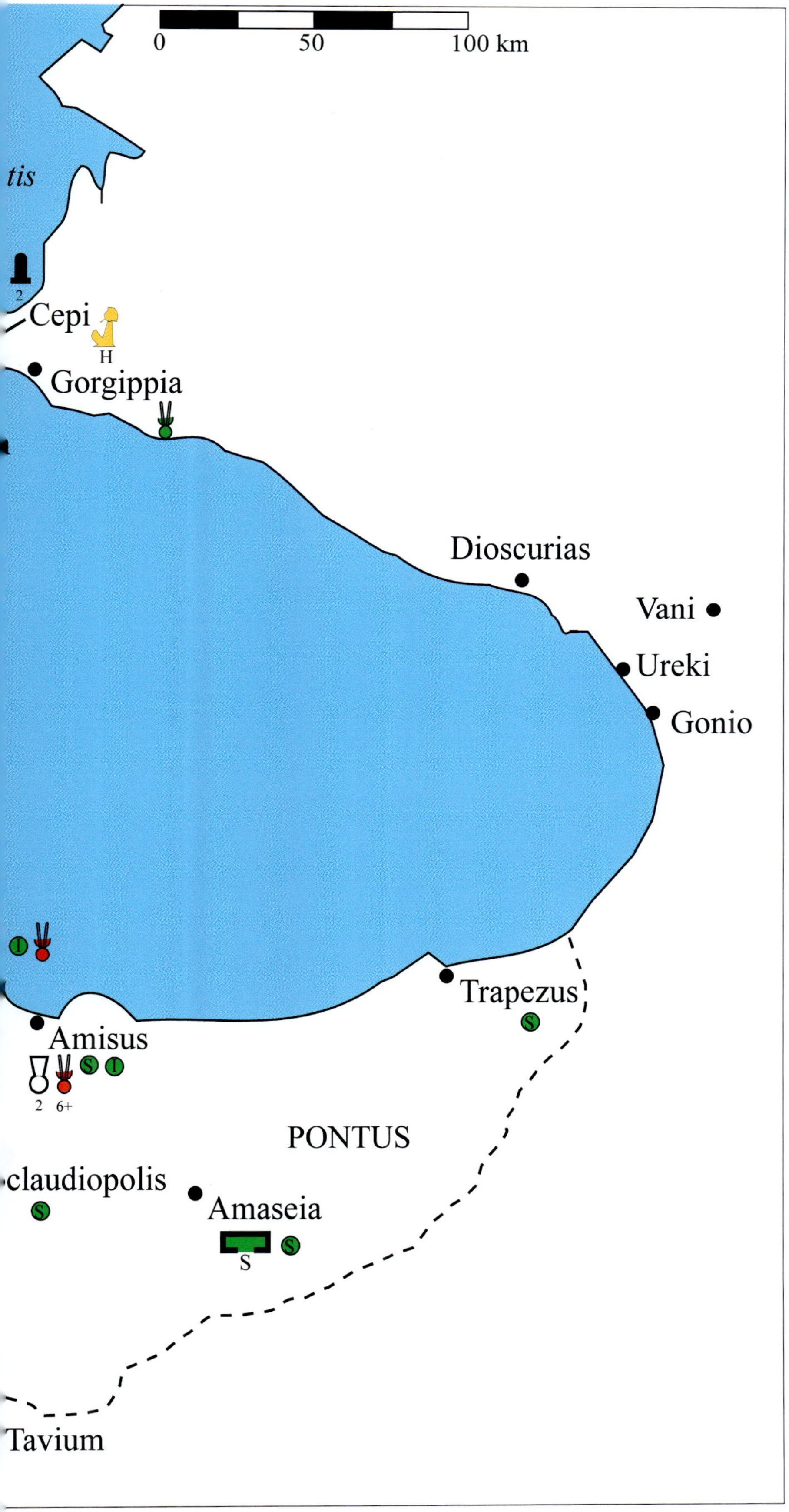

Diffusion of the Egyptian Cults
on the Black Sea Coast,
after Bricault 2001.

Разпространение на египетските култове
по крайбрежието на Черно море,
по Bricault 2001.

Egyptian Cults on the Black Sea Coast

Vessela Atanassova

Египетските култове по крайбрежието на Черно море

Весела Атанасова

Египетски артефакти с повече или по-малко култова стойност циркулират в някои от селищата по Черноморското крайбрежие от около I хилядолетие пр.Хр. Няма съмнение, че в началото те пристигат от Египет през Асирия и Финикия, а впоследствие се разпространяват основно през новосъздадените гръцки колонии по северните и южните брегове на Черно море (като Хераклея Понтика, Византион, Синопе, Аполония Понтика, Месамбрия, Одесос, Истрия, Олбия, Пантикапей, Колхида и др.), които поддържали активни връзки с гръко-египетския град Навкратис. Най-често срещаните египетски предмети от това време са амулетите във форма на скарабей или скарабоид с различни магически или божествени изображения, гравирани върху тях. Все още не се наблюдава предпочитание при избора на божество.

Чак при първите Птолемеи отношенията между черноморските гръцки колонии и Египет стават по-значими. След като Птолемей I Сотер и неговите съюзници побеждават Антигон в битката при Ипсала (Фригия) през 301 г. пр.Хр., той омъжва дъщеря си Арсиноя II за Лизимах, царя на Тракия, и си отваря морските пътища към Понта. Впечатляваща триера, наречена „Изида", достига до бреговете на Боспорското царство и вероятно въвежда египетските божества Изида, Сарапис и Анубис в местния Пантеон. В Пантикапей е открита базалтова статуя на Арсиноя II, донесена от триерата или от друг египетски кораб. Трако-египетската царица, чийто култ като покровителка на мореплавателите е засвидетелстван из редица градове по крайбрежието на Егейско море, явно е имала подобно влияние и в градовете на Северозападния Понт. Тази нейна роля е възприета също от наследничките ѝ царици Береника II и Арсиноя III, чиито образи са запечатани в многобройните портрети върху бронзови пръстени, принадлежали на техните последователи от региона.

Птолемейското присъствие в Понта спомага за разпространението на култа към египетските божества от семейството на Изида. Той е засвидетелстван в някои от най-важните гръцки колонии по Черноморието (Месамбрия, Одесос, Томи, Херсонес Таврически), както чрез епиграфски паметници, така и чрез различни произведения на пластиката. От последните прозира синкретизмът на египетските с местните божества, необходим за по-лесното им разбиране и приемане от понтийското население. Това явление продължава и по време на Римската империя, когато култът към египетските божества е под опеката на римските императори. Подобно на останалата част от Империята в крайбрежните градове на Западния и Северен Понт се срещат многобройни паметници, сред които официални монетни емисии с ликовете на божествата от Нил. Не е ясно кога точно египетските култове отмират, но това се случва с постепенното проникване на християнството. Знаем, че най-късно датираният надпис, свързан с тях, е от Рим от 25 май 390 г. Две години по-късно големият храм на Сарапис в Александрия изчезва в пламъците, а с него и дългата история на египетските култове в гръко-римския свят.

Introduction

Egyptian objects with more or less cultic value were circulating in the Black Sea Coastal Region from around the I[st] millennium BCE onward. This is first seen on the Southern coast of the Black Sea in the territory of today's countries of Armenia, Azerbaijan, Georgia, and Turkey. There is no doubt that they were coming from Egypt through Assyria and Phoenicia (Piotrovski 1958, 20). One of the oldest known among them was a scarab found in Armenia, inscribed with the throne name of Thutmose III (1479-1425 BCE) (**Fig. 1**). From the 7th century BCE onwards when the Greeks established their first colony in Egypt under the Saite Pharaoh Psammetichus I (c. 664-610), the so-called town Naucratis became the principal place for Greek and Egyptian trade (Hdt., 2.152). The mercenaries from Naucratis started to exchange goods with all the Greek colonies. They also reached the newly established Greek colonies along the northern and southern

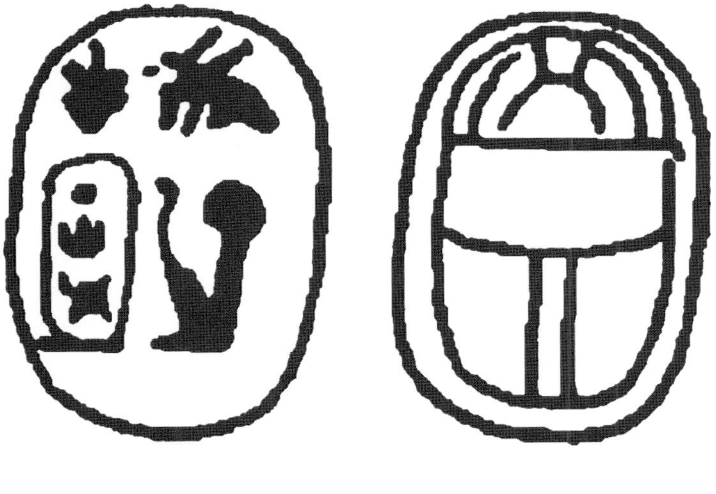

Fig. 1.
Scarab inscribed with the throne name of Thutmose III found in Armavir, Armenia (after Piotrovski 1958: fig. 1,1).

◄

Fig. 2.

Vase, Egyptian faience, tomb in the necropolis of Odessos, RHM-Varna inv. n° II 3218, early 3rd c. BCE.

shores of the Black Sea (such as Heraclea Pontica, Byzantium, Sinope, Apollonia Pontica, Mesambria, Odessos, Istria, Olbia, Panticapaeum, Colchis, etc.) exporting, there, a variety of exotic products (perfumes, spices, alabaster containers, glass, faience, etc.) (Archibald 2007, 264) (**Fig. 2**), including the Egyptian amulets bearing magical powers (Touraieff 1911, 20-24; Piotrovski 1958, 21-22). The last ones were small and easy to carry, which gave them the opportunity of being widespread. These ornaments were associated with popular Egyptian magic especially regarding fertility and the protection of women and children. For this reason, they were mainly found in sanctuaries or graves of women and children.

The most common Egyptian amulets were the scarabs and the scaraboids (**Figs. 3-5**). The scarab in Ancient Egypt was associated with the God Khepri, the morning manifestation of the God Re (the Sun). The Egyptians analogized the behavior of a scarab (*Scarabaeus sacer*) rolling a ball of manure on the ground to the God Khepri rolling the Sun in the sky (Wilkinson 2008, 11). The scarab was considered a symbol of health and protection of supreme powers, embodying life and immortality. Similar to the scarab, the scaraboid was an amulet with an engraved image but without the anatomical shape of the sacred Egyptian beetle. The images on the top of the scarabs and scaraboids usually represented creatures with magical powers (sphinxes, animals, deities, etc.) (Masson 2018, 24). In that period, the choice of a deity did not seem to follow certain specific rules.

Fig. 3.

Scaraboid with the image of a sphinx and a negroid, necropolis of Apollonia Pontica, AM-Sozopol, inv. n° 3694, 5th century BCE.

Fig. 4.

Scarab, carnelian, necropolis of Apollonia Pontica, AM-Sozopol, inv. n° 3656, 5th century BCE.

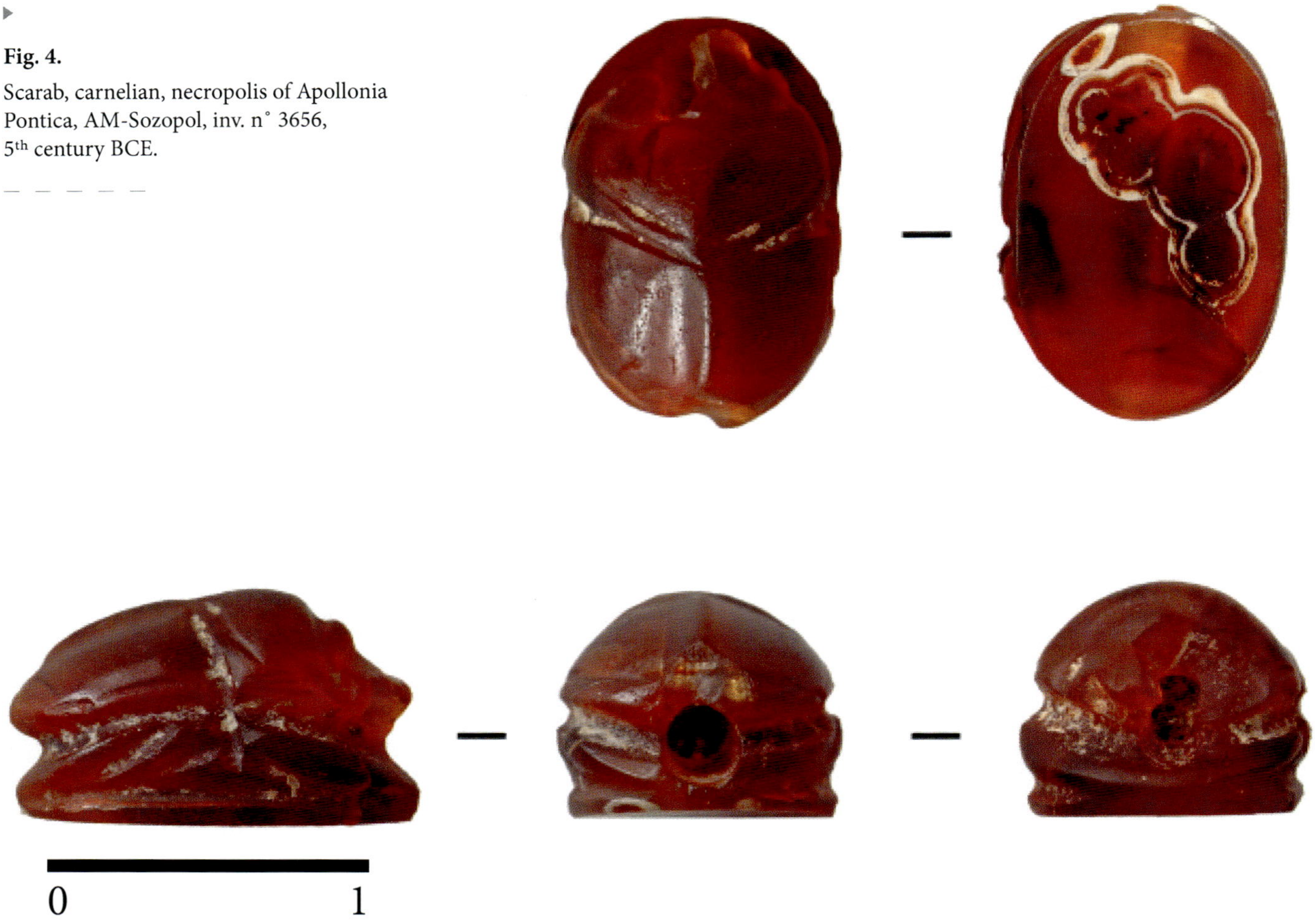

Fig. 5.

Scaraboid with an image of a sphinx, glass, necropolis of Apollonia Pontica, AM-Sozopol, inv. n° 3663, 5th century BCE.

First evidence of the spread of the Egyptian Cults

It was under the first Ptolemies that the relations between the Black Sea colonies and Egypt became more significant. According to some ancient authors, the statue of Sarapis was brought to Alexandria from Sinope, a town on the southern shore of the Black Sea, after it was dreamt by Ptolemy I Soter (323-282 BCE) (Plutarch, *De Iside et Osiride,* 28). The first official ruler of Egypt after Alexander the Great had his own interests in the lands of southern Thrace and Propontis. After he and his allies defeated Antigonos in the battle at Ipsus (Phyrgia) in 301 BCE (Hölbl 2001, 22) he married his daughter Arsinoe II to Lysimachus (Plut. *Vit. Demetr.* 31), the king of Thrace, and opened maritime routes to the Black Sea. During her time as Lysimachus' spouse, Arsinoe II received from her husband great honours, among them the cities of Heraclea, Amastris and Tium, all located on the southern shores of the Black Sea (Plut. *Vit. Demetr.* 31; Paus. 1. 10/ Memnon. 5.4-5; Jacoby, *Phot. bibl. cod.* 224, p. 225 a-b, see also Delev 2004, 320). Her influence in the Pontic region was important as bronze finger rings engraved with her portrait have been found as far as the Bosporan Kingdom (*see here M. Triester*). It is unknown whether Arsinoe II as queen of Thrace facilitated the spread of the Egyptian influences in the coastal cities of the Black Sea. According to the ancient auteurs, after the death of her husband and her two sons, she went to Samothrace and built the famous Rotunda of Arsinoe II (McCredie 1992). Lysimachus had already built a similar building in Odessos near the sacred area of the city and the temple of the Great Gods from Samothrace, presumably as a gift to his young wife (Stoyanov & Stoyanova 1997; Rabadjiev 2017)[1].

During her lifetime and after her death, Arsinoe II had an important religious role not only in Egypt but also in her first husband's lands. Apart from her close relationship with the Samothracian Gods, she was also simultaneously identified with both goddesses Isis and Aphrodite (Malaise 2005, 123; Bricault 2006, 27-33). Perhaps it was the expression of the syncretism of the two female Goddesses that was visible in the cities of the Black Sea. Several terracottas found in women's graves clearly represent the assimilation of Isis and Aphrodite (**Figs. 6-7** see also Kobilyna 1976, 48, II 16). The combined divinity was depicted naked, the hair falling on the shoulders in tiny Egyptian curls, with a flower crown topped with the Sun disk and a circle between the breasts representing the powerful "knot of Isis". The syncretism of the two female

[1] In fact, there are several indications of a temple in honour of the Samothracian gods at Odessos in the Hellenistic period (Cole 1984, 75-76; Rabadjiev 2017, 15). Their cult seems to be spread in many sites on the Black Sea coast (as Kallatis, Tomis, Dyonisopolis, Odessos, Olbia) (Rabadjiev 2017). The temple in Odessos was probably Doric in style, as proved by the architectural details discovered *in situ* (Mirchev 1967, 24-27, fig. 12), and dedicated to the cults of Theos Megas, the Dioskouroi, Demeter and Persephone (Mirchev 1967, 25).

Fig. 6.

Terracotta of Isis-Aphrodite, Apollonia Pontica, NAIM-Sofia, inv. n° 61/1285, the second half of 3rd century BCE.

Fig. 7.

Terracotta of Isis-Aphrodite, Apollonia Pontica, AM-Sozopol inv. n° 2120, the second half of 3rd century BCE.

Goddesses probably happened in Ancient Egypt before the Hellenistic period (Malaise 2014a, 250). It successfully combined the role of Aphrodite as the Goddess of love and fertility with the magical powers of Isis as the Goddess of revival and abundance.

This relation is also visible as far as the Bosporan Kingdom where a ship called "Isis" was depicted on the walls of the Aphrodite temple in Nymphaeum (Grač 1984) (**Fig. 8**). The latter was an important commercial centre, located about 17 kilometers to the south of Panticapeum (today's Kerch), the capital of the Bosporan Kingdom. The fresco represents a substantial trireme (1.20 m in length) of high quality using the "sgraffito" technique (Vinogradov 1999; Höckmann 1999; Murray 2001; Braund 2018, 160-177; Bricault 2020, 23-27, note 94 with bibliography; fig. 2). On the upper side of its prow was written the name "Isis" with deeply and meticulously incised large letters. Around the ship were carved multiple graffiti of lesser quality - among them the name of Paerisades, one of the kings of the Bosporan Kingdom, together with other local names which may relate to members of the dynasty and his entourage. According to the archaeological finds (small black-lacquered vessels, stamped tiles, etc.), the period of existence of the temple room with a plaster wall was the second quarter of the 3rd century BCE (Grač 1984), indicating that the king in question was Paerisades II, ruler of the Kingdom from 284 to 245 BCE (Vinogradov 1999, 272).

▲

Fig. 8.

Fresco from the temple of Aphrodite in Nymphaeum, Kerch, Hermitage Museum HΦ. 82-526.

To scholars, it is clear that the painting marks a historical event that occurred in the first half of the 3rd century BCE (Grač 1984; Basch 1985; Vinogradov 1999; Murray 2001; Bricault 2020, 23-27) and was related to the venue of a ship called "Isis" in a cultic place near the capital of the Bosporan Kingdom[2]. The impressive trireme was probably on a diplomatic mission in the region with political (Grač 1984; Basch 1985, Vinogradov 1999) but also religious purposes (Murray 2002, 551; Bricault 2006, 34)[3], especially the transportation of Egyptian cultic objects such as the black basalt head of a woman made in Egyptian style and found in Panticapeum (**Fig. 9**) (Touraieff 1911, 20, fig.14; Piotrovski 1958, 24). The woman wears a curved tripartite wig and a diadem with *uraeus*. The elongated face is plump; the eyes defined with long cosmetic lines are placed somewhat aslant. The eyebrows almost join each other over the very thin bridge of the nose. A ghost of a smile plays on the full lips. It certainly belonged to a royal woman, most probably the deified Arsinoe II-Isis (Touraieff 1911, 20, fig.14; Piotrovski 1958, 24; Lapis & Matthieu 1969, 126-127, 143, fig. 90) and it was exhibited in the capital of the Bosporan Kingdom. So it is unquestionably a very important evidence of the political interest of Ptolemy II in the northern coast of the Black Sea (Vinogradov & Zolotarev 1999, 365) as well as of the role of his sister and wife Arsinoe II. The latter was already worshipped in the Aegean region where a great number of maritime cities were founded in her name (Robert 1960, 156-157; Hauben 1983, 113; Bricault 2006, 28). This was also the moment when the thalassocracy of the Ptolemys started (Hauben 1983, 99).

That particular interest continued under the successors of Ptolemy II and again with the help of the Egyptian queens who continued to have influence in the cities on the Black Sea Coast. Berenice II, the queen and co-regent of Ptolemy III Euergetes from 246 to 222 BCE and her daughter, Arsinoe III, ruling as queen of Egypt and the wife of Ptolemy IV from 220 to 204 BCE were well known in this area and their images were carved on the bronze finger rings that spread to the Bosporan Kingdom (*see here M. Triester*). Both queens were equated to Aphrodite and Isis, as well as associated with the sailing and protection against shipwrecks (Hölbl 2001, 105). In fact, the whole 3rd century BCE was marked by the presence of the Ptolemies in the Black Sea region which more or less facilitated the penetration of the Egyptian cults (Bricault 2007, 245).

---

[2] According to other scholars the fresco was possibly showing the celebration of the *Ploiaphesia* of Isis (Braund 2018, 177).

[3] The presence of Bosporans in Egypt under the early Ptolemies was also attested (Vinogradov & Zolotarev 1999, 368; Braund 2018, 173) as well as that of Bosporan envoys to Ptolemy Philadelphus in a papyrus from Egypt (Plond VII, 1973 = Skeat 1974). The well-preserved papyrus is dated to 21 September 254 BCE. It contains a short letter of instruction sent in autumn 254 BCE by a high official of the Ptolemaic administration (the *dioecetes* Apollonius) to Zenon, his agent in the Arsinoite nome (in the Fayum), telling him to provide the necessary transport that the Bosporans will need when they reach the town of Ptolemais.

Fig. 9.

Basalt head in Egyptian style found in Kerch, Hermitage Museum inv. n° 3099.

The divine family of Isis, Sarapis, Anubis and Harpocrates

On the light of the new discovery from Odessos, nowadays Varna (*see here V. Tenekedjiev*), it is clear that the first spread of the Egyptian cults was that of the triad Isis, Sarapis and Anubis. That happened presumably in the last half of the 3rd century BCE according to the date of the sources. In fact, we dispose of four (even five?) very important epigraphic monuments coming from coastal cities in the Eastern Black Sea: Tauric Chersonese (**Fig. 10**), Mesambria (**Fig. 11**), Odessos (**Fig. 12**), Tomis (**Fig. 13**) and probably Tyras (**Fig. 14**) which, for the moment, are believed to be the most ancient found in the region. It is hard to determine the earliest of them. According to the editors of the marble plate from Chersonese, it was made in 254 BCE after the trireme "Isis" completed its diplomatic visit to the Bosporus and dropped its anchor in Chersonese where "Charmippos, son of Prytanis (dedicated) at the god's command to Sarapis, Isis and Anubis" an altar (Vinogradov & Zolotarev 1999, 372-373).

The monuments from Mesambria (**Fig. 11**) and Odessos (**Fig. 12**) are both dated to the end of the 3rd – beginning of the 2nd century BCE[4] (Mihailov 1970, 322; and *here V. Tenekedjiev*). The pilaster from Mesambria was dedicated by "Euelpistos, Apollônis, Athys, Lydos, Hermaios to Sarapis, to Isis, to Anubis and to Aphrodite, as a sign of recognition". The traces of small holes on the back suggest that it was attached to a wall. The names of the five mentioned individuals suggest a foreign origin probably from Asia Minor (Dunand 1973, 66). The marble pedestal from Odessos was a dedication to "Sarapis, Isis and Anubis, and the deities sharing the temple" and suggests the presence of an already existing temple of the Egyptian deities in the town. Almost the same dedication was found in Tomis "to Sarapis, to Isis, to Anubis and to all the gods" but was dated to the 1st c. BCE. It is probable that the marble base found in fragmentary condition in Tyras (**Fig. 14**) and dated to 2-1 c. BCE had a similar dedication "to Sarapis, to Isis, [to Anubis?] and to the gods sharing the temple, in recognition" (see *IOSPE* I^2 5; *RICIS* 618/1002).

In all of those dedicatory inscriptions the child god Harpocrates was replaced by Anubis in the divine triad. In fact, outside Egypt, Anubis is attested in epigraphic sources mostly from the island of Delos but also in some other places mainly in the Eastern Mediterranean and related with Ptolemaic Egypt (Gasparro 2018, 534). In Delos he appears to have been worshipped along with Isis, Sarapis and Harpocrates. He was mentioned there at least from the first half of the 3rd century BCE and certainly had a cult building called the Anubideion (Malaise 2014b, 81). Judging by the number of dedicatory inscriptions of the two triads that appear side by side at Delos Sarapis,

[4] Velkov 1969, 190, n°10 propose a later date in the 2-1 c. BCE.

▲

Fig. 10.

Marble plate with dedication to Sarapis, Isis and Anubis
State Chersonesus Museum

Size: 25.8 × 17.4 × 7.4 cm

Provenance: Excavations of the Temenos of ancient Tauric Chersonese (in 1993).

Date: 3rd century BCE (270-245 BCE?)

Inscription:
Charmippos, son of Prytanis (dedicated) at the god's command to Sarapis, Isis and Anubis.

Bibliography: Vinogradov, Zolotarev 1999.

▶

Fig. 11.

Marble pilaster dedicated to Sarapis, Isis, Anubis and Aphrodite
AM-Nessebar, inv. n°1738.

Size: 0,14 x 0,085 x 0,05 m.

Provenance: Mesambria

Date: 3rd century BCE (half?)

Inscription:
Euelpistos, Apollônis, Athys, Lydos, Hermaios to Sarapis, to Isis, to Anubis and to Aphrodite, as a sign of recognition

Bibliography: Mihailov 1962, 211-212, n°15, fig. 15; *SEG* XXIV [1969] 920; *RICIS* 114/1402.

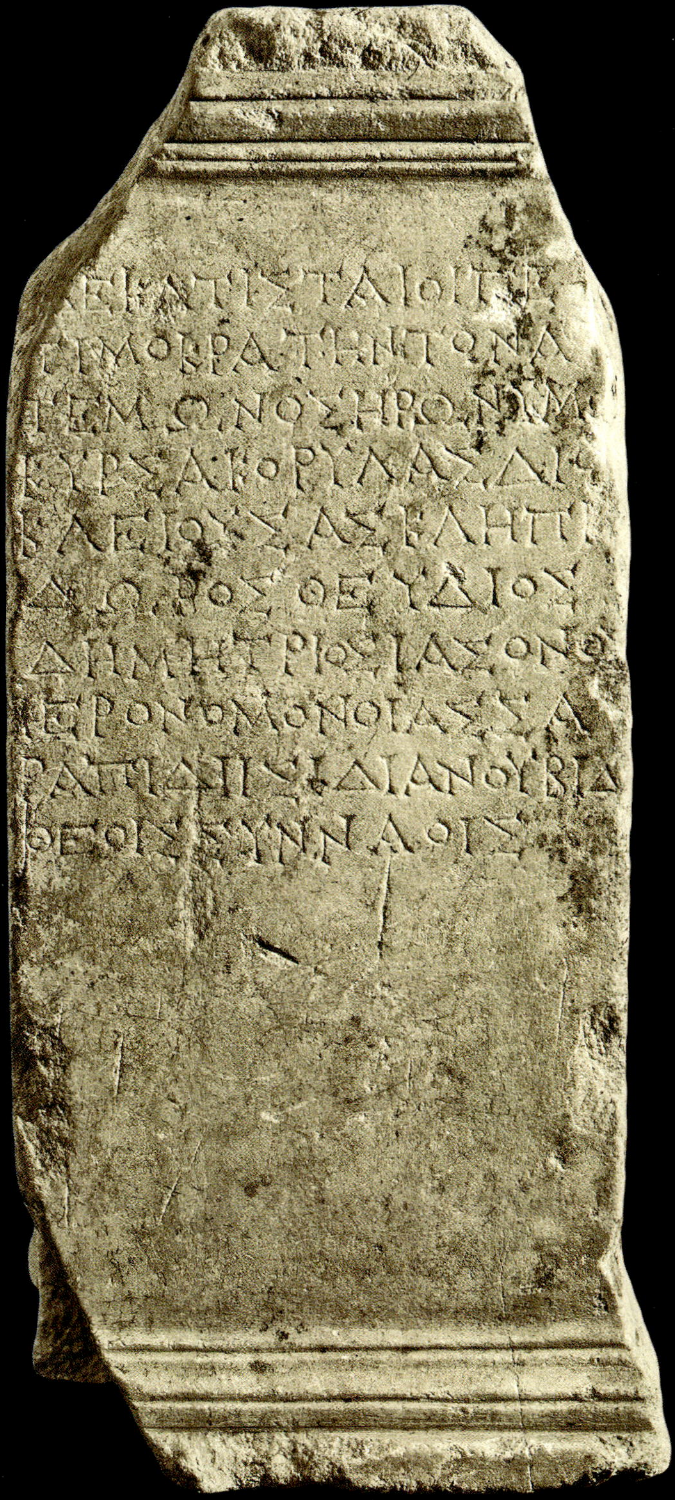

Fig. 12.

Marble pedestal with dedication to Sarapis, Isis and Anubis.
RHM-Varna

Size: 43 x 27 cm.

Provenance: Odessos, excavations from 2021 of Vassil Tenekedjiev

Date: 3-2nd century BCE

Inscription:
The dekatistai around Timokrates son of Artemon: Heronymos son of Kyrsas, Korylas son of Diokles, Asklepiodoros son of Theudis, Demetrios son of Iason, (dedicated this) sanctuary of their concord to Sarapis, Isis, Anubis, gods sharing the same temple.

Bibliography: (*see here Vassil Tenekedjiev*).

Fig. 13.

Marble plate with dedication to Isis, Sarapis and Anubis
National Archeological Museum, Bucurest № L 1600

Provenance: Tomis

Date: 1st century BCE

Inscription:
Good Fortune! Dionysios, son of Hedylos, from his own expense has built (this monument) through ... idoros also called Thea... and to Sarapis, and to Isis and to Anubis and to all the gods.

Bibliography: *IOSPE* I2 5; *RICIS* 618/1002.

Fig. 14.

Marble base broken in its left side with dedication to Sarapis, Isis (and Anubis?)
Tyras, Belgorod Dnjestrovski

Provenance: Tyras

Date: 2-1st century BCE

Inscription:
[…]*s, son of Kratinos, to Sarapis, to Isis, [to Anubis?] and the gods sharing the temple, in recognition.*

Bibliography: *RICIS* 115/0101.

Isis and Harpocrates/ Sarapis, Isis and Anubis the two deities appear to be equal by their importance within the sacred family. However as Harpocrates was considered the child in the triad, the role of Anubis is unclear. According to Plutarch, Anubis was born of the union of Osiris an Nephthys but brought up by Isis becoming "her guardian and attendant" (Plutarch, *De Iside et Osiride*, 14). In a unique hymn in honour of Anubis, found in Cius on the Propontis (nowadays Turkey) and dated to the 1st century CE, the dog-god was identified as the son of Osiris-Sarapis and Isis and called "king of all the Heavenly Gods" (*RICIS* 308/0302 = Louvre Ma 2862). For G. Sfameni Gasparro the role of the god was to serve as a dog / protector of the Gods and respectively to guide the faithful in worship-ceremonies (Gasparro 2018, 540, see also Bricault 2001). Together with Sarapis, Isis and Harpocrates he was perceived as a saviour god who offers salvation to his followers.

Furthermore, in Delos, Anubis was associated with Hermes, while Harpocrates with Apollo (Malaise 2014, 88). Anubis was compared to Hermes not because of his function as a mummifier, but because of that of Psychopomp, who, like the Greek god, takes the dead to the Underworld. This is probably the reason for the adoption of the cult of Anubis in the cities of the Black Sea, where the cult of Hermes was strongly spread (for Thrace see Draganov 2022, 18; for the Bosporan Kingdom see Gaidukevich 1971, 233). Maybe the objects as the gem found in Olbia with the image of Anubis cynocephal with a palm and caducei (Neverov 1978, 56, fig. 5 and here **Fig. 15**) and the lamp from Chersonese with the representation of Isis, Harpocrates and Anubis holding the caducei of Hermes (Kobilyna 1978, 39, II, 11) could be regarded as an echo of that assimilation.

Fig. 15.
Gem made of jasper found during excavations in Olbia with the image of Anubis cynocephal, 2nd century CE, Hermitage Museum, inv. n° 01.70 (Neverov 1978: pl. 48, fig. 5a-b).

Fig. 16.

Bone knife handle (?) with the image of Harpocrates, found in Tiritaka, 1st century BCE.

Fig. 17.

Terracotta lamp handle with the image of Isis Lactans, Odessos, RHM-Varna, inv. n° II. 5813, Roman period.

Harpocrates, the child in the divine family of Sarapis and Isis, seems to be worshipped in the Black Sea region from a later date (at least from the first century BCE on) and especially in the Crimea region. In Tiritaka, located immediately south of Panticapeum (today on the outskirts of the city of Kerch), in a sanctuary of Dionysos functioned at the end of the 2nd c. BCE to the beginning of the 1st c. CE was found a bone votive object with the image of Harpocrates (Zinako 2021; Kotina 2021) (**Fig. 16**). The last one was represented as a naked youth, whose body still retained childhood plumpness. He stands on a semi-circular profiled base cut vertically at the back, between two columns, with acanfa leaves. Harpocrates' left foot rests on a goose that is calmly sitting with its paws closed and its head raised with its beak wide open. A similar image of Harpocrates was engraved on an ivory handle of a ritual knife found during the excavation of the House of Dyonysus in Kato Paphos, Cyprus (Flourentzos 2007, 301, fig. 14). The ivory object from Tiritaka probably had the same purpose (Kotina 2021). What is interesting is the context of the findings – both were found in a building related to Dionysos. The deity was perceived in the Bosporan Kingdom as the patron of fertility and chthonic forces, as the embodiment of immortality and saviour god (Kobilyna 1978, 39; Zinako 2021) some of the qualities of Harpocrates as well. The relation between Dionysus and Harpocrates is shown again in a figurine with probable local production found in a tomb n°47 from Panticapeum (Kobilyna 1978, 39, II, 13). Furthermore Harpocrates is found in the North-West Black Sea littoral in most of his embodiments: with his mother Isis as a breastfed child (in Odessos, see here **Fig. 17**; Olbia, see Kobilyna 1978, 37, II, 9 and Panticapeum, see Kobilyna 1978, 37, II, 8), sitting on a lotus flower (from Mesambria, see here **Fig. 18** and from Panticapeum, see Kobilyna 1978, II, 12) or with a goose (from Chersonese, see Kobilyna 1978, 40, II, 15).

▲

Fig. 18.
Scarab with the image of Harpocrates sitting on a lotus found in a grave in Mesambria, second half of 2nd century BCE, AM-Nessebar (Chacheva 2021).

During the Early Hellenistic period (3rd century BCE), coins with images of Egyptian deities were minted only in the city of Perinthus (on the shores of the Sea of Marmara). There was a great variety of coin types with images such as the busts of Sarapis and Isis, the *basileion* of Isis, Anubis with a palm and the sacred bull Apis. It seems that during that period Perinthus became the most important point of exchange of Egyptian goods in Thrace (Peter 2008, 203-204). The *basileion* of Isis reappears again on the coins of Vani and Dioscurias (nowadays Sokhumi) in Ancient Colchis where it is represented upon two wheat flowers (*see here N. Phiphia,* fig. 2). These coins were probably minted by Mithridates the Younger, son of the king of Pontus Mithridates VI Eupator (120-63 BCE), probably while he was ruler of Colchis in the early 1st century BCE. At the end of the same century the queen of the Bosporan Kingdom Dynamis (21/20 BCE – 7/8 CE) and granddaughter of Mithridates VI minted coins with isiac images as well. At this period probably she was already married to Polemon I of Pontus and together they were Roman client kings and rulers over the Bosporan and Pontus Kingdoms (**Fig. 19**). One of the coins represents a head of Sarapis and a *cornucopia* on its reverse, while the other depicts a cobra with *basileion* on its head (Kobilyna 1976, 43, n° 1-2 ; Bricault 2007, 219-220). In Ancient Egypt Isis was associated at least from the New Kingdom (16-11th century BCE) on with the cobra-goddess Renenutet, which was a deity related

Fig. 19.
Stater from Bosporus with the monogram BAE and cobra with *basileion*,
End of 1st century BCE.

to agriculture and crops (known as Isis-Thermuthis by the Greeks). Together with the *cornucopia* the cobra on the Bosporan coins might reflect the abundance and nourishment. So, the coins from Bosporus as well as those from Colchis minted in the 1st century BCE maybe point out of trade contacts with Egypt established from the first Ptolemies (Bricault 2008, 220).

Egyptians Cults in the Roman Black Sea Coast

Slowly, but steadily the Roman presence in the Black Sea region increased from the 1st century BCE on. Even at the height of Roman power, political control was enforced through a variety of mechanisms, from outright annexation to alliances with native rulers. Some of the Kingdoms among its southern, western and eastern coasts became Roman provinces (Moesia, Dacia, Thracia, Bithynia, Paphlagonia, Pontus) other Roman client kings (Bosporus). From the time of the Flavians (69-96 CE), after the visit of Vespasian (69-79 CE) in the Serapeum of Alexandria in 69 CE (Henrichs 1968), the cult of Sarapis and Isis became imperial and spread all over the Roman Empire as well as in the Black Sea coastal cities already part of the Roman provinces. The most of them began to issue coins with the Egyptian gods images as a sign of agreement with the central government. Those cities were in Moesia Inferior (Istrus, Tomis, Callatis, Odessos), in Thracia (Mesambria, Anchialos, Deultum, Bizye, Byzantium), in Bithynia (Prusias, Heracleia, Tium) in Paphlagonia (Amastris, Abonuteichus, Sinope) and in Pontus (Amisus, Trapezus).

There were representations of Isis, Sarapis and Harpocrates in various postures while Anubis was represented only on one medallion minted by Philip the Arab (244-249) in Bizye among the other Isiac gods (Peter 2008, 218). Hence Sarapis was perceived as the protector of the emperor and his family. So the most frequently emitted were the coins with the image of Sarapis standing or sitting, with a *patera*, a horn of abundance or a sceptre. In several places (coins from Tomis, Anchialos, Deultum Odessos) Sarapis was seated on a throne inside a temple, which, according to most researchers, was a sure indication of the existence of Sarapeion (temple of Sarapis) in the city (Peter 2008, 2014). The images of Isis were lesser and were minted in a smaller number of cities (Callatis, Anchialos, Bizye, Byzantium, Tium, Amastris, Abonuteichus, Sinope and Amisus). In Amastris her bust was depicted (**Fig. 20**). On the coins from Callatis, Anchialos, Byzantium and Amastris the Egyptian goddess was represented with a sail as *Isis Navigans*, i.e. as the Patroness of sailors and Mistress of the seas, her important role in port cities (Bricault 2020, 54-57). In Sinope the busts of Isis and Sarapis were represented turned in the same direction on coins minted in the 2nd and 3rd century CE (Bricault, Delrieux, Leschhorn 2008, 102-103). During the Roman period the town “resurrected” the legend of the divine statue of Sarapis, brought from Sinope to Alexandria, probably to please the

princeps (Bricault 2020, 254). Harpocrates was shown naked, with finger in his mouth and a horn of abundance in his right hand in 5 of the Black Sea cities (Deultum, Bizye, Heracleia, Tium, Amastris). In Tium and Amastris the sacred bull Apis was depicted on the local emissions with the sun disk between his corns (Bricault, Delrieux, Leschhorn 2008, 100).

▲

Fig. 20.
Bust of Isis on coin minted in Amastris, 2nd century CE.

Together with the coins the objects of small plastic representing the Egyptian deities became frequent in the Black Sea coastal cities showing their importance among the local population. The busts and heads of Sarapis were in general his most common form of depiction (on glyptics, jewellery, numismatics, coroplastics) (Veymiers 2009, 23). He was most often depicted full face as a mature man with a *calathos* on his head, having on it a vegetable decoration composed of leaves or olive branches as a sign of his agrarian nature. An extremely well preserved bronze bust of Sarapis was discovered in nowadays Pomorie (ancient Anchialos) (**Fig. 21**, *see also here N. Phiphia*, fig. 3). The god is presented frontally, with his head slightly curved to the right. He is depicted as a man in adulthood with a beard and hair falling down to the shoulders. Facial features (eyes, nose, mouth) are marked and shown in detail. The hair falls into large wavy locks voluminously treated over the forehead, on the side of the face and on the neck. The beard is in small curls. On his head he wears a relatively high *calathos* decorated in front with a branch of

Fig. 21.
Bronze bust of Sarapis found in Anchialos, 2-3rd century CE, NAIM - Sofia, inv. n° 1196.

Fig. 20.

Oil lamp with the image of Sarapis, Isis-Thermuthis and Sarapis-Agathodemon, found in Tauric Chersonese, 2nd century CE, Hermitage museum inv. n° X. 1896, 47.

leaves presented in relief. He is wearing a *chiton*, with a *himation* over his left shoulder. The bust was placed on a pedestal, reminiscent of an altar, and below it there were holes for attachment, probably on some kind of pedestal (Tacheva-Hitova 1982, 27).

In the Black Sea region Sarapis was also depicted on tree oil lamps found in Tauric Chersonese (**Fig. 22**) and on one found in Deultum in a rare specimen attested exclusively in the Eastern Mediterranean representing a group of isiac deities (Kobilyna 1976, 44, II6; Podvin 2011, 89-90; Atanassova 2023). The god is shown from the front, dressed in a long robe and standing on an altar, holding a sceptre in his left hand, his right hand raised in salutation gesture (*adlocutio*). A garland of flowers descends from his neck under his torso. An admirer is kneeling before the altar. On his both sides are standing two cobras, positioned on circular altars, probably representing again Isis-Thermuthis and Sarapis-Agathodemon, syncretic forms of Isis and Sarapis with two serpent-like deities – Agathodemon and Thermuthis (Veymiers 2009, 88; Atanassova 2023, 11-12). Both of them wear a *basileion* on the head, which facilitate their identification. In this syncretic form, Sarapis-Agathodemon and Isis-Thermuthis were related to the crops, the harvest, the abundance and were considered to be the bearers of fertility and prosperity. They were also very often represented as the protectors of different deities of the Osirian cycle (Malaise 2005, 172-173). The whole scene records probably the ritual going out of the divine statue of Sarapis during an isiac festivity celebrated in the region.

From that period we find also small objects with the depictions of Isis, Anubis and Harpocrates (*see here J.-L. Podvin*) but also some other gods with Egyptian origin like Zeus-Amon, Bes, Ptah, Thot, most often represented on different kinds of amulets (Touraieff 1911, 21-22, 24-26; Kobilyna 1978, II, 17-21; see also Chacheva 2021, 101 for Mesambria) as well as the pseudo-*ushabtis* with the image of mummified Osiris (Touraieff 1911, 27-28 in the Bosporus, see also here **Fig. 23**). The last ones (called *shabti*, *ushabti* or *shawabti*) were group of Egyptian figurines that were placed in the tomb along with other burial equipment. These were usually small figurines made of wood or various types of soft stone. They depicted individuals in the form of mummies similar to Osiris with arms crossed over the chest or holding some tools. In rare cases, the personages were dressed in their everyday clothes performing some action. The purpose of these figurines in Egypt was to serve the deceased in the world beyond according to their various needs. The figurines were probably imported from Egypt during the Roman period and were perceived as the image of Osiris. The local isiac adepts probably used them during ritual and initiation processions that took place in temples dedicated to the Egyptian gods (Malaise 2005, 17-18).

Conclusion

So, it is clear that the cities on the Black Sea region and especially those on its western part were very accommodative with the deities coming from the Nile Valley from at least the end of the 4th century BCE on. Known partially from the magic objects circulating in the Eastern Mediterranean region from the 1st millinery BCE, the Egyptian beliefs easily penetrated in the Black Sea coastal cities through the established Greek colonies and with the direct or indirect intervention of the Ptolemies in the Hellenistic period. At the time of the Roman Empire they were once again introduced by the Roman imperial propaganda and were installed in the newly formed Roman provinces but also among the *amici populi Romani* (as the Bosporan Kingdom). The end of the Egyptian cults coincided with the fall of the Roman Empire and the gradual penetration of Christianity in the coastal cities of the Black Sea.

▶▶

Fig. 23.

Ushabti of Osiris, Dionysopolis, RHM-Varna, inv. n°II 2221, Roman period.

Ptolemaic Finger Rings in North Pontic Area: New Finds and Hypotheses

Mikhail Treister

Птолемейски пръстени в района на Северния Понт: нови находки и хипотези

Михаил Трейстер

Статията е посветена на анализа на бронзовите пръстени от така наречения Птолемейски вид, върху чиято лицева страна са изобразени предимно женски портрети. Въпросните пръстени произлизат главно от района на Северното Черноморие и най-вече от територията на Боспорското царство. Въз основа на анализ и сравнение с подобни портрети върху монети и пръстени са предложени възможни идентификации на изображенията с портретите на Арсиноя II, Береника II и Арсиноя III. Разгледани са спецификите в географското разпределение на находките, характеристиките и хронологията на погребалния контекст, в който са открити пръстените. В заключение се вземат под внимание проблемите около интерпретацията на пръстените, която би могла да обясни високата концентрация на местонамирането им в района на Северното Черноморие и най-вече на територията на Боспорското царство.

General information

To date, there is no single catalogue of the finger rings, on the bezels of which there are presumably represented the portraits of the rulers of the Ptolemaic dynasty, widespread in the North Pontic region, mainly in the Cimmerian Bosporus, in the middle – second half of the 3rd century BCE (**Figs. 1-5**). An attempt to make such a list by T. Schreiber in 2015, which includes 84 rings made of bronze, bone, glass and marble, more than two-thirds of which (54) are bronze rings, represented approximately in equal proportions by the images in intaglio and in relief (Schreiber 2015, 229, 273-276;

2018, 59), may be hardly considered as successful one. Of the extensive publications on this topic in Russia, the author was acquainted only with the mid 1970-s articles by O.Ya. Neverov (Neverov 1974, 106-115; 1976, 167-177), and correspondingly operated with about a half of known to date material with records of archaeological contexts. I also know quite a lot of rings (at least 20) that have been sold at the auctions in recent years or kept in private collections, which are also not included in the Schreiber's list. An example of unprovenanced rings, most probably of North Pontic origin are the objects from the Karisalovs' collection (**Figs. 2, 4-5; 3, 16; 5, 9. 16-17**), recently acquired by the Pushkin Museum of Fine Arts in Moscow (Cat. Moscow 2019, 113-116, nos. 43-49).

For comparison, gold Ptolemaic rings are extremely rare. These include the pieces from Mottola in the Tarentum region (Vollenweider 1958, 29, Nr. 1: Berenice II (?), Taf. II, 1; Cat. Milan 1984, 289-290, no. 210; Pfrommer 1990, 226, Anm. 1609; 228, FK 33, Taf. 10, *4*; Plantzos 1999, 48, pl. 88, 1; Gerring 2000, 174, Nr. XVII/17, Abb. 135; Boardman 2001, 362, 371, pl. 1008: Berenice II (?)), the portrait on which is comparable to that on the gold ring attributed as the portrait of Arsinoe II in the Hermitage (Furtwängler 1900, Bd. 1, Taf. XXXII, *33*; Bd. 2, 159; Vollenweider 1958, 30, Nr. 3; Cat. St. Petersburg 2007, 242, ΄no. 248; Cat. Amsterdam 2010, 172, no. 161; Arsent'eva & Gorskaya 2019, 53, no. 21), and an iron ring with a gold bezel inlay with a portrait, presumably, of Berenice I, allegedly found in a tomb on Corfu (Vollenweider 1958, 30, Nr. 6, Taf. II, *3*; Thompson 1973, 80; Boardman & Vollenweider 1978, 78-79, no. 282, pl. XLV; Plantzos 1999, 47-48, pl. 88, 1a–b; Gerring 2000, 174, Nr. XVII/17, Abb. 136; Boardman 2001, 362, 371, pl. 1009 (Berenice I?)). Another gold ring, presumably with a portrait of Arsinoe III, was sold in 2019 at the Bonhams auction in London (Bonhams. Antiquities. London, 28 Nov. 2019, lot 140: https://www.bonhams.com/auctions/25447/lot/140/). Finally, one silver ring is known, which originates from the Pichvnari necropolis in Georgia (**Fig. 2, 8**) (burial no. 217/2004: Vickers & Kakhidze 2004, 22; 2008a, 145; 2008b, 232; 2014, fig. 115, 3).

Attribution of the portraits on the finger rings

In the works devoted to the "Ptolemaic" finger rings published in Eastern Europe, as a rule, attributions made by Neverov (Neverov 1974, 106-115; 1976, 167-177), are not questioned. On the contrary, in modern studies in the West, with rare exceptions (Spier 1992, 48), skepticism reigns in this regard (Schreiber 2015, 232; 2018, 59-62). I agree that the images of the rulers of the Ptolemaic dynasty on coins (**Fig. 1, 2. 5-8**) should be considered as the main material for comparison. Another important material for analogies are the images of the queens of the Ptolemaic dynasty on the so-called Ptolemaic *oinochoai*, made of faience, on some of which there are written the names of the queens (Thompson 1973, 19-20; Waraksa 2018, 17-19), Arsinoe II as on the vessel

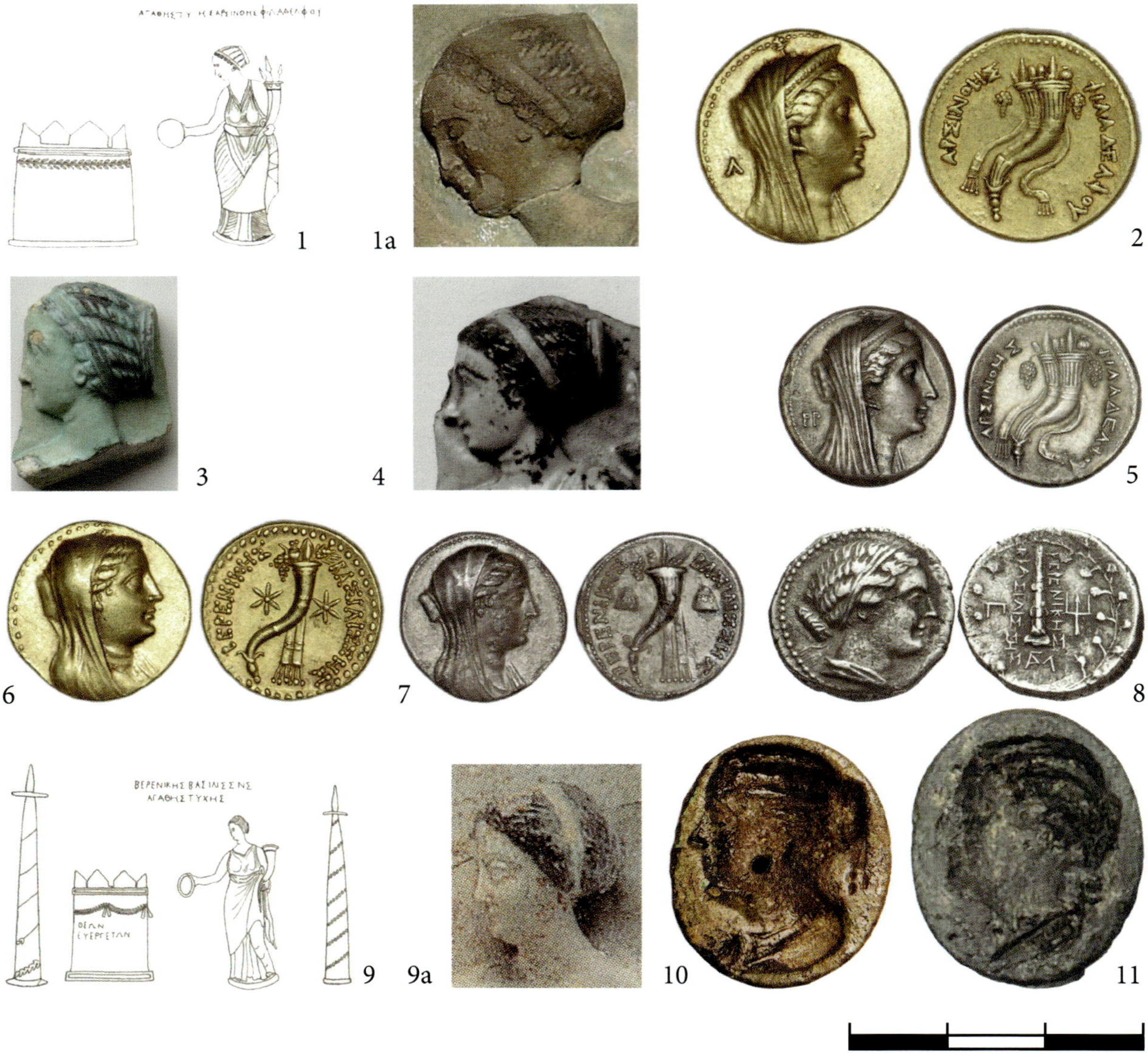

Fig. 1.

Portraits of Arsinoe II and Berenice II on the coins, *oinochoai* and finger rings.

1-2, 5-7 – London, British Museum
10-11 – Saint Petersburg, State Hermitage
1, 1a – *Oinochoe* from Canosa, inv. no. 1873,0820.389
2 – Gold octodrachm of Arsinoe II, inv. no. 1841,0726.516
3 – *Oinochoe* fragment. New York, Metropolitan Museum of Art, inv. no. 26.7.1017
4 – *Oinochoe* fragment. Baltimore, Walters Art Museum, inv. no. 48315;
5 – Silver decadrachm of Arsinoe II, inv. no. 1845,0705
6 – Gold 2,5 drachm of Berenice II, inv. no. 1867,0506.11
7 – Silver 2,5 drachm of Arsinoe II, inv. no. 1900,1204.9
8 – Silver didrachm of Berenice I or II. Cyrene (Svoronos 317)
9, 9a – *Oinochoe* from Xanthos. Antalya, Archaeological Museum, inv. no. A.514
10-11– bronze finger rings with the portrait of Arsinoe II (?)
10 – Chersonesos, inv. no. X.1900.40
11 – Gorgippia, inv. no. Гп.1881.8
Scale – to the finger rings nos. 10-11

from Canosa in the British Museum (**Fig. 1, 1-1a**) (Thompson 1973, 125-126, no. 1, pls. I–II; Pfrommer 1998, 58-59, Abb. 90-91), or Berenice II – from Xanthos – in Antalya (**Fig. 1, 9-9a**) (Demargne 1958, 54-58, no. 707, pl. XIV; Thompson 1973, 149-150, no. 75, pl. B, XXV–XXVII; Lindner 2013, 33-34, fig. 18a). On the contrary sculptural portraits, used by Neverov, often as decisive arguments, can be hardly serve as reasons in favor of one or another attribution due to the unreliability of the attribution of the portraits themselves.

Schreiber came to the conclusion that for most of the finger rings the term "Ptolemaic" is inapplicable, and in the absence of the diadem on the portrait, which was the main visual sign of the Hellenistic ruler, there is no reason to consider them otherwise than portraits of unknown persons, made in the typical for the 3rd century BCE style, albeit reflecting the portrait features of representatives of the Ptolemaic dynasty (Schreiber 2015, 271-272; 2018, 59-62).

However, there is hardly any reason to consider finger rings with portraits, but without diadems, only as images of private individuals. It is obvious that such portraits were recognizable regardless of whether they were wearing a diadem or not. It is also clear that the rings, although they were mass products, were made in various workshops, and in the process of reproduction, some elements of the portrait could be lost or distorted. Another argument is the fact that some portraits are repeated on rings made of different materials: bronze, bone, less often gold, silver, marble and glass. The serial manufacture is further supported by the fact that in some finger rings, the images were incised on the oval plates, which were inserted in the bezels. Finally, it is difficult to imagine that relatively large series of rings bearing portraits of unknown persons were distributed, the images on some of which find parallels precisely on the coins of the Ptolemaic queens. However, even if we generally acknowledge the connection between the portraits on the rings and the images of the Ptolemies, this does not save us from solving a number of problems, in particular, the attribution of images. Since the overwhelming majority of the rings feature female portraits, let us consider the possibility of attributing them as images of Arsinoe II, Berenice II, and Arsinoe III.

The portraits of Arsinoe II and Berenice II

There is often confusion with the definition of the portraits of Arsinoe II and Berenice II. They are characterized by the so-called *Melonenfrisur*, a hairstyle in which strands of hair are twisted into longitudinal rolls, resembling melon rolls, forming a knot at the back of the head. However, there are variations of this hairstyle, which are manifested primarily in the way the braided hair is styled into a knot. Variants of *Melonenfrisur*, including portraits of queens of the Ptolemaic dynasty of the 3rd century BCE, were analyzed in detail in the dissertation of Mairi Gkikaki (Gkikaki 2011).

For Berenice II after the parallels on coins, a hairstyle of the type "c" is distinguished, in which the hair on the back of the head is collected in a round wide knot (rear view, presented in side view as a rather wide roller) (Gkikaki 2011, 538, ZMc-M; on the coins MC- M5: Gkikaki 2011, 469-470, 541). It is also designated as a "disc knot" (Lindner 2013, 31). Not only the images on silver coins of Berenice II dated to ca. 250-246 BCE (**Fig. 1, 8**) (Poole 1883, 60, pl. 13, *7. 8*; Svoronos 1904, 51-52, Nr. 314-321, Taf. 3, 40-45; Willers 2007, 87-88, Taf. 11, *7-8*; van Oppen de Ruiter 2015, 42, pl. 3.2c (with the dating 258-252 BCE); Schreiber 2015, 244-247; Tonkova 2017, 556, fig. 4), but also on bronze rings, usually with relief images, one of the most numerous groups are in accord with this scheme.

Although the attribution of silver coins minted in Cyrene is often considered debatable, and the coins were attributed not only to Berenice II, but also to Berenice I (Lorber 2014, 139, fig. 48, note 189; Schreiber 2015, 246), but in recent works, in particular, Katharina Martin, tends to attributed them to Berenice II (Martin 2012, 413, 416, Anm. 104, Abb. 18). The rarest version of the portrait on bronze coins with the portrait and the inscription "Queen Berenice" and the image of eagle and the inscription "King Ptolemy" (meant Ptolemy III) on the reverse is attributed to the mints of various centers of the Middle East – in this case, it is obvious that this is a portrait of Berenice II on the front side, on the reverse side – an eagle) (Svoronos 1904, Nr. 1047-1050, Taf. 31, 11-20. 22-28; Martin 2012, 413, Anm. 93, Abb. 14; Lorber 2014, 158, fig. 86; 159, see also Cat. London 2001, 86, no. 83). In my opinion the portrait on the silver didrachms of Cyrene is very similar to those on bronze obols.

Neverov, although he proceeded from the fact that the portraits of Berenice II "have a tiny chignon", does not distinguish between the shape and size of the buns on the back of the head, in most cases defining portraits with both a disc knot and a rounded bun as images of Arsinoe II (Neverov 1974, 109-110, fig. 9-10; 1976, 169, pl. II, 1. 3). In one case, a portrait with *Melonenfrisur* and a rounded small bun is determined by him, however, as a portrait of Berenice II (Neverov 1974, 109, fig. 15; 1976, pl. II, *7*). However, if one looks at the coin portraits of Arsinoe II (**Fig. 1, 2. 5**) (Svoronos 1904, 73, Nr. 476, Taf. XV, *15*; 144, Nr. 952, Taf. XXVIII, *16*; Pfrommer 1998, 47, Abb. 77a; 2001, 40, fig. 28a) and Berenice II (**Fig. 1, 6-7**) (Svoronos 1904, 150, Nr. 979, Taf. XXIX, *4-5*; 152, Nr. 990, Taf. XXXV, 4; Pfrommer 1998, 80, Abb. 116a, 117a), in which they are shown with draped heads, it is obvious that there are no fundamental differences in the shape of the knot at the back of the head. They are distinguished, rather, by the number of rolls of twisted strands. On the portraits of Arsinoe II, as a rule, there are five of them, and on the portraits of Berenice II – four. This difference has already been noticed by some researchers (Thompson 1973, 82, 84; Finogenova 2001, 166; Gkikaki 2011, 470).

If this is really a significant feature, then the rings from Chersonesos (**Fig. 1, 10**) (Neverov 1974, 110, note 33, fig. 12; 1976, 168, pl. II, 4) and Gorgippia (**Fig. 1, 11**) (Neverov

1974, 110, note 31, fig. 11; 1976, 168, pl. II, *2*; 2010, 266, 267, fig. 5) really depict Arsinoe II, as Neverov believed (Neverov 1976, 168), and the ring from Pantikapaion (Neverov 1974, 110, fig. 15; 1976, 169, pl. II, 7; Cat. St. Petersburg 2007, 235, no. 256; Schreiber 2015, 273, Nr. Ia14) shows Berenice II. This is indirectly confirmed by the size of the knot on the back of the head, shown in the form of a roller: on the portraits of Arsinoe II it is clearly larger, which is also confirmed by the image on the *oinochoe* with the name of the queen from Canosa, now in London (**Fig. 1, 1-1a**) (Thompson 1973, 125-126, no. 1, pls. I–II; Pfrommer 1998, 58-59, Abb. 90-91), in comparison with the images of Berenice II on the vessels from Xanthus in the Museum of Antalya (**Fig. 1, 9-9a)** (Demargne 1958, 54-58, no. 707, pl. XIV; Thompson 1973, 149-150, no. 75, pl. B, XXV–XXVII; Lindner 2013, 33-34, fig. 18a) and in the J. Paul Getty Museum (Pfrommer 2001, 36, fig. 25; Lindner 2013, 33-34, fig. 18b; Cat. New York 2016, 228-229, no. 162; Hill 2019, 161, fig. 2o). D. Thompson also pointed out the decrease in the size of the knot in the portraits of Berenice II compared to the portraits of Arsinoe II (Thompson 1973, 86).

In this case, I would disagree with Neverov's attribution of the portraits on the finger rings from Olbia (**Fig. 2, 3**) (Neverov 1974, 109, note 23, fig. 9; 1976, 168, pl. II, *1*) and Pantikapaion (Neverov 1974, 110, note 32, fig. 10; 1976, 168, pl. II, *3*), which, rather depict Berenice II than Arsinoe II. Probably then (five rollers) of Arsinoe II is represented on the bezel of the ring from the vicinity of Smyrna (**Fig. 2, 7**), on which she is depicted with two pendants hanging from a knot at the back of her head (according to Jean Charbonneau, this is a portrait of Berenice II) (de Ridder 1924, 138, no 1461, MNC 2168; Charbonneaux 1958, 97-98, fig. 8). Comparable pendants are also shown on the finger rings from Chersonesos (**Fig. 1, 10**), Pantikapaion (Kerch Museum, KM-647, Cat. Kerch 2017, 323, no. 188) and Pichvnari (**Fig. 2, 8**) (Vickers & Kakhidze 2004, 22; 2008a, 145; 2008b, 232; 2014, fig. 115, *3*), on a ring supposedly from the North Pontic region from the Karisalovs collection in the Pushkin Museum (**Fig. 2, 4**) (Cat. Moscow 2019, 32, 113, no. 44), as well as on the rings in Toronto (**Fig. 2, 10**) (Denis 1996, 210, fig. 7) and Oxford (**Fig. 2, 11**) (Boardman & Vollenweider 1978, 81, no. 287, pl. XLVII), the images on which (with four and five rollers, respectively) are identified with the portrait of Berenice II.

Indirectly, the attribution of the portraits of Arsinoe II on the finger rings is confirmed by the seals depicting a female head with a *Melonenfrisur* hairstyle with a roller, reminiscent of the portrait images of Ptolemaic queen, on the papyri II and IV from Elephantine, dated to 285/284 and 284/283 BCE. In one case, this is the seal of the Syrian woman Elaphion, a prostitute or concubine (Rubensohn 1907, 29-30; cf. Grzybek 1989, 206-212) with four rollers (Rubensohn 1907, 15, IV. Nr. 24, Taf. 2; Vandorpe 1996, 259, no. 6, seal c; 2015, seal id 807; Plantzos 1999, 25, fig. 1, *24*; 26, no. IV.6; Schreiber 2015, 260-261, Taf. 30, *7*; 2018, 62; https://berlpap.smb.museum/03737/), in the other – Androsthenes

1 2 3 4 5 6 7 8 9 10 11

from Kos – with five (Rubensohn 1907, 12, II. Nr. 5, Taf. 2; Plantzos 1999, 25, fig. 1, 5; 26, no. II.1; Vandorpe 1996, 259, no. 8, seal a; 2015, seal id 794; Schreiber 2015, 260-261, Taf. 30, 7; 31, 1; 2018, 62). Given the dating of the seals, it is impossible to discuss them as images of Berenice II. In this case, there remains only a choice between Berenice I and Arsinoe II (during her marriage to Lysimachus). Accordingly, there is reason to consider the portraits with *Melonenfrisur* with a disc knot as earlier and attribute them to Berenice I or Arsinoe II, and the portraits with Melonenfrisur with a bun – to Berenice II.

Female portraits on massive bronze finger rings with relief images with a *Melonenfrisur* hairstyle (**Fig. 3, 1-9**), representing the most numerous group in question, are identified as images of Arsinoe II (Neverov 1974, 110; 1976, 168; Neverov, in: Cat. St. Petersburg 2007, 235, no. 258; Korovina 1987, 143; Limberis & Marchenko 1997, 53-55; 2007, 235), Arsinoe II or Berenice II (Tonkova 2017, 554-557), or Berenice II (Cat. London 2001, 63, nos. 33-34; Finogenova 2001, 165, 166; Krasnodubets 2018a, 108; 2018b, 105; Galbois 2018, 207, no. M8, fig. 61). In my opinion, those scholars who consider a significant part of them as portraits of Berenice II are right, because the vast majority of portraits have four rollers, although there are exceptions, for example: five rollers on portraits on the rings from Kiten to south of Apollonia Pontika (**Fig. 3, 3**) (Tonkova 2017, 556, fig. 7; Chacheva 2021, 96, fig. 1), Pantikapaion – from the collection of A.V. Novikov (**Fig. 3, 6**) (Neverov 1974, 110, note 35, fig. 13; 1976, 168, pl. II, *6*; Cat. St. Petersburg 2007, 235, no. 258; Schreiber 2015, 275, Nr. Ib. 24, Taf. 27, 1) (extremely similar is a ring, originating from burial mound no. 1/1977, tomb no. 2 of the necropolis of Pantikapaion, modern quarter Marat-2 in Kerch (Kerch Museum, KM-4018, Cat. Kerch 2017, 323, no. 187)), and presumably of Asia Minor origin – on the finger rings in the Getty Museum (**Fig. 3, 5**) (Spier 1992, 49, no. 89), six – on the finger rings from the collection of the University of Bern (Willers 2007, 87-88, Taf. 11, 4) and the J.Paul Getty Museum (**Fig. 4, 3**) (Spier 1992, 49, no. 88).

◄

Fig. 2.

Portraits of Berenice II in intaglio technique.

1 – Chersonesos, excavations before 1917 г. Chersonesos, Museum, inv. no. 35272/2
2 – Pantikapaion, Central section, 1987. Moscow, Pushkin State Museum of Fine Arts, inv. no. M1733, original and off-print
3 – Olbia, State Hermitage, inv. no. Ол.1010, original and off-print
4, 6 – Karisalov's collection, Moscow, Pushkin State Museum of Fine Arts, inv. no. II1e 3191-3192, originals and off-prints
5 – Bern, Antiquity collection of the University, inv. no. 243
7 – Louvre, inv. no. Bj1461; MNC 2168, original and off-print
8 – Pichvnari. Burial no. 217/2004. Silver. Batumi, Archaeological Museum
9 – Phanagoria. Eastern necropolis. Burial no. 74/2006. Institute of Archaeology, Russian Academy of Sciences
10 – Toronto, Royal Ontario Museum, inv. no. 991.169.1
11 – Oxford, Ashmolean Museum, inv. no. 1941.318

1
2
3
4
5
6
7
8
9
10
11
12
13
14
15
16
17

Portraits of Arsinoe III

Neverov singled out two types of portraits of Arsinoe III. The first type (Neverov 1974, 111; 1976, 169) is with a roller along the edge of the hairdo, turning into a chignon at the back of the head (*Schneckenförmigen Knoten* or *Schneckenknoten* / *Arsinoe-Knoten*, after the terminology of E. Gkikaki (Gkikaki 2011, 30-32, 55, 202, Z-Ha-P 5)). This type currently includes 10 pieces, the finger rings with relatively small bezels (2.3-2.6 x 1.8-2.1 cm) found only in the Cimmerian Bosporus (**Fig. 5, 5-8**) (Neverov 1974, fig. 17; 20; 1976, 169, pls. II, *9-10*; III, *1-3*; Cat. St. Petersburg 2007, 236, no. 259; Schreiber 2015, 265, 274, Nr. Ia17, Taf. 24, *4*), as well as the finger rings in the collections of the University College London (Petrie 1927, 20, no. 324, pl. XVI; Schneider 2015, 239, Anm. 71; 274, Nr. IA.24), the Archaeological Museum of the Münster University (Schneider 2015, 238-239, 272, Nr. 2; Taf. 24, *1*) and the Karisalov's family, now in the Pushkin Museum of fine arts, Moscow (**Fig. 5, 9**) (Cat. Moscow 2019, 114, no. 46). This variant finds close parallels on coins, in particular on the posthumous golden octadrachm (**Fig. 5, 2-2a**) (Svoronos 1904, 211, Nr. 1269, Taf. XLII, *1*; Neverov 1976, 171, pl. II, *8*; Pfrommer 1999, 104, Abb. 145a; 2001, 44, fig. 30a; Cat. London 2001, 84, no. 75; Gorrini 2006, 224, tav. I, 2a–b; Gkikaki 2011, 30, 156, Ha-M 15; Martin 2012, 403, Abb. 10; Lorber 2014, 149, fig. 64; Schreiber 2015, Taf. 24, 6; 25, *1*; Cat. New York 2016, 211-212, no. 136) and on the bronze portrait kept in Mantua (**Fig. 5, 1**) (Gorrini 2006, 221-237 with bibliography in note 1 on p. 221; tav. IV; Gkikaki 2011, 216, Ha-P 15; Butz 2017, 46-56) and this observation is supported by other researchers (Schreiber 2015, 265). A very close to the portrait on the octadrachm, including similar earrings

◄

Fig. 3.

Portraits of Berenice II and Arsinoe III in relief.

1 – Nicosia, Cyprus Museum, inv. no. 1993, VI-1/141
2 – Aphrodisias. Selifke, Archaeological Museum
3 – Kiten, Urdoviza. Primorsko, Historical Museum, inv. no. 61
4 – Steklen near Svishtov. Sofia, National Archaeological Museum, inv. no. 4206
5 – Asia Minor. Malibu, The J. Paul Getty Museum, inv. no. 83.AN.434.17
6 – Pantikapaion, A.V. Novikov collection, St. Petersburg, State Hermitage, inv. no. B.2673
7 – Phanagoria. Eastern necropolis. Burial no. 249/1965. Moscow, Pushkin State Museum of Fine Arts, inv. no. Ф-1193
8 – Vinogradnyy 7. Burial mound no. 2/1993. Burial no. 26. Taman, Archaeological Museum (photo by I.I. Marchenko)
9 – A. Merle de Massoneau collection, Berlin, Antiken, inv. no. Misc. 11863.228
10-12 – Chersonesos
10 – North Region. Quartier no. 9, 2002 excavations, inv. no. 37380/23
11 – XVth street, Hellenistic drain, 1970 excavations, inv. no. 36844/26
12 – From the excavations of K.K. Kostyushko-Valyuzhinich, inv. no. КП-6145
13 – Myrmekion, M.2013-480, probably from the ashlar layer, Kerch, East Crimean Historical-Archaeological Museum-Reserve, inv. КП-185463, KM-8559
14 – D.G. Burylin collection, Ivanovo, Art Museum, inv. no. A-560/1
15 – Vicinities of Smyrna, Louvre, Bj 1440
16 – Karisalov's collection, Moscow, State Pushkin Museum of Fine Arts, inv. П1е 3198
17 – Asia Minor. Malibu, The J. Paul Getty Museum, inv. no. 85.AN.370.22

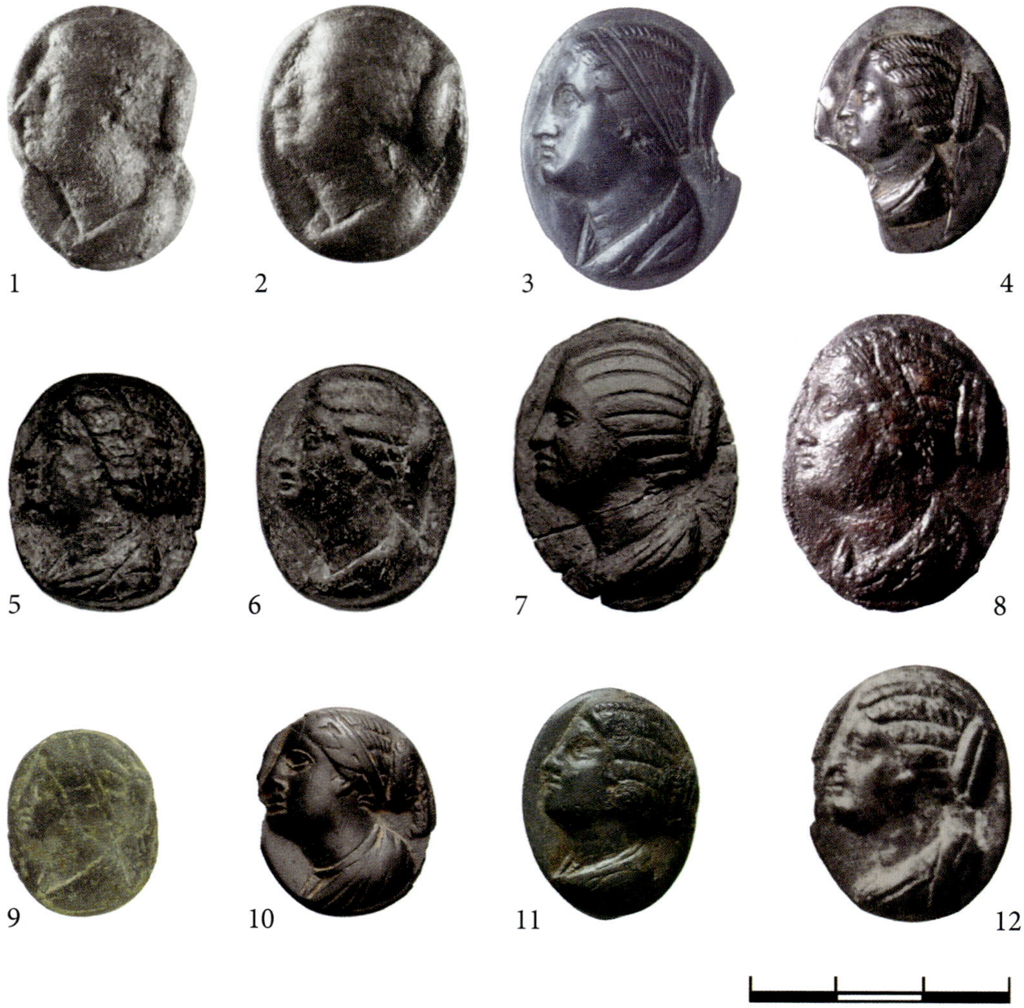

Fig. 4.

Portraits of Berenice II in relief from the museum collections and auctions (without known provenance).

1-2 – Berlin, Ägyptisches Museum, inv. no. 9336 and 11 380
3 – Malibu, The J. Paul Getty Museum, inv. no. 81.AN.76.208
4 – London, British Museum, inv. no. 1917,0501.1268
5-7 – Münster, Archäologisches Museum
5 – Inv. no. L428
6 – Inv. no. L427
7 – Inv. no. 2270
8 – London, British Museum, inv. no. 1917,0501.1267
9 – Auction Themis, Auction 8, lot 832
10 – Cngcoins.com2880746.jpg
11 – Zeus Numismatics, lot 2293
12 – Münzen und Medaillen AG Basel. September 1970. Sonderliste M, 39, Nr. 98; 41

and S-shaped curls on the cheek, is represented on a garnet gem found on the island of Cos and now in Vienna (**Fig. 5, 4**) (Zwierlein-Diehl 1973, 42, Nr. 32, Taf. 7; Meisterwerke Wien 1996, 108, Nr. 150, Abb. 133; Plantzos 1999, 114, no. 33, pl. 6; Galbois 2018, 58, 197, no. G21), as well as on a relief bezel of a bronze finger ring from the House IV of the Western Quarter of Eretria (Urfer 2020, 81-82, fig. 3, *a*).

This group of finger rings is adjoined by a series of small rings with portraits in relief (bezels ca. 2,1-2,3 x 1,7-1,8 cm) which are represented by the finds from Chersonesos (**Fig. 3, 10-12**) (Krasnodubets 2018a, 108, no. 6, fig. 1, *3*; 110, no. 9; 2018b, 105, fig. 1, *1-2*) and Myrmekion (Fig. 3, 13)[1]. The North Pontic provenance is also likely for the similar finger ring with gilded bronze bezel from the collection of D.G. Burylin, which is kept in the Ivanovo Art Museum (**Fig. 3, 14**) (inv. no. A-560/1, КП-3349/1; Treister 1992, 106, note 165) and for the ring from the Karisalov's collection in Moscow (**Fig. 3, 16**) (Cat. Moscow 2019, 115, no. 48). A comparaneous ring of allegedly Asian Minor origin was acquired by the Paul Getty Museum (**Fig. 3, 17**) (Spier 1992, 49, no. 90). One more finger ring, in the Louvre, was found in the vicinities of Smyrna (**Fig. 3, 15**) (de Ridder 1924, 136, no. 1440, MNC 2166). Recently a similar bronze finger ring was found during the excavations of the south palestra of Eretria on the island of Euboea (Urfer 2020, 80-82, fig. 2). The portraits on these rings are very generalized. The finds of such rings in Greece and Asia Minor do not allow us to consider the rings from the North Pontic region as items of local production.

Questions are raised by the second version of the portraits, which was attributed by O.Ya. Neverov (Neverov 1974, 111-112; 1976, 169, 172) to Arsinoe III. This is a fairly common variant of images on the finger rings (**Fig. 5, 10-13**) (10 pieces: mainly from the Bosporan Kingdom and the Trans-Kuban region), a distinctive feature of which is a narrow roller along the edge of the hairdo with oblique parallel strands. Long, slightly curved strands, descend from the crown to the roller. The rounded bun at the back of the head is tied at the base with a ribbon. The bun itself is decorated with numerous small rounded protrusions which represent either scrolls of the curls, or heads of hairpins, or a winding of threads with beads (?) (Neverov 1974, 111-112; 1976, 169, 172, pl. III, *4-7*; Cat. St. Petersburg 2007, 236, no. 261). O.Ya. Neverov cites no parallels to this variant. At the same time, a similar portrait with a similar bun on a finger ring of a different shape, kept in Oxford (Boardman & Vollenweider 1978, 81-82, no. 289, pl. XLVII), was attributed by J. Boardman and M.-L. Vollenweider precisely on the basis of Neverov's attribution, the fact to which attention has already been drawn (Schreiber 2015, 252).

Differences in the interpretation of hairstyles were explained by the long period of reign of Arsinoe III as the sister and wife of Ptolemy IV (Boardman & Vollenweider 1978,

[1] Field inventory M.2013-480. Kerch, Museum, КП-185463, КМ-8559. I am grateful to A.M. Butyagin for the information and the photograph of the finger ring.

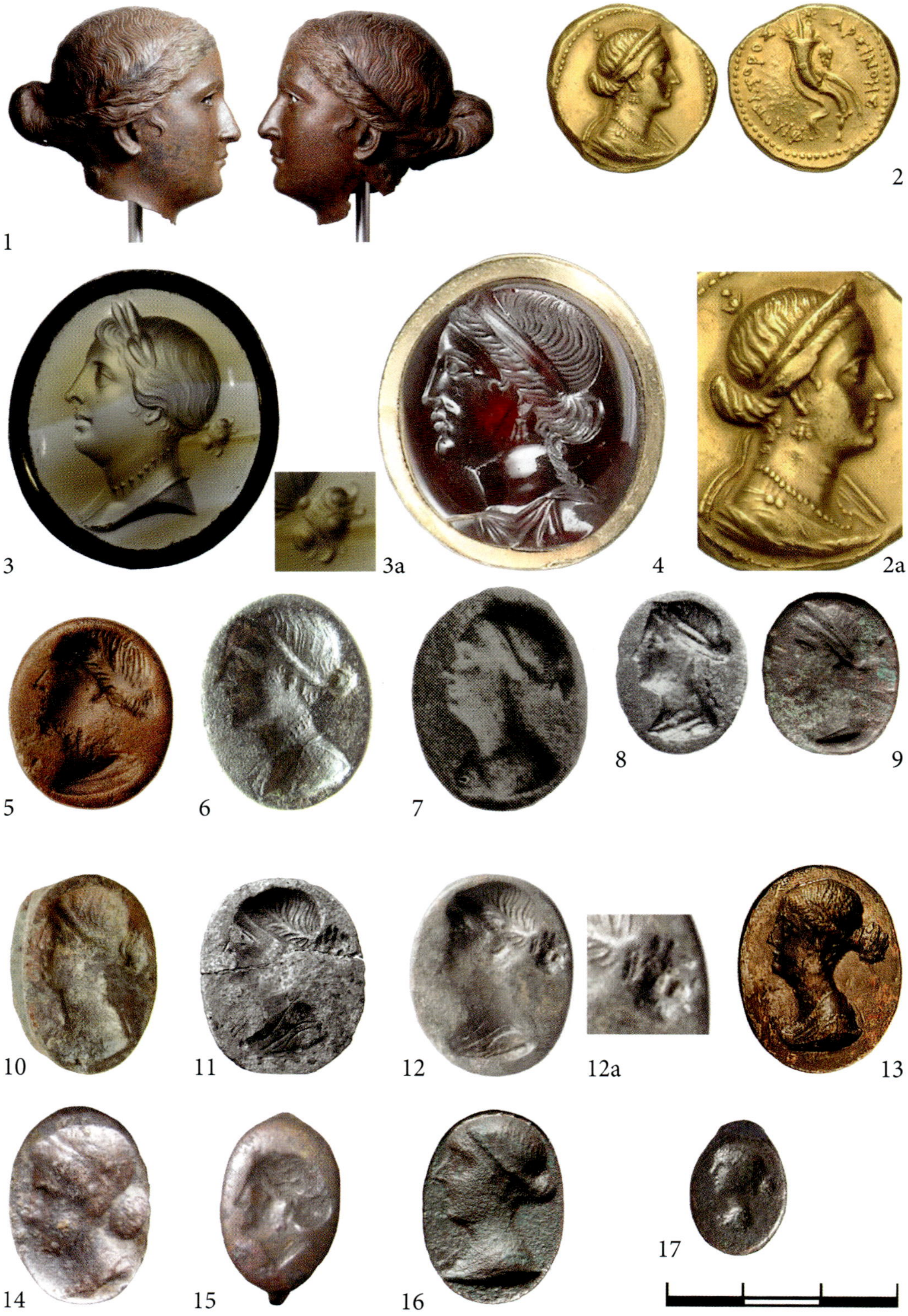
1
2
3
3a
4
2a
5
6
7
8
9
10
11
12
12a
13
14
15
16
17

◄
Fig. 5.

Portraits of Arsinoe III on coins, in bronze statuary, *oinochoai*, glyptics and bronze finger rings.
1 – Bronze portrait. Mantua Museo Civico di Palazzo Te, Acerbi Collection, inv. no. 96190279
2, 2a – Posthume gold octodrachm with the portrait of Arsinoe III (204-203 BCE). Berlin, Münzkabinett, Ident.-Nr. 182_7869
3, 3a – Gem (carnelian) with the portrait of Arsinoe III or Cleopatre II. Paris, Bibliothèque nationale, Cabinet des Médailles, inv. no. 58.2319, Chabouillet.2319
4 – Gem (garnet) with the portrait of Arsinoe III. Cos. Vienna, Kunsthistorisches Museum, inv. no. AS VII, 1016
5-12 – Bronze finger rings. Arsinoe III (?)
5, 8, 13 – Pantikapaion. St. Petersburg, State Hermitage
5 – Inv. no. П.1873.90
6 – Tanais. Burial no. 51/2008. Tanais, Archaelogical Museum-reserve
7 – "House of Chrysaliskos". Moscow, State Historical Museum
8 – Inv. no. ПАН.1849;
9 – Karisalov's collection, Moscow, State Pushkin Museum of Fine Arts, inv. IIIe 3190
10 – Vinogradnyy 7. Burial no. 21/2015. Phanagoria, Archaeological Museum (photo by N.I. Sudarev)
11 – «Maikop». Acquired in 1914-1915. Berlin, Antikenmuseum, inv. no. 30585. Lost
12, 12a – Tenginskaya. Burial no. 140/1998. Moscow, State Museum of Orient
13 – Inv. no. П.1867.27щ
14-15 – vicinities of Smyrna, Louvre
14 – Inv. no. Bj 1395
15 – Inv. no. Bj 1399
16-17 – Karisalov's collection, Moscow, State Pushkin Museum of Fine Arts
16 – Inv. no. IIIe 3193
17 – Inv. no. IIIe 3202. Scale – to finger rings nos. 5-17

81-82, no. 289) or by the non-obvious attribution (Plantzos 1999, 49). The parallels to the portrait with a bun on small anepigraphic bronze coins minted in Cyprus, which have already been pointed out (Boardman & Vollenweider 1978, 82), and which are traditionally associated with the coinage of Ptolemy IV, and the portrait was attributed as an image of Arsinoe III (Svoronos 1904, Nr. 1160-1162, Taf. 39, *4-10*) or Cleopatra VII (Kreuzer 2004, 41-45), can hardly be accepted without reservations – there is every reason to consider the female head on the obverse of the coins as the image of Aphrodite, the patroness of Cyprus (Lorber 2014, 160, fig. 89).

Similar portraits, but with a large rounded bun without protrusions and not constricted at the base, are presented on two bronze rings from the vicinity of Smyrna. One of them shows a diadem; on both – there are rollers with oblique parallel strands of hair (**Fig. 5, 14-15**) (de Ridder 1924, 131, no. 1395, 1399; Charbonneaux 1958, 97-98, fig. 9). The strands of hair vary in their treatment from the finds from the North Pontic region.

Among the rarest parallels to the portrait with a bun with rounded protrusions known to me is an image on the carnelian gem in the Cabinet des Médailles in Paris (**Fig. 5, 3-3a**), which was attributed by A. Furtwängler supposedly as the portrait of Arsinoe III (Furtwängler 1900, Bd. I, Taf. XXXI, 29; XXXII, 34; Bd. 2, 154-155; Plantzos 1999, 50, 114, no. 34, pl. 6; Galbois 2018, 198, no. G23), whereas by M.-L. Vollenweider – as the portrait of Cleopatra II dated to ca. 170 BCE (Vollenweider 1995, 119-120, no. 109).

E. Gkikaki considers the variant of the hairdo with a rounded bun at the back of the head as a further development of the *Haarkranz* hairstyle with *Schneckenknotten* in the Early Hellenistic period. The difference lies precisely in the shape of the knot at the back of the head - instead of *Schneckenknotten*, a rounded bun appears (Gkikaki 2011, 55). At the same time, the peculiarities of the hairstyle in the portraits with a bun at the back of the head do not find exact analogies in Hellenistic sculpture.

Thus, the attribution of the finger rings with such portraits as images of Arsinoe III is nothing more than an assumption. In favor of it is the closeness of the interpretation of the strands of hair on the crown and the roller, the obvious chronological closeness – in the earthen tomb No. 17/1873 on the Mithridates mound (CR St. Pétersbourg 1873, V–VI), there were found finger rings with the portraits both of the first (**Fig. 5, 5**) (State Hermitage, inv. no. П.1873.90: Neverov 1974, 111, note 44, fig. 17; 1976, 169, note 38, pl. II, 9) and the second (State Hermitage, inv. no. П.1873.89: Neverov 1974, 112, note 51; 1976, 169, note 45, pl. III, 4) variant, as well as the size of the rings. We can only guess, whether these images were some kind of modification of portraits with a roller and a chignon.

In general, the proposed attributions are also confirmed by the size of the rings. Rings with alleged portraits of Arsinoe III are smaller than rings with the portraits of Arsinoe II and Berenice II, thus reflecting the trend towards reduction in the size of the finger rings in the last quarter of the 3rd century BCE.

Geographical distribution of the finger rings

If the rings with portraits carved from bone (today 24 specimens are known[2], including those from Alexandria and Cyprus (Marangou 1971, 163-171; Alföldi-Rosenbaum 1980, 37-38, pl. 11, *1-5*; Spier 1992, 49, no. 91; Boussac & Starakis 1998, 160-161, figs. 1-2; Meyza 2012, 265-266, figs. 5-6; Koiner 2013, 127, fig. 9-10; Galbois 2018, 117, 119, 234-235, nos. O1-3; Michaelides & Papantoniou 2018, fig. 9; Schreiber 2015, 275-276)), presumably could even be made in Cyprus as an instrument of Ptolemaic propaganda, while being distributed, although very rarely, in the North Pontic area (Olbia), then a completely different distribution is demonstrated by the finger rings made of bronze. A significant part of them has no established provenance.

We are not aware of any confirmed case of find of the bronze finger rings in Egypt, although the Egyptian origin of some of them is very likely (University College London: Petrie 1927, 20, no. 324, pl. XVI; Schreiber 2015, 274, Nr. Ia21. – Ägyptisches Museum Berlin: Krug 1980, 39, fig. 5; Plantzos 1999, 48, note 56, pl. 89, 5-6; Schreiber 2015, 274, Nr. 1b.10-11). Let us also point out the already mentioned seals with portrait images

[2] T. Schreiber listed 22 specimens of bone finger rings (Schreiber 2015, 275-276), to which the 2008 find in Paphos, Cyprus (Meyza 2012, 265-266, figs. 5-6) and the find from Olbia (Maksimova 1958, 248-255, ill. on p. 248), unknown to him, must be added. Thus, the total number of currently known bone rings is 24.

with a *Melonenfrisur* hairstyle on the papyri from Elephantine, as well as on the seals found at Naucratis (British Museum, inv. no. 1888,0601.84: Gardner 1888, 87, pl. XIX, no. 12; Bailey 2008, 162, pls 112, 146, no. 3617; Masson 2018, 24, fig. 46) and Carthage (Berges 1997, 111, Nr. 176, Taf. 49). There are several evidences of finds of such rings in the west and south of Asia Minor, presumably in Smyrna or in its vicinities, some of which acquired by the Louvre (**Figs. 2, 7; 3, 15; 5, 14-15**) (de Ridder 1924, 131, nos. 1395, 1395bis, 1397, 1399; 136, no. 1440; 138, no. 1461; Charbonneaux 1958, 97-98, figs. 7-9), coming from the collection of the director of the Smyrna – Kasab railway, Paul Gaudin (1858-1921), the first explorer of Aphrodisias in Caria, who lived in Smyrna[3], from Aphrodisias, now in the Museum of Selifke (**Fig. 3, 2**) (Budde 1987, 13, Abb. 6; Schreiber 2015, 274, Nr. Ib9), from Northern Syria (Ras Ibn Hani to the north of Latakia (Bounni 1979, 284, fig. 6)) and allegedly from Rhodes (Cat. London 2001, 63, no. 34: British Museum, inv. no. 1930,0715.3), Lemnos (Plantzos 1999, 48, note 56) and Cyprus (**Fig. 3, 1**) (Erath-Koiner 2003, 108-110, Taf. 10, *1a–b*).

The few examples cited above, mostly with unconfirmed or alleged provenance, are opposed by at least 50 finger rings from the Black Sea region (Neverov listed only 23 rings, including two from Chersonesos and one from Olbia (Neverov 1974, 106-115; 1976, 166-183)). At least 45 examples of such finger rings originate from the North Pontic area (Treister 1982, 70-71, fig. 2; Korovina 1987, 137-148; Finogenova 2001, 164-167; Limberis & Marchenko 1997, 53-54, fig. 7, *9*; 2010, 153-155, fig. 3, 1; Medvedev 2014, 130, 131, fig. 5, 10; Krasnodubets 2018a, 105-112; 2018b, 105-109). As before, there is a significant predominance of such rings in the area of the Bosporan Kingdom, especially with the recent finds in Tanais (**Fig. 5, 6**) (Chernenko 2013, 128-129, fig. 1, *4*; 2015, fig. 1)[4] and in the Taman peninsula (**Figs. 2, 9; 5, 10; 6, 6; 7, 5**)[5], but also in Pantikapaion (**Fig. 2, 2**) (Finogenova 2001, 165, fig. 2; 166) and Myrmekion (**Fig. 3, 13**) (Field inventory M.2013-480. Kerch, Museum, КП-185463, КМ-8559), bringing the total amount in this region up to 30 items. The number of finds in Chersonesos also increased signif-

---

[3] See about him: Erim 1967, 233. https://doi.org/10.2307/501557; Guichard & Savoy 2018, 5.

[4] Unpublished finds: Tanais, western necropolis, burial nos. 590: Bespalyy 2016, vol. 2, 112-113, nos. 8-9; vol. 5, 64, nos. 1649-1650; vol. 11, figs. 3583-3586. – Burial no. 634/2012: Bespalyy 2016, vol. 12, figs. 3845-3846.

[5] Vinogradnyy-7: burial mound no. 2/1993, burial no. 26: Limberis & Marchenko 1997, 53-54, fig. 7, *9*; Ustaeva & Zhuravlev 2010, 88-89, 91, fig. 53. – Burial mound no. 2/2006, burial no. 10: Limberis & Marchenko 2010, 153-155, fig. 3, *1*. – Burial no. 21/2015: Sudarev 2017, 187, fig. 13, upper row, second from the left. – Phanagoria, Eastern necropolis. Burial no. 78/1964: Neverov 1974, 108, fig. 2; 1976, 167, pl. I. *4*; Korovina 1987, 140-142, fig. 3, *2*; Finogenova 2001, 165, 166, fig. 1; 2010, 367, fig. 27 (left); Cat. Moscow 2017, 302, no. 183A. – Burial no. 199/1965: Korovina 1987, 144 (as Arsinoe II); Finogenova 2001, 165, fig. 4; 166 (as Arsinoe III); Cat. Moscow 2017, 302-303, no. 183Г (as Arsinoe II). – Burial no. 249/1965: Neverov 1974, 108, fig. 2; Korovina 1987, 142-143 (as Arsinoe II), fig. 4, *1*; Finogenova 2001, 165, 166 (as Berenice II), fig. 3; 2010, 367, fig. 27 (right); Cat. Moscow 2017, 302-303, no. 183Б (as Arsinoe II). – Burial no. 74/2006: Medvedev 2009, 149; 169, fig. 9. *1*; 2014, 130, 131, fig. 5, *10* (as Arsinoe III); Abramzon 2015, 16, 17, fig. 4 (as Arsinoe II). – Beregovoy 4: Zavoykin 2017, 234, fig. 2, *1*.

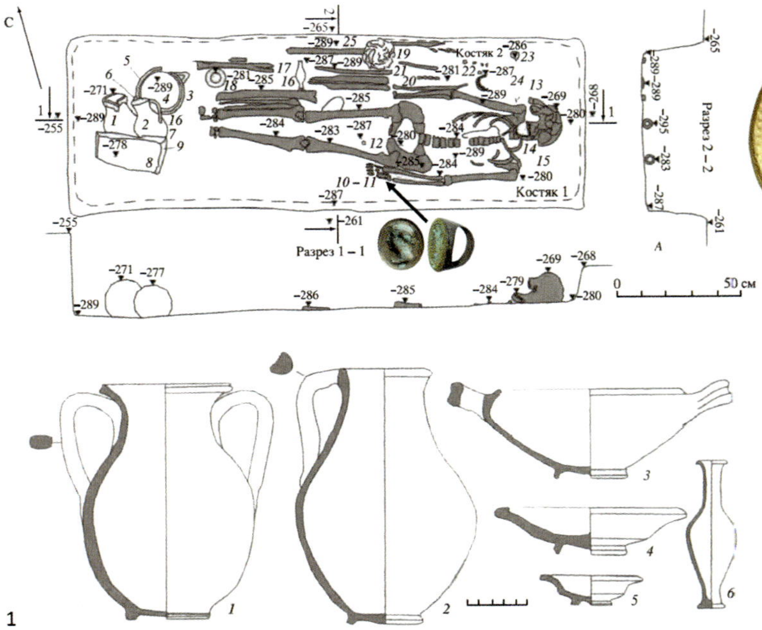
Костяк 2
Костяк 1
Разрез 1 – 1
Разрез 2 – 2
0
50 см

1

2

3

4

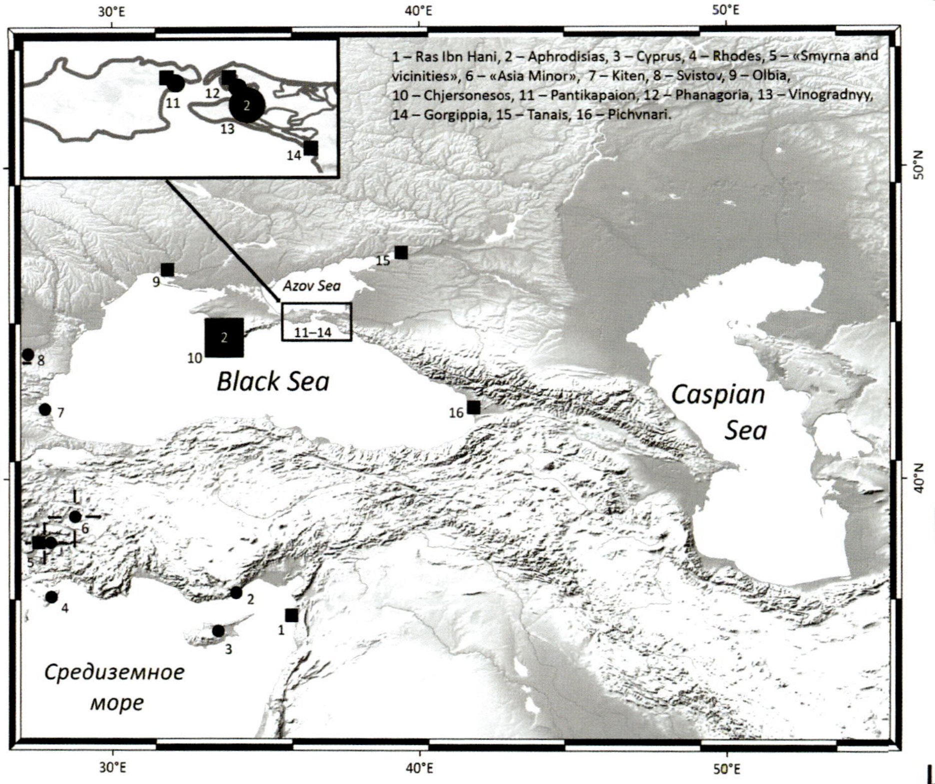
1 – Ras Ibn Hani, 2 – Aphrodisias, 3 – Cyprus, 4 – Rhodes, 5 – «Smyrna and vicinities», 6 – «Asia Minor», 7 – Kiten, 8 – Svistov, 9 – Olbia, 10 – Chjersonesos, 11 – Pantikapaion, 12 – Phanagoria, 13 – Vinogradnyy, 14 – Gorgippia, 15 – Tanais, 16 – Pichvnari.
Azov Sea
11–14
Black Sea
Caspian Sea
Средиземное море
30°E
40°E
50°E
50°N
40°N

5

6

Fig. 6.
Portraits of Arsinoe II and Berenice II in context, on coins and finger rings.

1 – Phanagoria. Eastern necropolis. Burial no. 74/2006. Plan, cross-section and finds of pottery
2 – Gold octodrachm of Arsionoe II. London, British Museum, inv. no. 1841,0726.516
3 – Silver didrachm of Berenice I or II. Cyrene (Svoronos. 1904. No. 317)
4 – Bronze obol. Ras Ibn Hani (Lorber 2014, fig. 86)
5 – Map of distribution of bronze and silver finger rings with the portraits of Arsinoe II and Berenice II (circles – finger rings with images in relief, quadrates – in intaglio)
6 – Phanagoria. Eastern necropolis. Burial no. 74/2006. Moscow, Institute of archaeology, Russian Academy of Sciences.
Scale – to finger ring no. 6

icantly (**Figs. 2, 1; 3, 10-13**) (Krasnodubets 2018a, 105-112; 2018b, 105-109). Another point, previously unknown, is the discovery of such rings in the Maiotian burial grounds in the Trans-Kuban region (**Fig. 5, 12**)[6]. Finally, three recently published finds of such rings in the Western Black Sea region (**Fig. 3, 3-4**) (Tonkova 2017, 554-557, fig. 1; 7; Chacheva 2021, 96, fig. 1) and in the Eastern Rhodopes (Manov 2018, 23) should be pointed out.

Such a distribution of bronze finger rings with portrait images (as opposed to bone ones), in my opinion, gives an obvious basis for the assumption that these rings were made exclusively (or mainly) for distribution outside the Ptolemaic state, and were distributed in Asia Minor (de Ridder 1924, 131, nos. 1395, 1395bis, 1397, 1399; 136, no. 1440; 138, no. 1461; Charbonneaux 1958, 97-98, figs. 7-9; Budde 1987, 13, Abb. 6; Spier 1992, 49, nos. 89-90), Syria (Bounni 1979, 284, fig. 6) and Cyprus (Erath-Koiner 2003, 108-110, Taf. 10, 1), but much more often in the North Pontic region, mainly in Bosporan Kingdom and even outside its borders.

Noteworthy is the difference in the distribution of the finger rings with portraits, which may be attributed as those of Arsinoe II and Berenice II (**Fig. 6, 5**), on the one hand, and Arsinoe III (**Fig. 7, 1**), on the other. If the former are represented also by rather rare finds in the Eastern Mediterranean (**Fig. 3, 1-2**), including Rhodes and Cyprus, and in the Western Black Sea region (**Fig. 3, 3-4**), as well as in Olbia (**Fig. 2, 3**), despite the fact that a fairly significant number of them originate from Chersonesos (**Fig. 2, 1**), with the predominance of finds in the Bosporan Kingdom, than the latter, with the exception of one find from Chersonesos, were distributed only in the Bosporus and in the Trans-Kuban region.

[6] Psenafa, burial mound no. 1, burial no. 70: Cat. Maikop 2014, 34-35; 43, ill. 19; 44; 100-102, no. 177; Erlikh 2017, 16-17, no. 3; 34-35, fig. III, *3*. – Tenginskaya, burial no. 140: Beglova 2002, 303, Abb. 8, *1*; 2010, 417, 418, fig. 12; Beglova & Erlikh 2018, 62, no. 122; 170. fig. 80, *5*; Treister 2022a, 328, fig. 2, *12*; 2022b, 282, fig. 2, *12*. – Psif 3: Ivanov & Trubnikov 2018, 72. see also a finger ring, which originate allegedly from the so-called Maikop Treasure, earlier in the Antikenmuseum Berlin, inv. no. 30585: Treister 2022a, 328, fig. 2, *11*; 2022b, 282, fig. 2, *11*.

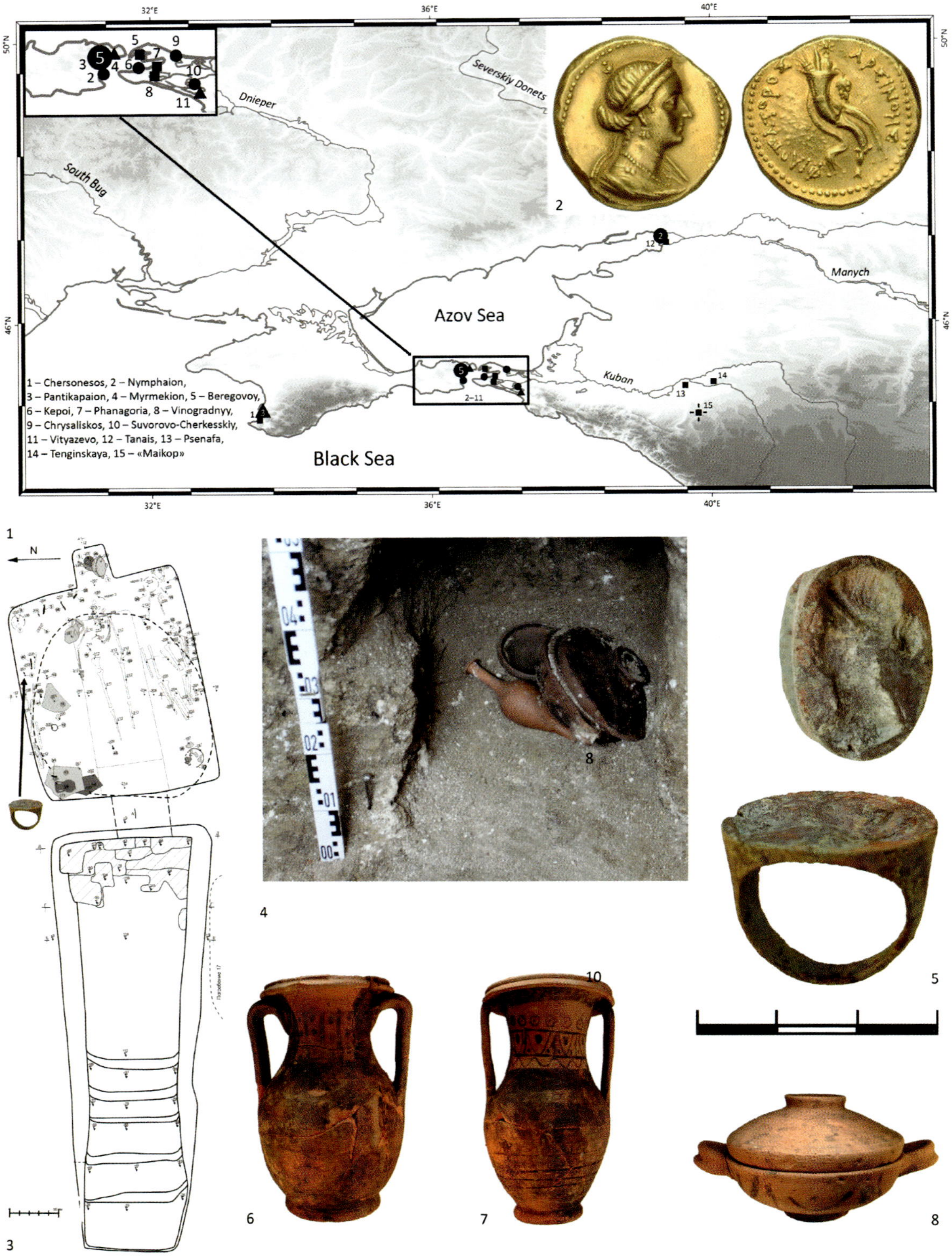
32°E
36°E
40°E
50°N
46°N
Severskiy Donets
Dnieper
South Bug
Azov Sea
Black Sea
Kuban
Manych
1 – Chersonesos, 2 – Nymphaion,
3 – Pantikapaion, 4 – Myrmekion, 5 – Beregovoy,
6 – Kepoi, 7 – Phanagoria, 8 – Vinogradnyy,
9 – Chrysaliskos, 10 – Suvorovo-Cherkesskiy,
11 – Vityazevo, 12 – Tanais, 13 – Psenafa,
14 – Tenginskaya, 15 – «Maikop»
2–11
N
1
2
3
4
5
6
7
8

◂

Fig. 7.

Portraits of Arsinoe III in context, on coins and finger rings.

1 – map of the distribution of bronze finger rings with the portraits of Arsinoe III in the North Pontic area (circles – with a chignon, quadrates – with a bun, triangles – relief portraits)
2 – posthume gold octodrachm with the portrait of Arsinoe III (204-203 BCE). Berlin, Münzkabinett, Ident.-Nr. 18217869
3-7 – Vinogradnyy. Burial no. 21/2015
3 – plan
4 – photo, detail
5 – finger ring
6-8 – pottery (plan and photographs by N.I. Sudarev)
Scale – to finger ring no. 5

While finger rings are often considered as elements of Ptolemaic propaganda, like faience *oinochoai* depicting Ptolemaic queens, they have different areas of distribution: oinochoai originate mainly from Egypt, primarily from Alexandria, and only 11% of vessels with a known origin were found in North Africa, Italy, Greece, Asia Minor and the Near East (Nenna & Seif El-Din 2000, 432-434; Lund 2014, 299; Waraksa 2018, 30-31, figs. 2-3). In the Black Sea region, where finds of Alexandrine pottery of the Hellenistic period are registered (Lungu 2007, 149-163) (*see here V. Kotenko*), such *oinochoai* with a reliable provenance are unknown, although such an origin of *oinochoe* fragments from the collection of Pierre Mavrogordato, now in the Antikensammlung Berlin (Kriseleit 1990, 61-64), cannot be ruled out.

Contexts of finds. Who were the recipients of the "Ptolemaic" rings in the Northern Black Sea region?

Finger rings with portraits similar to those of the representatives of the Ptolemaic dynasty are interpreted either as belonging to the servants of their cult (Kleiner & Ohly 1951, 27; Pfrommer 1998, 128), officials and courtiers, military men (Spier 1992, 48; Plantzos 1999, 49), or as a massive imitation of the official seals of palace officials, priests and priestesses (Müller 2009, 285, Anm. 843). Finger rings made of bone are considered to be made for servants (Boardman & Vollenweider 1978, 81) or as "nostalgic souvenirs" (Reeder 1988, 215; Erath-Koiner 2003, 110). According to Dietrich Willers, with whom I cannot but agree, the very material from which the rings are made, bronze, and their mass production do not give reason to assume that these rings were intended for high-ranking persons (Willers 2007, 89).

Who were the recipients of the „Ptolemaic" finger rings in the North Pontic region? The deceased wore from one to three rings, quite often – two or three. They were found in paired burials of a man and a woman with rings on the hands of each of the deceased or one of them, usually a woman (**Fig. 6, 1**). The finger rings were also found in neighboring burials arranged under the same barrow mound. The bronze rings under discussion are found in female, male burials and in those of teenagers. Burial structures belong to several types. These are ordinary soil graves (**Fig. 6, 1**) and burials under kurgans, earthen crypts, graves with side catacombs (**Fig. 7, 3**), tombs made of mudbricks as well as stone cists (Treister 1985, 131-132).

It is hardly possible to determine accurately and, most importantly, unambiguously, the social status of the people who wore rings of the "Ptolemaic" type in the Cimmerian Bosporus. Nevertheless, it is impossible to imagine that all of them were representatives of the "aristocracy of the Bosporus", as Y.A. Vinogradov recently suggested (Vinogradov 2017, 9; 2019, 10). Perhaps, such a definition is valid only for the burials discovered in 1881 in the burial mound in Anapa. Rather, they belonged to different, mostly "middle" strata of the Bosporan society (which is evidenced, in particular, by a rather standard and often modest set of grave goods **(Figs. 6, 1. 1-6; 7, 4. 6-8)**. This is indirectly confirmed by the fact that the ring with a portrait very similar to that of Berenice I or Arsinoe II belonged to the Syrian prostitute or concubine Elaphion, who wore it in Egyptian Elephantine (Rubensohn 1907, 29-30; cf. Grzybek 1989, 206-212). Moreover, the finger rings could be given as gifts or inherited. In some cases, this is confirmed by the degree of preservation of the rings and the dating of the complexes.

The chronology of the find contexts

With rare exceptions, Neverov did not analyze the contexts of the finds of the finger rings in terms of the chronology. In some cases, finds are said to be accompanied by "clay balsamaria of the 3rd century BCE" (Neverov 1974, 109, note 24; 110, note 31; 112, note 52; 1976, 180, note 18, 25; 181, note 46), but since these vessels have not been published, it is difficult to analyze critically the possibility of dating of these complexes. If we consider finds from complexes excavated in recent decades in the Taman Peninsula and in Tanais, for instance a female skeleton in the pair burial of the grave no. 74/2006 in the Eastern necropolis of Phanagoria (**Fig. 6, 1**) (Medvedev 2014, 128, nos. 1-4; 131, fig. 5Б, 1-4); the unpublished female burials, each with Rhodian amphoras, bronze mirrors, pairs of bronze finger rings and various necklaces in the western necropolis of Tanais[7], then it is clear the earliest of them may be dated already to the late 3rd century BCE. Of interest are the finds in the earthen crypt no. 21/2015 of the Vinogradny-7 necropolis, in which burials were made many times, while the finger ring with the portrait of Arsinoe III (**Fig. 7, 5**) was found among the bones belonging to the early burials in the crypt (**Fig. 7, 3**) (Sudarev 2017, 187, fig. 13, upper row, second from the left; 188) and in other similar earthen crypts of the same Taman necropolis, in which the finds of rings were accompanied by a standard set of pottery: unguentaria, painted pelikes, lagynoi, lekanoi

[7] Tanais, western necropolis, burial nos. 590: Bespalyy 2016, vol. 2, 112-113, nos. 8-9; vol. 5, 64, nos. 1649-1650; vol. 11, figs. 3583-3586. – Burial no. 634/2012: Bespalyy 2016, vol. 12, figs. 3845-3846.

(**Figs. 6, 1. 1-6; 7, 6-8**)[8]. Close in date are also contexts of the burials with the finger rings bearing the portraits of Arsinoe III in the Maiotian cemeteries in the Trans-Kuban region (Tenginskaya burial ground, burial no. 140: Beglova & Erlikh 2018, 60, no. 68; 168, fig. 75, 1; 194, 1), for instance in one of the burial-mounds of Psenafa necropolis (Erlikh 2017, 17-18, no. 17; 32, fig. IV, 7). It is obvious that in most cases they date from the first, less often the second half of the 2nd century BCE, and occasionally, can also come from contexts of the 1st century BCE, judging by the find in the residence of Chrysaliskos in the Taman Peninsula (**Fig. 5, 7**), which was destroyed at the end of the third or at the beginning of the last quarter of the 1st century BCE (Lomtadze & Zhuravlev 2020, 549, 551).

Interpretation

The question of the reasons for the wide distribution of the Ptolemaic finger rings in the North Pontic region has been discussed many times, mainly in Russian-language literature. Many serious publications on this topic in Western European literature remained unknown to the authors from Russia and Ukraine, as well as to the Western European scholars – the publications on this topic by the researchers from Eastern Europe.

According to my point of view, expressed in the articles of 1982 and 1985, it is explained by the fact that the images on the rings, as well as on the coins, most likely served the purposes of political propaganda of the Ptolemies, and the rings could be presented during ceremonies at the court of the Lagids or by Ptolemaic ambassadors outside of Egypt, thus reflecting the close political contacts between Egypt and the Bosporan Kingdom (Treister 1985, 137-139) (*see here V. Atanassova*). This point of view about the connection between the distribution of rings and the political contacts of the Ptolemies with the Bosporan Kingdom was supported by some other researchers (Vinogradov 1999, 300; Avram 2007, 130, note 11; Archibald 2007, 162; Dan 2011, 218, note 45; Galbois 2018, 66, 86-87).

Other hypotheses based on the private-representative nature of such gifts associated them with the spread of Egyptian cults among a narrow circle of seafaring merchants (Neverov 1974, 112-114; Molev 1994, 101-103; Marchenko & Limberis 1997, 54-55). However, they do not correlate, in my opinion, with the fact that the Egyptian cults spread almost everywhere in the Eastern Mediterranean and the Black Sea region[9], whereas the rings were found mainly in the Cimmerian Bosporus and to less extent in Chersonesos, in spite of the fact that both in Pantikapaion and in Chersonesos there is evidence of the penetration of Egyptian cults since the middle of the 3rd century BCE (Vinogradov & Zolotarev 1999, 357-381).

---

8 Vinogradnyi-7. Burial mound no. 2/2005, plundered earthen crypt (burial no. 12) (after: Marchenko *et alii* 2007, 162-166; fig. 14-19). See also burial no. 13 of the same burial mound with comparable set of pottery (Marchenko *et alii* 2007, 166-168, fig. 21, *1-2. 5-6*).

9 For instance, in the Aegean Sea basin: Grabowski 2014, 21-41; 2020, 131-148; Glomb *et alii* 2018.

The point of view was also expressed that the finger rings found their way to the Cimmerian Bosporus with Bosporan mercenary warriors or civilians who were in the service of the Ptolemies (Boardman &Vollenweider 1978, 82; Litvinenko 1991, 12-26; Zelinskyi 2020, 10-11). In my opinion, given the fact that the Ptolemies were mostly hiring mercenaries from other parts of the ancient world, extremely rare from the Bosporus[10], this point of view is in no way consistent with the predominant distribution of bronze rings in the North Pontic area.

It is quite obvious that when explaining the reasons for such a distribution of finger rings, one should proceed from some features of the contacts of the Ptolemaic state with this particular region. In this regard, it would seem that the point of view of Ivan Ladynin (Ladynin 2007, 247-248; 2011, 245-260), who was followed by some other scholars (Zavoykin 2010, 45; Krasnodubets 2018a, 107), that the rings could be presented "as prestigious, though inexpensive representative gifts to the Bosporites connected to the grain exports as a recompense for their cooperation in providing for the bread supplies to the Ptolemaic outposts and allied cities. Judging from the role of the Bosporan kings in the bread export, one can easily guess who the beneficiaries of those gifts must have been: probably, that were the state agents taking some part in the grain export. They must have accepted the gift not as officials but personally, though their service to the Ptolemies could be rendered only from their public positions".

This hypothesis, according to Ladynin, also explains why the finger rings were brought to Olbia and Chersonesos by an attempt to achieve similar agreements on the grain trade here, or by the fact that the finger rings were brought here via the Bosporan Kingdom. I fully admit the possibility that the finger rings, the finds of which were unknown to Ladynin, could also reached the Maiotians of the Trans-Kuban region through the Bosporus. But, in my opinion, this hypothesis is not very convincing, otherwise one should recognize the unsuccessful attempts of the Ptolemies to conclude such agreements in the West Pontus or consider the finger rings found in the area of Apollonia Pontika, and even more so in the area of the Roman fortress Nove on the Danube or in the rocky sanctuary of Perperikon in the Eastern Rhodopes, as brought through the Bosporan Kingdom. Moreover, the pattern of the distribution of finger rings in the burial complexes in the Bosporus shows that they were often found in the burials that were relatively poor in terms of inventory, which in no way correlates with the alleged distribution of rings to the participants on the Bosporan export trade, i.e. *naukleroi*, the ship-owning merchantmen and grain merchants.

The beginning of the mass distribution of the finger rings in the Bosporan Kingdom roughly coincides as it has been already stressed (Treister 1985, 137; Vinogradov 1999, 300), with the visit of the ship "Isis", represented in sgraffito on the wall of the sanctuary of Aphrodite in Nymphaion (Grach 1984, 81-88; Grač 1987, 86-95, Abb. 2, Taf.

[10] E.A. Molev (1994, 100) paid attention to this.

39; Vinogradov 1999, 274-275, fig. 1; Höckmann 1999, 306-307, fig. 1, pl. 1; 2010, 348, Abb. 3, *2-3*; 359-362, Anm. 109 with bibliography; Murray 2001, 251, fig. 1; 253, fig. 2; Braund 2018, 160-177; Bricault 2020, 23-27, note 94 with bibliography; fig. 2) (*see here V. Atanassova*, fig. 8). In this case, it does not matter what type of ship it was[11]. Few doubt the nature of the ship's visit, although here too there are various kinds of assumptions, from an official state visit to an embassy with the specific purpose of introducing the cult of Isis or Arsinoe-Aphrodite here.

The dating of the graffiti from Nymphaion is determined within the framework of 250/249-240 BCE (Tokhtas'ev 2006, 419-423; 2011, 677), either a broad dating of the visit (270-245 BCE) (Bricault 2020, 25, 39) or exact – spring 254 BCE (Avram 2003, 1207-1208; 2007, 132) is assumed, the answer to which was the embassy of King Peri-sades II to Egypt in september of that year. In general, the proposed dating correlates with the archaeological dating of the complex (Grač 1987, 90; Sokolova 2004, 183).

Taking into account the fact, that among the portraits on the finger rings there prevail those of Berenice II, the queen and co-regent of Ptolemy III Eurgetes III from 246 to 222 BCE and her daughter, Arsinoe III, ruling as queen of Egypt and the wife of Ptolemy IV from 220 to 204 BCE, then, if one accept the visit of the ship Isis to the Cimmerian Bosporus in 254 BCE, the finger rings under discussion could not find the way to the Bosporan Kingdom during this event. However, it cannot be ruled out that such embassies could be sent to the North Pontic region also later during the second half of the century.

Thus, none of the hypotheses proposed so far explains with 100% certainty the concentration of finds of bronze finger rings in the North Pontic area, however, the connection between the distribution of such rings and the diplomatic contacts of the Bosporan Kingdom with Egypt that we once proposed, remains, as it seems, quite likely, of course, in the broadest sense of the word. Undoubtedly, it is difficult to imagine that an Egyptian envoy could distribute such finger rings to the court officials of the Bosporan king, but such distributions cannot be ruled out during some mass events related to the arrival of Egyptian representatives to the Bosporus, which would explain the widespread distribution of rings precisely in the "middle layers" of the Bosporan society, especially among women. However, it cannot be ruled out that with the growing fashion for such rings, they could be massively reproduced in local workshops.

Acknowledgements. I would like to express my sincere gratitude to the colleagues, who supplied me with information and illustrative materials: Mikhail Abramzon (Magnitogorsk - Moscow), Alexander Butyagin (St. Petersburg), Ivan Marchenko (Krasnodar), Nikolai Sudarev (Moscow), Olga Tugusheva (Moscow), and Michael Vickers (Tiflis).

---

[11] Trireme: Murray 2001, 254; 2002, 548; Strootman 2019, 113-114, note 4; cf. Pisarevskiy 2020, 455-471. Most likely, it was a large ship: an *oktére* or even an *enneéra* (Höckmann 2010, 361), possibly the flagship of the fleet of Ptolemy II (*SEG* xlv (1995), 997 ad (5); Vinogradov 1999, 289, 293, 297, 300; Höckmann 1999, 322-323.

Isiaca du Bosphore cimmérien

Jean-Louis Podvin

Isiaca от Кимерийския Боспор

Жан-Луи Подван

Продължавайки работата, представена в предходни изследвания, които се отнасят до южната (Троада, Понт, Витиния, Пафлагония) и западната част на Понта (южен Дунав), представяме тук преглед на материали, свързани с египетските култове от Кимерийския Боспор, за да обогатим важните за времето си научни разработки, проведени от Мария Кобилина (Kobilyna 1976) и впоследствие разширени от Лоран Брико в неговия *Атлас на разпространението на египетските култове* (Bricault 2001).

La présence de divinités isiaques sur la côte méridionale de la Mer Noire est connue et nous avons pour notre part eu l'occasion de la mettre en évidence que ce soit dans sa partie orientale, dans le secteur du Pont et de la Paphlagonie, ou occidentale, de la Troade à la Bithynie (Podvin 2012b ; Podvin 2013). Elle s'explique largement par l'existence sur place de communautés, de royaumes, de principautés marquées par la civilisation hellénistique, même si les témoignages d'époque romaine paraissent les plus nombreux. Sur la côte ouest de la mer Noire, le colloque *Egyptian Cults on the Black Sea Coast* vise à souligner leur existence[1]. Mais qu'en est-il au nord du Pont Euxin, en particulier dans le secteur du Bosphore cimmérien, dont l'actualité récente souligne une fois encore l'importance géostratégique.

Sur un plan chronologique, nous nous plaçons donc aux époques hellénistique et romaine[2]. De ce fait, il convient d'exclure la plus grande partie des objets égyptiens et égyptisants (scarabées et amulettes notamment) étudiés par B. Touraieff, retrouvés sur la côte

[1] Pour l'exemple des lampes, voir Podvin 2016.
[2] Pour un aperçu général, cf. Podosinov 2012.

où ils étaient arrivés aux siècles précédents (Touraieff 1911), à l'instar de ce qui s'est produit jusqu'à l'extrémité occidentale de la Méditerranée, sur les côtes de l'Espagne par exemple (Padró i Parcerisa 1980-1985). Il n'est cependant pas exclu qu'une partie de ces amulettes aient été importées bien après l'époque de leur production ou qu'elles aient été réutilisées dans un contexte nouveau, connaissant ainsi une sorte de seconde vie.

D'un point de vue géographique, nous étudions ici le territoire de la Crimée, celui de la péninsule de Taman en face, et le détroit de Kertch qui les sépare et permet l'accès de l'antique Pont Euxin au lac Maéotis ou Méotide, soit de l'actuelle mer Noire à la mer d'Azov. Dans son étude fondamentale, le chercheur russe M. Kobilyna a dressé un état de la présence des divinités orientales dans cet espace (Kobilyna 1978). Plus récemment, L. Bricault a complété les informations dans son *Atlas* (Bricault 2001, 48-53). Compte tenu de la difficulté pour accéder à des informations nouvelles, nous voudrions ici reprendre cette documentation, la curiosité aiguisée par la présence de petits objets particulièrement mobiles, lampes, statuettes et gemmes notamment (Podvin 2015a ; Podvin 2015b).

Quelques rares documents remontent à l'époque hellénistique. C'est le cas notamment de la fresque polychrome de *Nymphaeum*, décortiquée par L. Bricault dans son étude sur les liens entre Isis et l'élément maritime (Bricault 2006, 22-36 ; Bricault 2020, 23-27 ; voir, dans ce volume, *V. Atanassova*, fig. 8). Rappelons que sur cette fresque découverte il y a maintenant quarante ans dans une chapelle d'Aphrodite à *Nymphaeum*, à une quinzaine de kilomètres de Panticapée (Kertch), plusieurs navires sont dessinés et peints sur le stuc ; l'un, bien que portant sur le parsème l'image d'un des Dioscures avec son cheval, est inscrit du nom d'*Isis*. La question souvent posée est de savoir si ce document, daté du 2ᵉ quart du IIIᵉ s. a.C., est à mettre en relation avec une ambassade de Ptolémée II, répondant à celle du roi bosporan Parisadès II en 254, à qui Zénon, intendant du diocète Apollonios, a pu faire visiter le Fayoum dans la lointaine Égypte (Orrieux 1985, 96, d'après P Lond. 1953 ; voir Will 1979, 189). Ce navire est-il un navire militaire ou une nef consacrée à la déesse Isis qui aurait apporté des objets cultuels[3] ? Il est bien difficile d'y répondre avec certitude. L'existence de navires militaires portant le nom d'Isis est attestée à l'époque romaine, à Rome et à Misène (fin Iᵉʳ s.- IVᵉ) (*RICIS* 501/0218 ; 504/0501-3). On trouve aussi des navires de commerce nommés Isis à Phoenix en Crète (début IIᵉ s.) (*RICIS* 203/0701), à Ostie (IIᵉ-IIIᵉ s.) (*RICIS* 503/1132) et dans le célèbre récit de Lucien de Samosate (IIᵉ s.) (Lucien de Samosate, *Le navire*), mais il en existait en Égypte dès l'époque hellénistique – et sans doute avant.

[3] Bricault 2006 ; 2020, avec la bibliographie antérieure. Citons cependant Murray 2002. Bricault 2008, 55, évoque la possibilité que ce navire aurait pu transporter la statue d'Arsinoé identifiée à Isis, dont un fragment supérieur a justement été retrouvé à Panticapée (*voir ici l'article de V. Atanassova*, fig. 9). Un pendant en verre bleu de Ptolémée II et Arsinoé II a été découvert à Eupatoria, à l'ouest de la Crimée : Ladynin & Popova 2010. La reine est identifiée par l'uraeus frontal.

▲

Fig. 1.
Isis et Sarapis en buste à gauche sur une bague en bronze, Phanagoria (©Musée de l'Ermitage).

Notons qu'en face de Panticapée, de l'autre côté du détroit de Kertch, à Phanagoria, une bague en bronze, réputée d'époque hellénistique, figure les têtes conjuguées à gauche d'Isis et de Sarapis (**Fig. 1**) (Veymiers 2009, 306, V.AAA 48, pl. 4 ; Ermitage, Saint-Pétersbourg, T 1872-52).

Les graffiti mentionnés sur des poteries de Kerkenitis (IVe a.C. ?) et sur des amphores de *Chersonesos* (IIIe a.C. ?), censés se rapporter à Isis pour les premières, à Isis et Sarapis pour les secondes, sont trop partiels pour pouvoir en déduire quoi que ce soit[4]. En revanche, l'inscription « Sarapis » sur un os d'astragale trouvé à *Chersonesos* et conservé au musée de l'Ermitage pourrait se rapporter à une association isiaque de cette époque des IIIe-IIe s a.C. (**Fig. 2**)[5].

Enfin, une inscription sur un bloc de marbre réutilisé dans une citerne, ayant peut-être appartenu à un autel, trouvée à *Chersonesos* en 1993 et datée du milieu du IIIe s. a.C., évoque la dédicace d'un membre de l'élite locale : « Charmippos, fils de Prytanis, sur leur ordre, à Sarapis, à Isis, à Anubis » (*RICIS* 115/0302 et ici *V. Atanassova*, fig. 10), preuve de la présence précoce de la triade dans le port de commerce.

▸

Fig. 2.
Os d'astragale avec graffito de Sarapis, *Chersonesos* (©Musée de l'Ermitage).

[4] *RICIS* 115/0301. Ne figurent que les lettres IS ou S, ce qui est bien fragile.
[5] Musée de l'Ermitage, X. 1990-25. Il mesure 3,6 cm sur 2,4 cm. On pourrait la rapprocher des tessères de Panticapée évoquées plus loin, même si l'époque est différente, et mettre ces objets en relation avec les banquets isiaques : cf. Podvin 2014, 129.

Le bilan pour l'époque hellénistique est donc des plus réduits (Archibald 2007 ; Avram 2007). Pour autant, cela ne doit guère étonner, car les témoignages de ces époques les plus anciennes sont également réduits ailleurs dans le Pont Euxin, et ils ne deviennent plus nombreux qu'aux alentours de l'ère chrétienne. C'est à ce moment-là que des attestations de sanctuaires sont conservées dans la zone des détroits (Cios, Cyzique) mais aussi plus au nord à Tyras et, face au Bosphore, à Olbia du Pont, autre grand port au nord du Pont Euxin. De même, c'est à ce moment, dans les années qui précèdent l'ère chrétienne, que Dynamis, descendante de Mithridate VI Eupator, frappe des monnaies présentant pour les unes Sarapis en buste à droite, pour les autres un *uraeus* coiffé du *basileion* (Kobilyna 1976, 43, n° 1-2 ; Bricault, *SNRIS*, 219-220 ; Bricault 2017).

Arrivons à l'époque romaine. C'est Panticapée qui apparaît comme le principal lieu de découverte, devant le site de *Chersonesos*.

Panticapée

Une peinture (**Fig. 3**) ornant un mur d'un tombeau présente un personnage masculin barbu et un autre féminin aux longs cheveux bouclés, tous deux coiffés d'un *calathos* et tenant du bras gauche une *cornucopia*, de part et d'autre d'un autel central vers lequel ils tendent le bras droit. Il est tentant d'y voir Isis et Sarapis, ou les défunts en Isis et Sarapis (Kater-Sibbes 1973, 178, n° 901 ; Tran tam Tinh 1983, 158, *III 18 et fig. 107 ; Clerc & Leclant 1994, 679, n° 122 ; Rostovtzeff *et alii* 2003, 244-245, pl. LII). Les autres scènes de la même paroi de la tombe montrent un cavalier et ses compagnons à l'arrière, une fête funéraire à droite, et des paons buvant dans un calice à gauche, au-dessus d'une niche.

Un relief en calcaire de 53 cm sur 39 cm découvert dans le mur d'un marché aux poissons montrerait Sarapis trônant, flanqué à sa droite d'Hermès et à sa gauche d'une femme, peut-être Isis (Kater-Sibbes 1973, 178, n° 899, d'après Pharmakowsky 1912, 346-347), mais cette attribution demeure hypothétique en l'absence de photographie.

Une tête en marbre d'un homme à la chevelure et à la barbe fournies, coiffé d'un *calathos* décoré d'une branche, pourrait représenter Sarapis[6].

Plusieurs gemmes ont été découvertes à Panticapée. Les bustes conjugués d'Isis et de Sarapis apparaissent sur une bague en bronze et sur une cornaline, datées des Ier a.C-Ier p.C. (Névérov 1976, 57, n° 7-8 pl. XLVIII ; Veymiers 2009, 305, V.AAA 46-47, pl. 42). Toujours à Panticapée, Sarapis debout tenant le long sceptre, face à Isis debout et au sistre dirigé vers le bas, est attesté (Névérov 1976, 56, n° 1 pl. XLVIII ; Veymiers 2009, 322, V.ACB 9, pl. 50) sur une pâte de verre du Ier s. Plus remarquable, une bague en or

---

6 Kater-Sibbes 1973, 178, n° 900. Malheureusement, nous n'avons pas vu de photographie de ce marbre conservé au musée Pushkin de Moscou.

d'époque impériale montre Isis et Sarapis en buste de face, avec le petit Harpocrate entre eux (Névérov 1976, 56-57, n° 6 pl. XLVIII ; Veymiers 2009, 132, 325, V.BAA 9, pl. 52). Les bustes affrontés des deux mêmes divinités figurent sur une cornaline du IIe s. (Névérov 1976, 57, n° 9 ; Veymiers 2009, 322, V.AAB 15, 106, 310-311, pl. 45 ; Moscou, musée historique d'État), alors que le buste du seul Sarapis orne une cornaline et un jaspe rouge du IIe s. probablement de Panticapée (Névérov 1976, 58, n° 17 et 15 ; Veymiers 2009, 243, I.AB 110-111, pl. 13).

Les fouilles de Panticapée ont encore révélé une cornaline du Ier s. d'Isis Fortuna – en l'absence de photographie, rien ne permet d'indiquer si c'est Isis, Fortuna ou Isis-Fortuna – et une autre, de même époque, qui montre Isis debout à droite, sistre à la main gauche et long bâton ou sceptre à la droite (Névérov 1976, 56, n° 3-4 pl. XLVIII.). Toujours du Ier s., un très beau buste sur cornaline d'Isis à gauche, le chef surmonté d'un haut *basileion*, est réputé provenir de Kertch (**Fig. 4**)[7]. On ajoutera à cet ensemble un *basileion* sur un grenat serti dans une bague en or (Névérov 1976, 59, n° 19 pl. XLIX).

▲

Fig. 3.

Sarapis et Isis sur une peinture d'un tombeau, Panticapée (d'après Tran tam Tinh 1983, fig. 107).

[7] Ermitage, G414 d'après Névérov 1976, 57, n° 10 pl. XLVIII. Ce *basileion* semble réalisé en épis de blé, et le style peut être rapproché de représentations de la déesse sur les lampes de Marathon (Fotiadi, 2011, 65-77), ou des épis entre Isis et Sarapis se regardant sur des lampes (Jovanova 2020) ou des médaillons, plus tardifs (Podvin 2014).

Fig. 4.
Buste d'Isis à gauche (d'après Névérov 1976, pl XLVIII, 10).

Fig. 5.
Isis en pied à droite sur une cornaline, *Nymphaeum* (©Musée de l'Ermitage).

À quelques kilomètres au sud de Panticapée, la catacombe n° 18 de la nécropole de *Nymphaeum* a livré une bague en bronze des Ier-IIe s., avec intaille en cornaline d'Isis en pied, à droite, tenant le sistre de la main gauche et une cruche de la dextre (**Fig. 5**) (Ermitage, ННФ.74-339). Un camée du IIe s. orné du buste de Sarapis de face et une intaille en cornaline des IIe-IIIe s., décorée de la tête de Sarapis à gauche, entre le soleil et la lune, le tout au-dessus d'un aigle aux ailes éployées, proviennent de deux autres sépultures (Névérov 1976, 58, n° 12 pl. XLIX ; Veymiers 2009, I.AA 43, 215, 227, pl. 4 ; I.BB 16, 215, 271, pl. 27 ; Ermitage, P. 1879.13 et P. 1910.70).

Une tessère en os frappée du buste d'Isis et du nom de la déesse a été trouvée en 1903 en compagnie de 14 autres tessères au nom et à l'effigie d'autres divinités au nom grec dans une boîte de jeu déposée aux Ier-IIe s. dans une tombe d'enfant, à Panticapée/Kertch (Rostovtszeff 1904, p. 109, pl. III-IV ; Rostovtszeff 1905, 114 n° 14. Depuis au musée de l'Ermitage : *RICIS* 115/0501).

C'est encore Isis qui apparaîtrait sur un petit buste en bronze de fin IIe-début IIIe s.[8], que M. Kobilyna évoque en comparaison avec un autre bronze, trouvé en face, à Gorgippia (*infra*).

8 Le bronze de Panticapée est publié par Bitch 1959, 311, ill. 8, 2 ; 312 n. 89.

Une statuette creuse en terre cuite brun foncé d'Isis *lactans* datée du Ier s. est signalée dans la cité de Panticapée (h. 17,5 cm) (Kobilyna 1976, 45 n° 8 et pl. XXXVI, II,8 ; musée d'Odessa, inv. 20531). La déesse est assise sur un haut trône rectangulaire évasé, dont les deux extrémités supérieures sont relevées. La tête ornée d'une couronne végétale et surmontée d'un *basileion*, sur lequel les cornes et les épis de blé sont visibles, dépasse le haut du trône. Comme c'est souvent le cas, la déesse surélève légèrement la jambe gauche – le *scabellum* est de biais – afin de mieux accueillir de ce côté l'enfant Harpocrate qu'elle allaite. C'est une statuette du même type mais plus petite (h. 7 cm) et en argile rouge vernissée, de meilleure qualité, qui a été trouvée un peu plus loin à Olbia (Kobilyna 1976, 45 n° 9 et pl. XXXVII, II,9 ; Podvin 2011, 252, pl. 54, Itf-Hc.ap(1) ; musée d'Odessa, inv. 22166) : même si la tête fait défaut, le reste du corps permet d'y reconnaître la déesse et son fils, avec un modelé plus fin, notamment pour les plis du *chiton* et de l'*himation* ; la présence d'une anse à l'arrière permet de l'attribuer à une anse plastique de lampe, mais il n'est pas exclu que l'exemplaire de Panticapée en soit également une.

Un petit bronze d'Harpocrate fort usé (h. 5,8 cm) figure le dieu assis sur ce qui paraît être une fleur de lotus, la jambe gauche pliée, la droite allongée. Sur la tête s'élève un élément – un pschent ? – et le dieu porte l'index droit à la bouche (Kobilyna 1976, 47 n°12 et pl. XXXIX, II,12 ; musée d'Odessa, inv. 45926).

C'est encore Harpocrate qui accompagne Aphrodite sur une intéressante terre cuite cassée en trois morceaux, réputée du Ier s. (h. 18 cm). La déesse est nue, ornée d'un collier et de bracelets aux bras et aux jambes, elle remonte le bras droit vers sa chevelure tandis qu'elle pose la main gauche sur la tête du jeune dieu. Celui-ci, potelé, est dans la nudité de l'enfance, il porte l'index droit aux lèvres et tient du côté gauche une corne d'abondance. Un hermès fait le pendant d'Harpocrate (Kobilyna 1976, 48 n°16 et pl. XLI, II,16 ; Tran tam Tinh *et alii* 1988, 441, n° 399 ; musée d'Odessa, inv. 20357, 20403, 21073).

D'une autre tombe de Panticapée provient une statuette d'Harpocrate, haute de 10 cm. Cette fois, le dieu est un jeune homme, dont la nudité n'est réduite que par un manteau jeté sur les épaules. Il porte une fois encore l'index droit aux lèvres et tient du côté gauche une corne d'abondance, tout en s'appuyant négligemment sur un pilier hermaïque. L'ensemble est posé sur un socle rectangulaire. Ses inventeurs précisent qu'il est fabriqué en argile de Kertch et qu'il serait du Ier s. a.C. (Kobilyna 1976, 47 n°13 et pl. XXXIX, II,13 ; Ermitage, inv. P 1866).

Pour compléter cet ensemble, des lampes ont également été relevées. L'une, bilychne, large de 10 cm, est décorée du buste de Sarapis de face aux traits bien incisés sur une anse delta à volutes (Kobilyna 1976, 43 n°4 et pl. XXXII, II,4 ; Podvin 2011, 220, pl. 16, Sbf5. adv(3)). Elle provient d'une tombe. Dans notre étude consacrée au luminaire isiaque, nous avons identifié deux exemplaires exactement du même type, retrouvés dans le temple de Déméter à Cnide, que l'on peut dater des années 80-120 (Podvin 2011, 220, pl. 16, Sbf5.adv(1-2)).

Une lampe figurant Harpocrate seul sur le médaillon est également connue (Tran tam Tinh *et alii* 1988, n°31d ; Podvin 2011, 235 et pl. 33, Hdf.m.E(10) ; Saint-Pétersbourg, Ermitage, inv. 1729). Le dieu est nu, index droit à la bouche, corne d'abondance du côté gauche.

Face à Panticapée, de l'autre côté du détroit de Kertch

À proximité, mais, à Cepi, a été relevée une statuette d'Harpocrate en terre cuite du Ier s. (Kobilyna 1976, 47 n° 14 et pl. XL, II,14 ; Tran tam Tinh *et alii* 1988, 423, n° 103e). Fragmentaire, elle a perdu les jambes à partir des genoux et la tête ce qui ne permet pas de savoir ce qui la couronnait. Cependant, la nudité, le déhanché et le bras droit replié vers le visage alors que le gauche enserre un pilier ou une corde d'abondance, le rattachent sans ambiguïté à l'iconographie du dieu enfant, bien attestée en Égypte comme hors d'Égypte, notamment en Asie Mineure (Podvin 2015, 213-215).

À Gorgippia (Anapa), c'est un buste d'Isis, bronze de 9 cm sur lequel la déesse est identifiable par son haut *basileion* aux cornes bien marquées qui a été découvert (Kobilyna 1976, 46, n° 10, pl. XXXVII, II,10 ; Tran tam Tinh 1990, 770, n°116, qui évoque Derksen & Vermaseren 1984, 432, pl. 76,7 ; Saint-Pétersbourg, Ermitage) ; une guirlande florale court en biais depuis l'épaule gauche[9] ; le buste est posé sur un globe, une caractéristique que l'on retrouve aussi bien avec la déesse qu'avec Sarapis et qui leur confère un aspect de *kosmokrator*[10].

Chersonesos

Un vase miniature en terre cuite trouvé à Chersonesos présente le dieu enfant à la coiffure florale, surmontée d'un large *calathos*, la main droite ramenée au visage. Cette fois, il est assis en amazone, la jambe gauche repliée, la droite en partie étirée, et il chevauche un animal dont il enserre la tête du bras gauche (Kobilyna 1976, 48, n°15 et pl. XL, II,15). Il serait du Ier s. a.C.

Le musée archéologique d'Odessa conserve une belle statuette de Sarapis trônant, en pierre (marbre ?), sur laquelle nous n'avons pas d'informations précise sinon qu'elle provient de la Chersonèse taurique (**Fig. 6**) (Reinach 1908, 19, n° 5 ; Kater-Sibbes 1973, 91, n° 504). Le dieu à la barbe et à la chevelure abondantes (mèches sur le front) est coiffé d'un très haut *calathos* fort évasé, qui dépasse la pointe triangulaire centrale du trône.

---

9 Voir par exemple Bricault & Podvin 2008, 20-21.

10 Par exemple Podvin 2011, 44, 58.

Fig. 6.

Statue en pierre figurant Sarapis trônant, Chersonèse (©Musée d'Odessa).

Même si les bras sont cassés, le gauche était relevé et tenait vraisemblablement le sceptre, alors que le droit était abaissé. La jambe gauche est un peu plus haute que la droite, ce qui laisse supposer l'existence du traditionnel *scabellum*, lui aussi cassé. Les plis du *chiton* et de l'*himation* sont soigneusement travaillés.

Une série de lampes à motifs isiaques a été découverte à *Chersonesos*. Un premier exemplaire concerne la triade Isis, Anubis, Harpocrate. Harpocrate, nu, tient la *cornucopia* du côté gauche ; Isis porte le *chiton* et l'*himation* ; Anubis, vêtu de la chlamyde, tient une palme du côté gauche. Son style maladroit (**Fig. 7**) témoigne de manière évidente d'une copie d'un modèle par ailleurs bien connu en Occident, puisque son origine est campanienne (Waldhauer 1914, 49, n° 315, pl. XXXIII ; Kobilyna 1976, 46-47 n°11 et pl. XXXVIII, II,11 ; Podvin 2011, 256, pl. 58, Hdf-Idf-Adg1.m.C(1) ; Podvin 2012a, 298).

Fig. 7.

Lampe ornée de la triade Harpocrate, Isis, Anubis, *Chersonesos* (d'après Kobilyna 1976, pl. XXXVIII, II,11).

Une autre lampe mais plus fruste est décorée sur le médaillon du buste de Sarapis posé sur une corolle de fleurs (Kobilyna 1976, 43 n°3 et pl. XXXII, II,3 ; Podvin 2011, 142-143, 216 et pl. 10, Sbf4b.m(3) ; musée de Chersonesos, inv. 1584), selon un type attesté en Orient par trois autres exemplaires du IIe s. (deux à Éphèse, un à Sidi Khrebish). Elle est conservée au musée local (d. 5,7).

Sarapis, en buste à gauche cette fois, apparaît enfin sur le médaillon d'une lampe de la seconde moitié du IIe s. (L. 8,1) (Chrzanovski & Zhuravlev 1998, 101-102 ; Podvin 2011, 142-143, 223, pl. 20, Sbg2a.m(1) ; musée historique de Moscou, inv. 33081). Le décor est de bonne qualité.

Sarapis debout sur une estrade limitée par deux défenses d'éléphant, bras droit levé en signe de salut, bras gauche tenant le sceptre, flanqué de deux serpents, avec Harpocrate dans le coin inférieur droit, figure sur trois lampes locales (Waldhauer 1914, 49, n° 312, pl. XXXIII ; Kobilyna 1976, 44 n°6 et pl. XXXIV, II,6 ; Tran tam Tinh 1983, 179-180, IVB 14-16 et fig. 141-142 ; Kater-Sibbes 1973, 898 ; Clerc & Leclant 1994, n°49d-f ; Podvin 2011, 260 et pl. 62, ITdd-Sdf-SAdg- Hdg(1-3), *voir ici V. Atanassova*, fig.21). Il s'agit ici d'un modèle typiquement oriental, que l'on retrouve aussi à Sardes et à Athènes. Une de ces lampes porte la marque d'un fabricant, Markou, et a été trouvée dans une sépulture. Ces modèles sont plutôt tardifs (IIIe s.).

On retiendra enfin deux intailles en cornaline de Sarapis du IIe s. La première montre le buste de Sarapis à gauche (Névérov 1976, 58, n° 16 ; Veymiers 2009, 322, I.AB 112, 243-244), et la seconde, plus complexe, figure celui de Sarapis-Ammon-Hélios radié à gauche, coiffé d'un haut *calathos* orné de feuillages et les tempes flanquées de grandes cornes enroulées de bélier (Veymiers 2009, 209, 361, VI.EAA 13, pl. 67).

Une intaille en jaspe des IIe-IIIe s., insérée dans une bague en argent, montre le buste d'Harpocrate adolescent à gauche, un pschent réalisé maladroitement posé sur la tête, index droit vers la bouche, une corne d'abondance derrière lui et une étoile devant lui[11].

Ce rapide inventaire – sans aucun doute incomplet car l'accès à la documentation, déjà compliqué, l'est devenu davantage avec la conjoncture actuelle, où il est impossible de contacter les musées du secteur – nous invite à avancer plusieurs remarques.

Les documents les plus nombreux sont d'époque romaine, c'est-à-dire au moment où les Romains contrôlent cet espace (mi Ier s. a.C. – mi IVe s. p.C.), et cette diffusion paraît donc liée à leur présence ou à leur protectorat, ainsi qu'au commerce actif que le Bosphore assurait avec la Méditerranée et l'Asie Mineure.

[11] Névérov 1976, 58, n° 18 pl. XLIX ; Ermitage, Ch. 1908.24. Une intaille en onyx du même type a été découverte à l'autre extrémité de la Méditerranée, près de Segobriva, en Tarraconaise : Fernández 2006, 259-270.

On ne dispose pas d'élément probant attestant l'existence de sanctuaires dédiés aux divinités isiaques dans le Bosphore cimmérien, alors que des sanctuaires de Zeus, Apollon, Artémis, Aphrodite, Asclépios, Déméter, Arès, Héraclès existent à Panticapée. Cela peut bien entendu être dû au hasard des découvertes, mais on n'oubliera pas qu'il est de même sur la rive méridionale du Pont Euxin, alors que les choses sont quelque peu différentes sur la côte occidentale.

Plusieurs des petites pièces découvertes sur place témoignent d'une volonté de produire localement des artéfacts isiaques. On le voit par exemple pour les terres cuites, mais aussi pour des luminaires. Or, si l'on décide de produire de tels objets localement, c'est parce que cela correspond à des demandes, à des besoins, nous dirions aujourd'hui à un marché. Cette clientèle ne paraît pas être d'une grande exigence, peut-être parce que ses connaissances sur ces divinités ne sont pas d'une grande précision, à moins qu'il ne faille incriminer celle des artistes ou des artisans locaux. Cela semble aussi indiquer que l'on se trouve aux extrémités du monde romain.

Le contexte funéraire doit être enfin souligné. Il est régulièrement mentionné, comme c'est le cas dans d'autres espaces[12], en Afrique notamment, et privilégie Sarapis. Cette prévalence de Sarapis dans la documentation peut être mise en relation avec les réseaux d'échanges en mer Noire, qui relie, entre autres, Sinope à Panticapée (Dan 2009). Or, Sinope a été, sans doute à l'époque flavienne, un espace de diffusion de la religiosité sarapiaque. On n'oubliera pas qu'à l'échelle méditerranéenne, Sarapis est également plus présent qu'Isis dans les inscriptions, mais aussi sur certains supports iconographiques (les lampes par exemple) (Podvin 2011, 144-146).

[12] Mais pas dans d'autres, comme à Tarse : Picaud & Podvin 2011.

Isis and Serapis in Ancient Colchis in the Greco-Roman period

Natia Phiphia

Изида и Сарапис в Древна Колхида през гръко-римската епоха

Натия Фифия

Колхида е достатъчно отдалечена територия, за да бъде пряко повлияна от Египет. Въпреки това активните отношения между колхите и понтийските гърци, както и римското присъствие в източното Черноморие все пак оставят своите следи. Няма съмнение, че в Древна Колхида култът към двете египетски божества Изида и Сарапис може да бъде проследен. Атрибутите на Изида са изобразени върху така наречените „Анонимни медни монети, сечени във Вани (?)". Тези монети изглежда са емитирани от Митридат Младши, син на Митридат Евпатор, вероятно докато е бил владетел на Колхида в началото на 1 век пр.Хр. Друго сериозно доказателство идва от римско време – култът към Сарапис е засвидетелстван в римската крепост Апсарус (съвременен Гонио) и в Уреки. Дали египетските култове са били почитани на местно ниво или са били основно свързани с чуждестранни жители, които не са живели тук постоянно? Това е въпрос от голямо значение, който всъщност съдържа няколко други въпроса: каква е степента на тяхното почитане, по какъв начин са се разпространили в Колхида и какъв е бил социалният статут на населението, което ги е почитало. Докладът е опит да се отговори на тези въпроси.

Georgia in antiquity was divided into two economic-geographic regions and two states existed here – Colchis and Iberia (**Fig. 1**). Both regions were heavily affected by surrounding civilizations. Colchian pagan pantheon was a recipient of substantial outside influence and the local cults also influenced the Greeks living here – the merge of outside and local elements characteristic to similar cults is vivid on the artifacts.

Fig. 1.
Map of ancient Georgia.

First we will make a general overview of the pre-Christian, pagan beliefs in Colchis in Hellenistic Age and in Roman era in order to understand to what extent Egyptian cults were popular in Colchis. The Greek colonists starting from the 6th cent. BCE brought the Greek cults, for example the cult of Apollo (*SEG* XLI (1991):1421, 1; Kaukhchishvili 2019, 235; Dundua *et al.* 2013, 150-156), Artemis (Zos. 1.32.3; Dundua *et al.* 2013, 150-156), Hecate (Dundua *et al.* 2013, 155). Later the Greco-Roman influence can be traced in the worship of Hermes-Mercury near Dioscurias (Kaukhchishvili 2009, 77). On the other hand, locals worshipped astral deities too – the Sun and the Moon alongside with the Earth – Vani decree is a clear evidence of it (Kaukhchishvili 1987; Kaukhchishvili 2009, 150; Vinogradov 1997, 583). Local inclination towards synthesis of the similar cults is vividly illustrated in the hermaphrodite nature of astral deities. Symbols of Apollo, like lion on Phasian coinage is hermaphrodite (Dundua *et al.* 2013, 150-156), while symbols associated with the Moon god, also have synthesis of male and female moon gods (Dundua *et al.* 2013, 155). Colchians believed that the Sun was female deity while the Moon was male unlike the Greeks, who believed otherwise. The hermaphrodite nature of the elements of astral deities served as a solution to the problem of discrepancies between the beliefs of the locals and the migrants – the Greeks who struck the coins found the way to meet the local taste.

Now we will discuss in details what we know on an empiric level about Egyptian cults and then analysis will follow.

The artifacts

1. The *basileion* of Isis on anonymous coins found in Vani (ancient Surion)

In 1967, during Vani archaeological excavations, a hoard of coins was discovered close to the altar of the temple. It was inside a broken Colchian wine vessel (*kvevri*). The soil was fully black with the signs of fire. Mosaic stones, iron nail, fragments of Colchian amphora were discovered here also (Khoshtaria *et al.* 1972, 177). The hoard consisted of 119 coins and almost all of them – except one were identical (Dundua *et al.* 2013, 258). The different coin was struck in Amisus in 111-105 BCE or in 105-90 BCE and this gave the scholars possibility to date the other coins (Dundua *et al.* 2013, 258). The coins from Vani hoard are considered to be unique (Dundua *et al.* 2013, 258-259). Two other samples of such coins are known from archaeological excavations, one was found in Eshera, near ancient Dioscurias (modern Sokhumi) and another one in Tsebelda, 35 km. from Sokhumi (Lordkipanidze 2001, 99).The description of the coins is as follows (**Fig. 2**):

Obv.: basileion of Isis or styled effigy of lotus (see discussion below)
Rv.: Eight-pointed star

Fig. 2.
Anonymous coins from Vani with the *basileion* of Isis.

1.2. A statuette of Serapis from Apsaros

An artifact connected with the cult of Serapis is a small bronze statuette found in Gonio-Apsarosi (**Fig. 3**) (Kakhidze *et al.* 2002). The artifact was unearthed near the south gates of the fortress in a well-dated archaeological layer and belongs to the 3rd cent. CE (Mshvildaze & Mamuladze 2009, 69). The description of the artifact is as follows: Serapis has a long beard, *calathos*, *himation* on his shoulders.

Fig. 3.
Statuette of Serapis from Apsaros (Gonio).

▲

Fig. 4.

Serapis on an intaglio from Ureki.

1.3- Serapis on an intaglio from Ureki

In 1942 a hoard of different types of artifacts – jewelry, coins, beads – was found in Ureki (Western Georgia, 20 km. south of Phasis/Photi). The hoard was dated by an archaeologist Andria Apakidze back to the 3rd-4th cent. CE (Apakidze 1947, 110). One silver ring was found among the artifacts of Ureki hoard which has the depiction of Serapis (**Fig. 4**). A. Apakidze described the artifact as follows: The ring is oval, with gallery, and nicolo/onyx stone is inside the gallery. Nicolo/onyx stone has the polished depiction of Serapis, right, crescent is around his neck and some necklace in a form of a star, he also has a long and curled hair, twisted beard, moustache and some clothes on his shoulders (Apakidze 1947, 104). There is no preciseness in Apakidze's description of Serapis's image. Serapis is in profile, left, with thick twisted beard, *calathos* and *himation* on his shoulders.

1.4. Municipal copper coins of Trapezus

Municipal copper coins of Trapezus also reveal the cult of Serapis. Trapezus in the Roman Era was populated by or was directly neighbouring Colchians and is considered to be the part of historical Colchis (Melikishvili 1970, 273; Pipia 2011), therefore effigy of Serapis on these coins serves as an evidence for the study of pagan pantheon of Colchis.

Today up to 350 samples of these coins were found. Majority of them are discovered on the territory of historical Colchis. Obverse of these coins usually have the effigy of different roman emperors, while the reverse shows the depiction of different gods – "Mithras, the god of the Sun and light, is portrayed on the reverse of 210-220 coins out of 340-350 samples, Tyche – on 50-55 samples, Dionysus – on 17 samples, Serapis – on 12 samples, Abundantia – on 12 samples, Apollo – on 6 samples, Hermes – on 2 samples, Hercules – on 1 sample, Rhea Cybele – on 1 sample, Pales – on 1 sample" (Dundua *et al.* 2015, 10).

Analysis

The description of copper coins from Vani needs clarification. N. Khoshtaria, O. Lordkipanidze and R. Puturidze first published the information about the discovery in 1972 but they did not specify the description (Khoshtaria *et al.* 1972). Later, G. Dundua and O. Lordkipanidze insisted on the idea that the obverse of these coins have an image of "head-dress of Isis, a stylized lotus" (Dundua & Lodkipanidze 1979, 4), and later T. Dundua agreed with them. They all also connected the image on the reverse with the symbol of Mithridatic dynasty (Dundua *et al.* 2013, 257). Additionally, G. Lordkipanidze also agreed with them (Lordkipanidze 2001, 96). However, such image appears on different coins connected with the cult of Isis and is specified as *basileion* of Isis (Bricault 2008, 16-17), as for specifically the coins from Vani, R. Veymiers also identified the image on the obverse of the coins as a *basileion* of Isis (Veymiers 2014, 216).

Historical circumstances how the symbol of Isis appeared in Colchis was also addressed by scholars. The copper coins found in Vani are anonymous emission and it is strongly believed among Georgian scholars, that they are the result of the collisions between the King of Pontus – Mithridates VI (120-63 BCE) and his son Mithridates Junior, whom he appointed as a ruler of Colchis on the demand of Colchians and later jailed him (App. Mith. 9.64). This should have happened in 85 BCE (Dundua & Lodkipanidze 1979, 3; Dundua 1996). It seems, Mithridates did not trust his own son completely, possibly soon became suspicious about his involvement in Colchian rebellion and soon got rid of him. Appian's full account of the event is the following:

> "Mithridates, after his return to Pontus, went to war with the Colchians and the tribes around the Cimmerian Bosporus who had revolted from him. The Colchians asked him to give them his son, Mithridates, as their ruler, and when he did so they at once returned to their allegiance. The king suspected that this was brought about by his son through his own ambition to be king. Accordingly, he sent for him and first bound him with golden fetters, and soon afterward put him to death, although he had served him well in Asia in the battles with Fimbria."
>
> (App. *Mith.* 9.64).

As for the possibility whether Colchians worshipped Egyptian cults or not, initially, in 1978 E. Pokhitonov expressed his opinion about it and believed that such reality is not expected in Ancient Colchis, which was later rejected by G. Lodkipanidze (Lordkipanidze 2001, 99) and M. Mshvildadze in her doctoral thesis (Mshvildadze 2002, 39). G. Lordkipanidze suggested the connection between ithyphallic iron statues found in Vani (2nd-1st cent. BCE) with the mysteries connected with the cult of Isis and Osiris (Lordkipanidze 2001, 96), so the cult of Isis for him seemed to be spread among the population living around Vani, the city of temples, while M. Mshvildadze pointed out that cult of Isis syncretized with the previously established cults in Colchis which were associated with fertility, specifically, with Demeter, Hecate, Rhea-Cybele, Phasian goddess seen by Arrian in Phasis and "Great Mother of Gods" worshipped in western Georgia (Mshvildadze 2002, 39-40).

R. Veymiers pointed out that the appearance of artifacts connected with the cult of Isis, specifically, coins from Vani was not a result of direct contacts of Colchis with Alexandria, Egypt. He assumed, that the iconography appeared as a result of commercial contacts of Colchis with the Aegean world (Veymiers 2014, 216). We agree that it is not a result of direct contacts with Egypt, however, one aspect should be pointed out – direct commercial contacts of Aegean world with Colchis declined after 4th cent. BCE, Sinope played more important role as a mediator between Aegean world and Colchis (Phiphia 2014, 66-67). On the eve of Mithridatic wars there is a crisis in Colchis, no foreign coins are discovered here and they started to reappear only after the reign of Mithridates VI of Pontus and till the end of his wars, are always connected with him, therefore, if we see any new foreign influence in Colchis at this point, it should be connected with the kingdom of Pontus. In fact, this is an additional argument to the claim that these coins are connected to Mithridates Junior and his father.

One more aspect should be addressed too. On the reverse of some samples of coins from Vani, the image of wheat as a part of *basileion* may be distinguished, which should not be very unusual since we are dealing with the cult connected with fertility and agriculture. We definitely know that wheat was not a popular crop in western Georgia, however the remains of wheat are discovered in Vani and they are dated back to the late Hellenistic Age (Bokeria *et al.* 2009, 144). This is a rare case and an interesting coincidence with the context of the rebellion of Mihtridates Junior. Why did the Colchians demand him as a ruler? Could it be tentatively suggested that he introduced some new crops to the locals which could "boost" agricultural output, at least for a while and the Colchians supported him? Perhaps, Mithridates Junior may have introduced new crops alongside with new elements of the goddess of fertility and agriculture to raise his legitimacy and increase his support among Colchians – his ambitions seem to be a contributing factor. Wheat is not found in archaeological layers of Western Georgia neither before 2nd – 1st cent.

BCE nor after it, which may serve as an additional argument to argue that Mithridates the Junior could have tried to bring some novelties in local agriculture. Additionally, it should be noted, that the discovery of wheat is very unusual and rare in western Georgia, including Vani, usually millet was used as a sacrifice grain in the city of temples. This again seems to support the idea that production of wheat was quite ephemeral in Western Georgia, unlike the Eastern Georgia, where it was abundant.

The cult of Serapis can be traced in Ancient Colchis exclusively during the Roman Era. Unlike the cult of Isis whose worship seemed to have been institutionalized and having to serve the purpose to increase the legitimacy of the ruler – Mithridates Junior, the spread of the cult of Serapis seems to have more different form. The evidences are not enough to argue its widespread worship, especially among the local population, however still they suggest different situation about it.

The image of Serapis from Ureki hoard is more closely related to four samples published in R. Veymiers' catalogue, specifically to I.AB 26, I AB 28, I AB 31, I.AB 132, more closely to the latter (Veymiers 2009, 236-236, 246). Also, even more similarity we can find with two other samples published by the same scholar, specifically to I.AB 323 and I.AB 349 (Veymiers 2011, 247, 249). They are dated back to 1st, 2nd or 3rd cent. CE. The last two samples, which reveal more similarity with Ureki one, are dated back to 2nd-3rd cent. CE (Veymiers 2009, 236-236, 246) which is aligned with A. Apakidze's dating of the artifact and the whole hoard. A. Apakidze connected the other elements of the hoard stylistically to the materials of Armazi and Samtavro (Eastern Georgia) and gave more broad dating of the other artifacts in the hoard – 3rd-5th cent. CE. (Apakidze 1947, 104), however, since some artifacts, specifically, a golden coin of Claudius Tacitus (275-276 CE) gave him a chance to suggest more precise date and chronology of the silver ring with Serapis, he limited the date to 3rd-4th cent CE. He believed that the hoard could be the part of a burial (Apakidze 1947, 104), however, no remains of bones were discovered there. Although, it is widely known that humidity in the Western Georgia, especially in coastal line prevents bones to survive. Good illustration of this is Pichvnari cemetery, located 15 km. away from Ureki, here among several hundreds of Greek and Colchian burials almost none had the bones preserved (Kakhidze 2004). However, A. Apakidze believed that ashes were buried in Ureki burial (Apakidze 1947).

For the interpretation of these material and the understanding of the spread of Serapis' cult, we should take into consideration the context in which they were found. A. Apakidze indicated on one interesting fact – the Ureki hoard consisted of golden jewelry, the absolute majority of the artifacts stylistically are closely related to the discoveries from Iberia, specifically, to materials found in Armazi and Samtavro (Apakidze 1947, 104), thus hinting on the local mastery. This would suggest that locals worshipped Serapis. The burial does not seem to be connected with the Romans – the place of its discovery is not located near any of the places where roman garrison stood – neither Gonio, nor Phasis, not to mention Dioscurias and Pytius, are located very close, thus the ring from Ureki hoard with the depiction of Serapis may belong to the locals, rather than to Roman soldiers.

M. Mshvildadze and Sh. Mamuladze emphasized that Serapis from Ureki hoard should have cosmic characteristics, since he is depicted with astral elements – star and crescent. The authors also believe that this is a manifestation of Serapis whose cult is merged with the cult of Men – the moon god (Mshvildaze & Mamuladze 2009, 68). Astral attributes of Serapis from Ureki could be a reflection of a local religion – Vani decree reveals the worship of astral deities (Kaukhchishvili 1987; Kaukhchishvili 2009, 150).

Unlike the ring with the image of Serapis from Ureki, the artefact found in Gonio cannot argue the spread of the cult among the locals, it definitely should reflect the religious views of a roman soldier who was stationed here. The specific legion which served in Gonio in the 3rd cent. CE was *legio XV Appolinaris*. The soldiers of this legions are considered to be influenced by oriental cults, especially by Mithraism. One Carnuntine gravestone dated back to the first half of the 1st cent. CE and which belongs to a certain C. Pedusius, a veteran of the *Apollinaris*, displays a half-moon and stars, which is considered to be the Mithraic symbolism (Wheeler 2000, 279), however since crescent and star is depicted with Serapis on a ring from Ureki hoard, it seems, this symbol can be connected with Serapis as well.

The statuette of Serapis from Gonio is believed to reveal the similarity with the effigy of Serapis on municipal copper coins of Trapezus (Mshvildaze & Mamuladze 2009, 70).

Since Trapezus is considered to be the part of historical Colchis the evidences from this territory also should be taken into account for the understanding of the religion of Colchians. This region seems to be more influenced by the cult of Serapis. 12 samples of municipal copper coins from Trapezus have Serapis on reverse. However, Serapis was worshipped among other gods and was of lesser importance than Mithras. The relative statistics of the images of gods on the reverse of Trapezuntine coins vividly illustrate the prevalence of the cult of Mithras, however, Serapis is also present. Both cults, Mithras and Serapis should be considered as a part of roman influence, however the local taste also seems to be taken into account while designing the coins.

Trapezus was identified as a Greek city by Arrian in the middle of the 2nd cent. CE, Colchians were the immediate neighbors of Trapezuntines (Arr. *Perip*. 11). The image of Mithras on Trapezuntine coins is stylistically connected with different gems found in Iberia and Colchis (Dundua *et al.* 2015, 173-174). The cult of Mithras later merged with the worship of Saint George and the evidences about the worship of "Jege/Jgege-Misaroni" described by S. Makalatia are connected with this syncretization (Makalatia 1938).

The scholar firmly established the idea of the popularity of cult of Mithras in Ancient Colchis and all Georgian scholars later shared this opinion. Also, it should be noted that very few samples of Municipal copper coins of Trapezus were discovered before the excavations of Bichvnita and Sokhumi, which proved to be a strong argument to percept Trapezus as a part of Colchian realm (Dundua *et al.* 2015, 175-176). Thus, the cult worshipped in Trapezus, including Serapis is a part of a Colchian history and municipal copper coins of Trapezus serve as evidence to prove the popularity of the cult of Serapis in Colchis.

Conclusion

Greco-Roman civilization brought Egyptian cults in Colchis – cult of Serapis and Isis. While the cult of Isis was popular at the end of the Hellenistic Age possibly only among the elites of Colchian society, Serapis is known exclusively from the Roman era. If the emission of anonymous copper coins struck in Vani is associated with Mithridates Junior, we may tentatively argue that he brought the cult of Isis here and institutionalized it, however it is hard to say to what extent it was popular among lower classes of Colchis. On the other hand, the cult of Serapis seems to be more popular – while one artifact from Gonio can be connected to Roman soldiers, other evidences seems to be connected with the locals and since Colchis is considered to be quite wide territory at this point and not only modern western Georgia, Trapezuntine coins seems to be connected with Colchian history and reveal worship of Serapis.

Recently Discovered Hellenistic Dedication to Serapis, Isis and Anubis from Odessos[1]

Vassil Tenekedjiev

Новооткрит елинистически надпис посвещение на Серапис, Изида и Анубис от Одесос

Васил Тенекеджиев

През 2021 г. в античния град Одесос (днешна Варна), разположен на Българското Черноморие, беше открит блок във формата на ара с надпис. Той е бил използван като сполиум в градежа на ранновизантийска сграда. Блокът е с ширина 20 см, дължина 27 см и височина 43 см. Върху горната му страна има пет отвора за метални щифтове, като в даден момент тя е била преработена. Надписът съдържа посвещение на три египетски божества от елинистическата епоха: Серапис, Изида и Анубис. Посвещението е направено от религиозна група от Одесос наречена „декатисти" и в него се споменава за все още неизвестно светилище на същите богове в града. Първият превод на надписа е на епиграфа д-р Николай Шаранков. Той датира посвещението в края на 3 или първата половина на 2 в. пр. Хр., като отбелязва, че това е едно от най-ранните свидетелства за култа към египетските божества в района на Западния Понт, както и най-старото епиграфско сведение за него от територията на България.

On the 5th of July 2021, a rare archaeological discovery was made in the ancient city of Odessos (today's Varna) on the Bulgarian Black Sea coast. The find was a marble *ara*-like block with a Greek inscription on it – a dedication to three Egyptian deities from the Hellenistic Age: Serapis, Isis, and Anubis. The artefact was found during a rescue

[1] I would like to thank cordially Dr Nikolay Sharankov from Sofia University St. Kliment Ohridski for the translation and the interpretation of the text. Without his consultation, this publication would have been impossible.

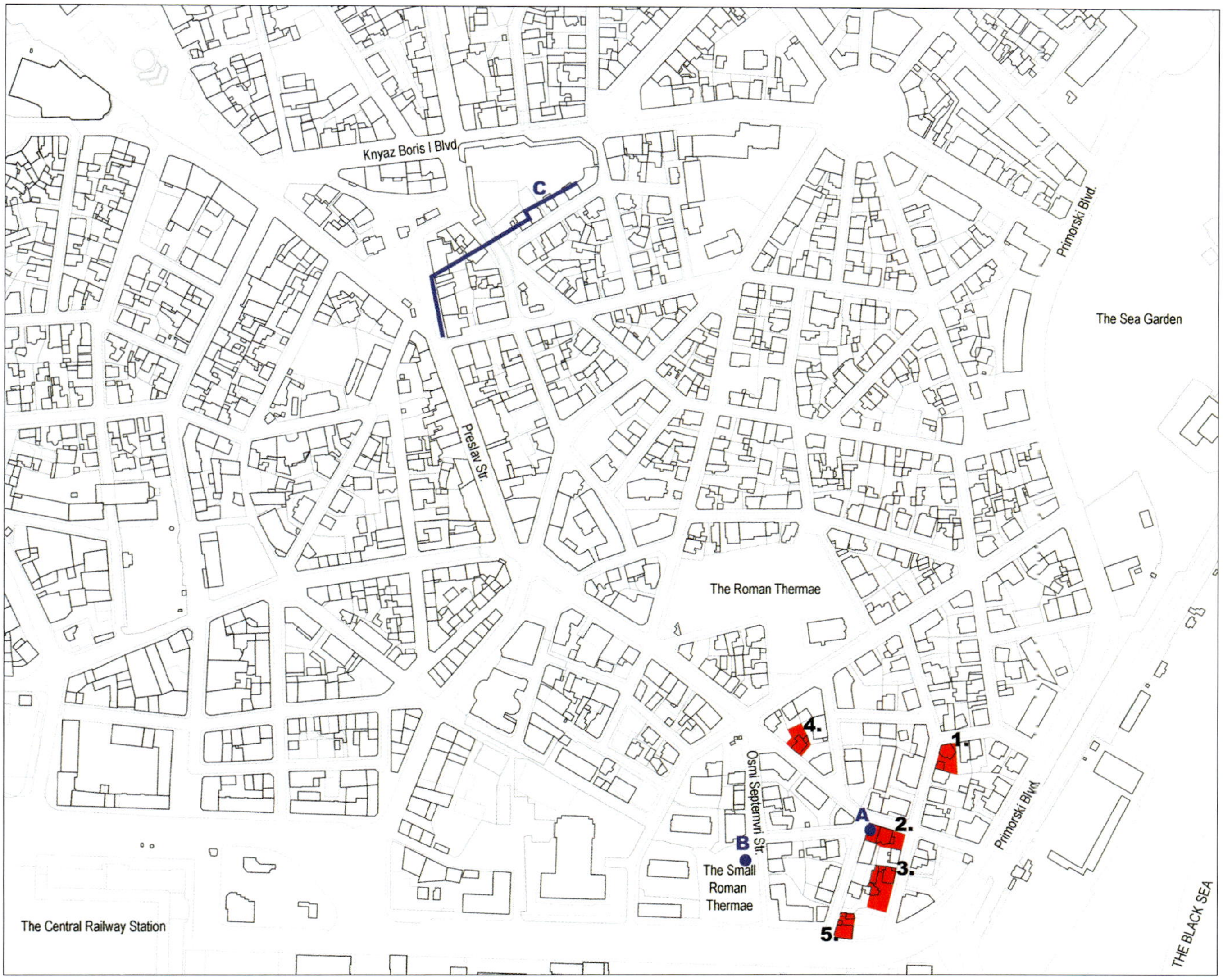

Fig.1.

Map of the old part of Varna with the location of the sites mentioned in the article (Author: Vassil Tenekedjiev)

A. The Temple at the corner of (36) San Stefano and Chernorizets Hrabar Streets

B. The Temple of Heros Karabasmos and Phosphoros

C. Hypothetical reconstruction of a part of the Hellenistic wall of Odessos based on several preserved sections.

1. 18 Tsar Ivan Shishman Str.
2. 36 San Stefano Str.
3. 3-5 Tsar Ivan Shishman Str.
4. 25 San Stefano Str.
5. 21 Primorski Blvd.

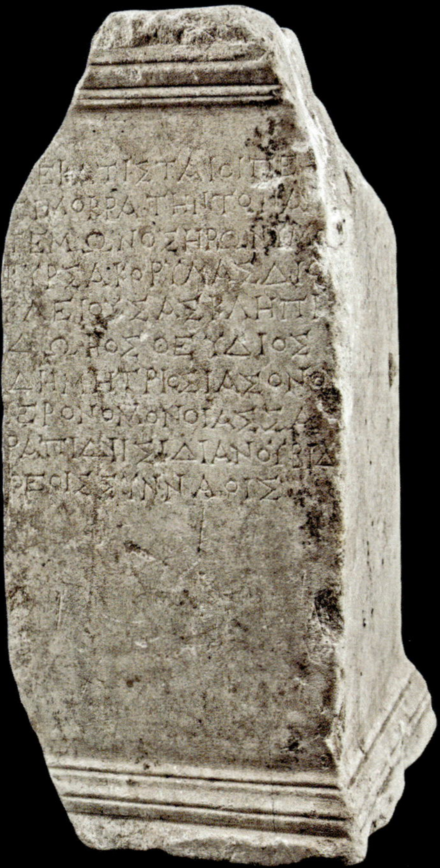

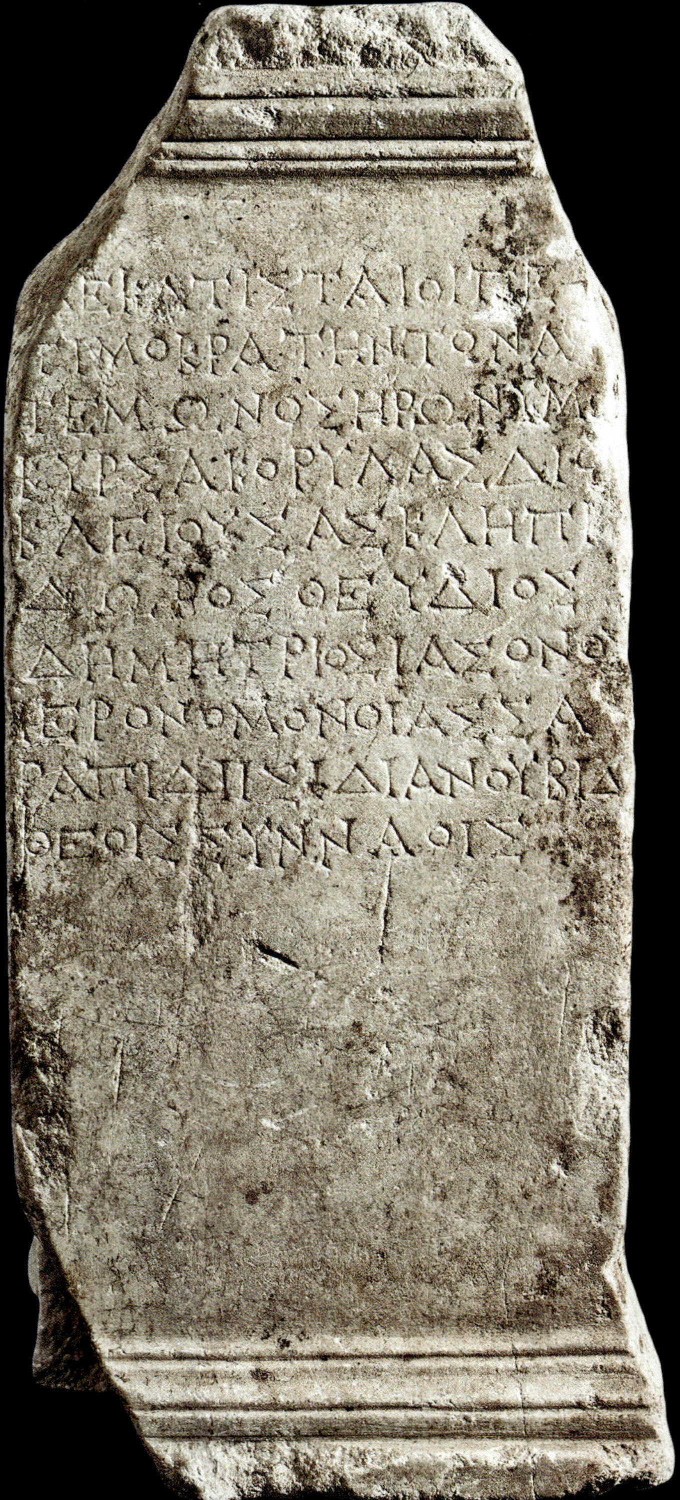

▲

Fig. 2.

The marble block with the dedication (Photograph: Rumyana Kostadinova).

▶

Fig. 3.

The marble block with the dedication: the front side (Photograph: Rumyana Kostadinova).

excavation conducted by the Department of Archaeology of Varna Regional Museum of History, and led by the author. The site was at 18 Tsar Ivan Shishman Street, which is situated in the south-eastern corner of Ancient City of Odessos-Varna Archaeological Reserve (Tenekedjiev 2022, 40-41 and here **Fig. 1**)

Description

Upon discovery the block was almost entirely preserved and in good condition (**Fig. 2-6**). Only small pieces from the bottom and the top edges have been chopped out. It has a rectangular shape with simple decorative profiles at the base and at the top. The dimensions of the block are 20 cm wide, 27 cm long and 43 cm high. The piece is made of fine light grey marble, and the quality of the work reveals a high level of craftsmanship. The inscription is engraved on one of the narrow vertical sides of the block, which therefore could be considered as the front side. All four vertical sides including the profiles were well smoothed during production. Perhaps in its original state the surface was polished, but having being buried underground for centuries, the block has now lost its polished appearance. The top and bottom sides are flat, and only roughly worked with a chisel.

Fig. 4.
The marble block with the dedication: the back side (Photograph: Rumyana Kostadinova).

Fig. 5.
The marble block with the dedication: the left side (Photograph: Rumyana Kostadinova).

Fig. 6.
The marble block with the dedication: the right side (Photograph: Rumyana Kostadinova).

The top of the block shows traces of later remodelling. The upper parts of the two lateral vertical sides were chopped symmetrically (but not very carefully) at some point, thus reducing the top side to a narrow irregular strip (ca. 13 cm wide). Five approximately rectangular holes for metal joints were made in it (**Fig. 7**). Their dimensions are: 1st hole (from the front) 3 x 2 cm, 2nd hole 2.4 x 1.6 cm, 3rd hole 3.2 x 2 x 3.1 cm, 4th hole 1.2 x 1.8 x 2.9 cm, 5th hole 2 x 3.8 x 3.5 cm. The depth of the first two holes cannot be measured because there are remains of lead inside. The five holes are not in a line. Nos. 1, 3 and 5 are closer to the left edge of the strip, and the other two – to the right. Distance between the holes is as follows: 3.3 cm, 1.8 cm, 1.8 cm, 3.3 cm, and 1.5 cm. Nos. 4 and 5 are partly damaged, maybe (although not certainly) this occurred when the top of the block was reworked. It is difficult to determine when the holes were made. At least three options could be proposed. All the holes could belong to the original design of the block; some of the holes could be from the original design, and the others could be added later, or all the holes could be connected with the remodelling of the artefact. The last option is hardly credible because of the damage to holes 4 and 5.

The inscription roughly occupies the upper half of the front side, starting at 2.6 cm under the top profile, and leaving an empty field (24.3 cm high) underneath. The text consists of ten lines filling the space from edge to edge, except for the bottom line which is 3 cm shorter. The letters are carefully engraved, and with a height which varies for different letters, between 0.8 and 1.4 cm. The inscription is almost completely preserved, with only a small amount of damage to some letters along the right edge.

Fig. 7.
The marble block with the dedication: the top side (Photograph: Rumyana Kostadinova).

The first specialist in epigraphy to study the text was Dr Nikolay Sharankov from Sofia University St. Kliment Ohridski. He made the first translation, which is presented here.

> Δεκατισταὶ οἱ πε[ρὶ]
> Τιμοκράτην τὸν Ἀ[ρ]-
> τέμωνος: Ἡρώνυμο[ς]
> Κύρσα, Κορύλας Διο-
> κλείους, Ἀσκληπι[ό]-
> δωρος Θεύδιος,
> Δημήτριος Ἰάσονος,
> ἱερὸν ὁμονοίας Σα-
> ράπιδι, Ἴσιδι, Ἀνούβιδι
> θεοῖς συννάοις.

> "The dekatistai around Timokrates son of Artemon: Heronymos son of Kyrsas, Korylas son of Diokles, Asklepiodoros son of Theudis, Demetrios son of Iason, (dedicated this) sanctuary of their concord to Sarapis, Isis, Anubis, gods sharing the same temple."

Archaeological context [2]

The artefact was not found in its original archaeological context, but reused as material in the construction of a later building.

The site of the rescue excavation is a plot of land located in a densely built-up neighbourhood of Varna. The archaeological work was confined to the limits of the property, and synchronised with the parameters of the architectural project for the new residential building. At least two serious practical obstacles hindered the work. Firstly, the area had been part of an urbanized area for many centuries, and a series of subsequent building activities had compromised the earlier archaeological layers. Secondly, it was not possible to expand the survey to the neighbouring areas, nor to dig to the bedrock in the whole plot of land in order to study completely some of the archaeological contexts. Therefore, the exploration of the site revealed only a small glimpse from the larger picture of ancient Odessos and mediaeval Varna, and in many aspects, the results from the rescue excavation were partial and inconclusive.

During the archaeological work, remains of several historical periods were discovered. Starting from the top layers and proceeding downwards, there were archaeological materials and structures from the late 19th – early 20th centuries, from the period of the

---

2 The results from the excavation at 18 Tsar Ivan Shishman Str. have not been published yet. See a short report in: Tenekedjiev, Stefanova *in print*.

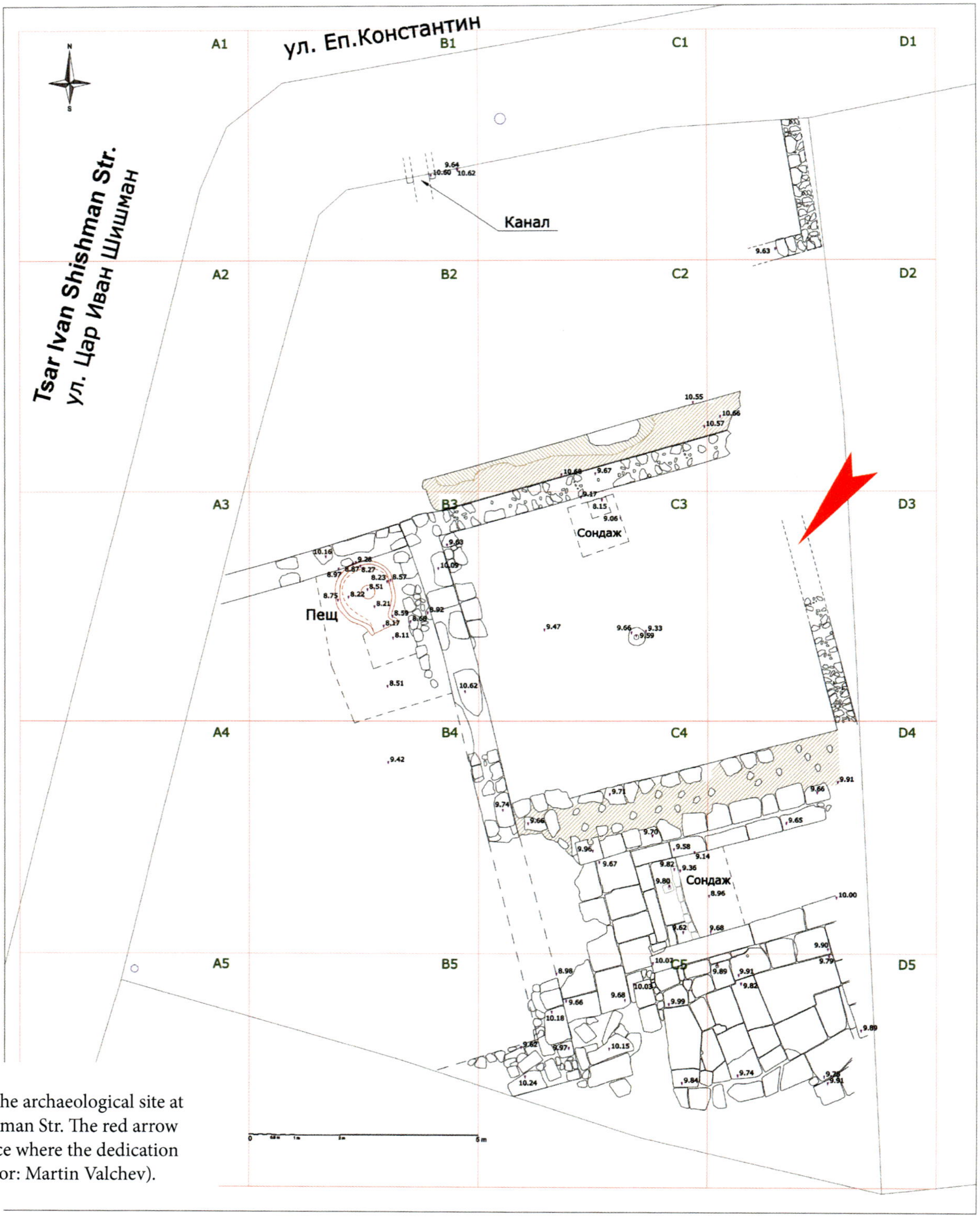

Fig. 8.

General plan of the archaeological site at 18 Tsar Ivan Shisman Str. The red arrow points to the place where the dedication was found (Author: Martin Valchev).

Ottoman domination of Bulgaria (the late 14th – second half of the 19th centuries), and from the Middle Ages (more precisely from the period 12th – 14th centuries). The most significant structures were discovered underneath (**Fig. 8, 9**). Those were the ruins of a large building with spacious rooms organised around a small rectangular yard paved with massive stone flags. The complete ground plan of the building remains uncertain because large parts of it were (and hopefully still are) under the neighbouring houses (assuming that there were any preserved parts of the construction there). Careful inspection of the remains of the building showed that it experienced several serious repairs and renovations, however the archaeological materials found in the debris indicated clearly that the building, with all of its architectural phases, should be dated to the Late Antique/Early Byzantine period (4th – 6th centuries CE). Any attempts at more precise dating would be purely hypothetical, if possible at all.

The walls of the building were constructed with roughly hewn stones. Only their front-facing side was worked better to approximate the form of a block. Most of the stones were of relatively small size (around 25 x 30 x 35 cm with variations). Apart from those there were some significantly larger block-like stones used in various parts of the walls without any specific pattern. One could assume that they were taken from earlier edifices. Except for one very unusual wall with stones and mortar (which probably functioned not as a proper wall but as a reinforcement for the construction of the building), all the others were bonded with mud.

Fig. 9.
The inner yard of the late antique/early byzantine building (Photograph: Asya Stefanova).

The marble block with the dedication to the three Egyptian deities was used as building material in the lower part of one of these mud-bonded walls (**Fig. 10**). It was oriented north – south, with a width of 53 cm, and functioned as the eastern wall of a room. Maybe on its other side, which currently lies under the neighbours' property, there was another premise. The position of the block in the masonry was around the level of the floor. Unfortunately, having in mind all the repairs and the state of preservation of the building it is difficult to say whether the block was part of the foundation, or it was in one of the bottom tiers of the superstructure. It is important to note that there were only two marble *spolia* in all the preserved part of the edifice. The block with the dedication, and a fragment of a marble stele with an inscription – a Hellenistic decree (**Fig. 11, 12**). The latter was reused as building material in the above-mentioned 'unusual wall' with mortar. The location of the decree's fragment was only a few meters from that of the block with the dedication.

▲

Fig. 10.
The marble block with the dedication when it was discovered (Photograph: Asya Stefanova).

▲▲

Fig. 11.
The fragment of the Hellenistic decree when it was discovered (Photograph: Asya Stefanova).

The technical specifics of the site and the architectural project for the future building did not allow the team to excavate further down, or in a larger area under the Late Antique/ Early Byzantine edifice. Nevertheless, several small test trenches were dug in selected places throughout the site. No earlier architecture, nor distinct cultural layers from the Classical Roman, the Hellenistic, or any historical period preceding them were discovered there. In some of the trenches however, there were small deposits of archaeological materials the characteristics of which were the same: fragments of Hellenistic pottery, animal bones, seashells, and fragments of charcoal.

Fig. 12.
The fragment of the Hellenistic decree (Photograph: Lumyana Kostadinova).

Discussion

Beyond any doubt, the most interesting aspect of the new discovery is the content of the text. Its detailed publication with commentary by N. Sharankov is expected in the future. Therefore, only some important notes on the topic are presented here, they were provided by Dr Sharankov in personal communication with the author of this paper:

> 1. "The lettering points towards a date at the end of the 3rd or the first half of the 2nd century BCE."
>
> 2. "The dedication was made by members of a cult association designated as *dekatistai* – a rather rare word attested only in two other dedications to the Egyptian deities – one from Kos, dated to the 1st century BCE (*RICIS* 204/1002), and one from Prusa ad Olympum, with a date in the 2nd century CE (*RICIS* 308/0401)."
>
> 3. Concerning the exact meaning of the term, N. Sharankov's "personal opinion favours the understanding of *dekatistai* as worshippers celebrating on the tenth day of the month."
>
> 4. "This is one of the earliest pieces of evidence about the cult of the Egyptian deities in the Western Pontic area, as well as the oldest epigraphic witness from the territory of Bulgaria. Moreover, while most other dedications to the Egyptian deities from the region in this period were made by individuals, here we see a religious association of a rare type."
>
> 5. "The object of the dedication is referred to as ἱερὸν ὁμονοίας, *sanctuary of concord*, which must have been the temple – or rather a sanctuary – of the Egyptian deities where the association of the dekatistai gathered. The word ὁμόνοια is seemingly an allusion to the association itself, as in other inscriptions of religious associations, and not the personified goddess of that name."
>
> (*pers. comm.*)

The next important question that needs discussion concerns the original function of the block with the dedication. Not much can be said about it with certainty, however the holes in the upper side of the block (if at least some of them, if not all, were part of the original design) suggest that probably this was a pedestal for a statue. One would expect that this was a representation of the Egyptian triad from the inscription. It should be noted though that no image of the deities was mentioned in the text. It remains also obscure why the top of the block was remodelled, and when exactly all of the holes there were made.

The immediate archaeological context did not give direct information about the original place of the marble block with the dedication. As was mentioned earlier, the artefact was found as a *spolium* in a wall of a building from the 4th – 6th century CE. Although there were significant repairs and changes to its architectural construction, no archaeological evidence collected during the excavation suggested that any of the walls belonged to an earlier (and more precisely Hellenistic) edifice. Nevertheless, one would theorise that most likely the marble block was originally taken from a place somewhere nearby. The location of the dedication's original site, apparently a temple or a sanctuary, could have been very near, even under some of the unexplored areas of the Late Antique/Early Byzantine building that still lie under the neighbouring plots.

Another important find discovered nearby also deserves attention. That is the above-mentioned second marble *spolium* – a fragment from the middle part of a stele with a text of a proxeny decree. The preserved width of the marble piece is 25 cm, and the preserved height – 28 cm. It is 16 – 17 cm thick. Parts of 15 lines of an Ancient Greek text (with 1.1 cm high letters) are still legible on the front side. According to N. Sharankov who first studied the artefact, it can be dated generally to the 3rd – 2nd century BCE.[3] It can be assumed that the decree was also on display, together with the dedication to the Egyptian deities, in the hypothetical temple or sanctuary under discussion. The fact that the two spolia were discovered close to one another reused in the Late Antique/Early Byzantine masonry makes even more probable the hypothesis that the Hellenistic sacred site was somewhere close by in the area.

The inscriptions found at 18 Tsar Ivan Shishman Street now need to be analysed in their broader archaeological context. The location of the site was close to a small promontory, usually called the 'Varna Cape', which existed in its natural state until the early 20th century. At that time the coastal line was artificially altered, and today from the area of the former cape starts the breakwater of the eastern harbour of Varna (Gochev 1987, 349-353). Several rescue excavations have been conducted so far in the south-eastern corner of the archaeological reserve and more precisely in the area of the old cape. Some of the results may contribute to the discussion of religious life in this part of the ancient Odessos in Antiquity.

1. In 1963, the ruins of a temple with four Doric columns on its northern façade was excavated at the corner of (36) San Stefano and Chernorizets Hrabar Streets (Mirchev 1967, 21-24). This was around 100 m to the south, south-west of 18 Tsar Ivan Shishman Str. No specific archaeological material that could contribute to the precise dating of the building was reported, however Doric order suggested an early date. Taking into account that the city of Odessos was founded in the second quarter of the 6th century BCE (Minchev 2006, 61), the temple could be dated hypothetically and broadly to the period of the mid-6th – 5th centuries BCE.[4]

---

3 The decree has not been published yet.

4 There is an opinion however that these particular Doric columns should be dated to the 3rd century BCE (Stoyanov, Soyanova 1997, 30).

2. In 2021, a fragment of a Hellenistic marble statue and a small piece of a marble Doric column were found in close proximity to the temple. That happened during a rescue excavation in the other, at that time still archaeologically unexplored, part of the same plot of land, located at 36 San Stefano Street (Tenekedjiev, Mircheva *in print*). The statue was of particular interest. It was discovered reused in the stone foundation of a building from the 20th century. This is a fragment of a sculpture in the round representing a young woman in expressive, forward motion emphasized by her flowing garments (Tenekedjiev 2022, 40 and here **Fig. 13**). Only the torso and the legs down to the knees are preserved. The piece is 55 cm tall. It is of fine marble in an off-white, yellowish shade. The execution is of very high artistic quality. The image resembles very much the renowned statue of Nike from Samothrace but with some key differences. Firstly, on the back of the figure, which is well preserved, there are no wings. Secondly, a close inspection of the bottom end of the fragment and of the shape of the folds of the *chiton* reveals that the latter is knee-length. This observation could explain why the sculpture was broken at that particular place, which would have been the most solid part of the figure if the *chiton* was floor length.

The identification of the statue is still disputable, however parallels from the islands of Delos and Paros suggest that probably the statue from Odessos represents the goddess Artemis. The style of the sculpture points to a date in the period of the 3rd – 2nd centuries BCE.

It seems logical to connect the statue with the nearby temple. Although it is not sufficient evidence to identify the dedication of the sacred site, it is a solid indication that the temple was still in use during the Hellenistic age.

3. Around the middle of the 20th century, during digging works for a sewer on Chervenoarmeyski Blvd. (today Primorski Blvd.) a fragment of a stele of a proxeny decree was found (Mihailov 1970 No.43. Mirchev 1967, 21). It was not in a clear archaeological context. The exact spot of the discovery was not specified in the available publications, but Milko Mirchev implied in his article about the ancient temples of Odessos, that it was in the section of the boulevard that was near the temple at 36 San Stefano Street and the former Varna Cape (Mirchev 1967, 21-24) At the end of the decree, there was an instruction that the stele should be displayed in the temple of Apollo. M. Mirchev suspected that maybe the temple mentioned in the decree was the one on San Stefano Street (Mirchev 1967, 24).

4. During rescue excavations in several plots of land in a large area near the Varna Cape (roughly around 500 – 600 m in diameter) deposits of similar materials have been found: fragments of Archaic, Classical Greek or Hellenistic pottery, animal bones, seashells, and charcoal fragments. Stratigraphically, these deposits belonged to the deepest cultural layer in the area. In most cases, such as at 25 San Stefano Str. (Manolova-Voykova,

Fig. 13.
The sculpture found at 36 San Stefano Str. (Photograph: Rumyana Kostadinova).

Tenekedjiev 2021), at 36 San Stefano Str. (Tenekedjiev, Mircheva *in print*), and at 18 Tsar Ivan Shishman Str. (Tenekedjiev, Stefanova *in print*), the exact nature of the deposits was not clear because they had been damaged by later building interventions. The situation was more informative in the archaeological site at 3 – 5 Tsar Ivan Shishman Str. (Manolova-Voykova, Tenekedjiev, Mircheva 2018, 223). More than 20 of those deposits were discovered there, revealing that they were in fact remains of ritual pits. There, the bedrock is not deep, and the bottoms of some of the pits were cut into it, thus remaining partly preserved. Recently, in the nearby site at 21 Primorski Blvd., where the bedrock is even more shallow, several more and better preserved ritual pits were found. So far, three of them were completely explored, and one more has been detected and awaits excavation, as the site is still in progress.[5]

Remains of an interesting, partly destroyed structure was also discovered at 3 – 5 Tsar Ivan Shishman Str. It was part of an underground *dromos* oriented east – west, and constructed of limestone blocks. The dromos used to provide access to an unknown structure that was located at its western end, in the area that today is in the neighbouring plot. There is no archaeological record on this matter from the time of the construction of the new building there. Even if there had been remains of a chamber or some other structure, the new foundations destroyed them. In the fill of the *dromos* there was a pit with the typical content, described above (Manolova-Voykova, Tenekedjiev, Mircheva 2018, 223) The analysis of the pottery has not been completed yet nor published, but it is already safe to conclude that the structure had ritual function and could be dated to the Hellenistic or to the Classical Greek period. The exact purpose of the underground structure with the *dromos* is highly hypothetical. To reconstruct it as a tomb or a *heroon* is tempting, but it would be just a speculation that cannot be proved.

It is not known yet in what exact territory the ritual pits had been distributed. The westernmost of them were abutting Osmi Septemvri Str. and near it, in the area of the so-called “Small Roman Thermae” (Toncheva 1967, 157-159).

5. Those last pits were discovered in close proximity to a small temple dedicated to the Thracian god Heros Karabazmos and the goddess Phosphoros (Toncheva 1969b). Marble votive reliefs of the two deities were found in the debris (Toncheva 1969a, 23, fig. 27, 28). The temple was built in the Hellenistic period, more precisely in the late 4th century BCE, (Toncheva 1969b, 364).[6]

The temple and the pits near it were on the upper part of a natural slope that marks the west end of the elevated ground located eastward and reaching out to the Varna Cape.

---

[5] The results from the excavation have not been published yet.

[6] Later, commenting the reliefs found in the building A. Minchev dated its construction to the 2nd – 1st century BCE (Minchev 2007, 74).

The archaeological information from excavations in that whole area is not yet sufficient for general conclusions. On one hand, it is not certain that the area between the cape and the temple of Karabazmos and Phosphoros was actually within the walls of Odessos during the first five – six centuries of its history. On the other hand, there is enough evidence that the area was used extensively for ritual purposes. At this stage, these are nothing but vague observations, but they should be taken into consideration when the excavations in this part of Varna continue in the future.

Conclusion

The marble block with a dedication to Serapis, Isis and Anubis found recently in Odessos is an important discovery most of all because of the information that the inscription contains. The dedication that dated to end of the 3rd or the first half of the 2nd century BCE is one of the earliest pieces of evidence about the cult of these deities in the Western Black Sea region, and the earliest known example from the territory of today's Bulgaria (*see here V. Atanassova*). The inscription also mentions a special religious group connected with the cult – the so-called *dekatistai*. Finally yet importantly, the text reveals that as early as end of the 3rd or the first half of the 2nd century BCE, in Odessos existed a sanctuary (possibly a temple) of the three deities from Egypt.

From the perspective of archaeology, many important questions remain without an answer. What was the original purpose of the block? Was it a pedestal of a statue, or it served in different way? Why was the block reworked, and what was its subsequent function? It is certain only that eventually in the Early Byzantine period the block became a *spolium* in the wall of a building.

The location of the sanctuary of Serapis, Isis and Anubis remains unknown, but perhaps it was somewhere not far from the place where the block was found. It should be added that the site is in a large area, maybe out of the earlier city, with noticeable evidence of religious activity from the time of the foundation of Odessos to the Hellenistic period at least. Apart from the ritual pits scattered around in that area, two temples and one underground structure with a *dromos* were excavated. Therefore, this would be a suitable place for another sacred site – the sanctuary of the Egyptian triad.

Undoubtedly, the block with the dedication will continue to attract the attention of the experts in the future, and one hopes that the information it provides would help for the better understanding of religious life in Hellenistic Odessos. The artefact also will motivate the archaeologists that excavate in this part of Varna to look for the sanctuary or temple of Serapis, Isis and Anubis, and clarify the earlier periods in the history of the area around the former Varna Cape.

Ce que le séjour d'Ovide à Tomes nous apprend sur le culte d'Isis au début de l'Empire

Mina Tasseva-Bencheva

Овидий в Томи и култът на Изида от периода на началото на Империята

Мина Тасева-Бенчева

Заточен в град Томи, на брега на Евксинския понт, около 8 г. сл. Хр. по заповед на Август, римският поет Овидий създава поредица поеми, които адресира до близките си. Част от тях е събрана в съчинението „Писма от Понта“ в четири книги. Първата поема от книга I на това съчинение описва наблюдавана от Овидий сцена: двама души, единият от които признал, че е разгневил богинята Изида, седнал пред нейния олтар, а другият, чието зрение било отнето по подобна причина, крещял посред улицата, че е заслужил съдбата си (Ov., *Pont*., 1.1.51–54). Споменатата от Овидий сцена е интересна, тъй като редица археологически и епиграфски данни от Томи, където Овидий пише тези стихове, сочат, че в този град действително се е практикувал култ към египетските божества. Настоящата статия разглежда първата поема от книга I на „Писма от Понта“ и по-конкретно стихове 51 – 54 от нея в светлината на литературни произведения от периода, както и на епиграфските данни за египетските култове, които са значително обогатени и систематизирани през последните години. Изложението е развито в четири части, които проследяват съответно контекста, в който се вписват стихове 51 – 54 и замисъла на поемата, сведенията за египетските култове в Томи, темите за властта на Изида върху човешкото зрение и за практиката на изповедта в нейния култ и посланието, предадено чрез поетичния език на Овидий в анализирания текст.

Relégué à Tomes par Auguste vers le mois de décembre de l'an 8 p.C., le poète latin Ovide rédigea, depuis cette ville sur la côte du Pont Euxin, une série de textes en vers qu'il adressa à ses proches. Une partie de ces textes est rassemblée dans la collection dite des *Pontiques*, composée de quatre livres. L'auteur de l'*Art d'aimer* y décrit à la fois des éléments de sa vie aux confins de l'Empire, des détails d'événements contemporains et des réflexions sur son passé et sur son destin.

Le poème I de cette collection, adressé à Brutus, évoque l'image de deux personnages que le poète dit avoir aperçus, l'un ayant fait la confession d'avoir outragé Isis, assis devant son autel, et un autre, privé de vue pour une raison similaire, criant dans la rue qu'il a bien mérité son destin (Ov., *Pont.*, 1. 1.51-54). Les quatre vers contenant cette description ne comportent pas de précisions relatives à l'espace et au temps : Ovide s'abstient d'indiquer s'il décrit une scène qui s'est déroulée durant la période de sa relégation à Tomes, ou s'il parle, d'une manière plus abstraite, d'un événement du passé ou d'une image qu'il a forgée dans son esprit. Ce passage est pourtant intéressant pour l'étude des cultes isiaques sur le littoral du Pont Euxin, puisque la ville de Tomes où était installé Ovide sur ordre d'Auguste, fut, d'après les données archéologiques et épigraphiques que nous possédons, un centre de ces cultes.

Le passage en question a fait l'objet d'études ponctuelles parues dans les éditions et dans les commentaires des *Pontiques* que nous reprenons dans ce texte. Ces études permettent de replacer les vers dans le cadre de l'œuvre ovidienne et, plus globalement, dans le domaine de la poésie du début de l'Empire. En revanche, on a rarement considéré, à notre connaissance, ces vers à la lumière des données épigraphiques sur les cultes isiaques. L'ouvrage de M. Tacheva-Hitova *Les cultes orientaux en Mésie inférieure et en Thrace* est une exception notable à cet égard, la chercheuse y envisageant notre texte, dans quelques passages, comme un témoignage possible des pratiques religieuses à Tomes (Tacheva-Hitova 1983, 40 et 64). L'occasion se présente, avec ce volume, de revenir sur ce sujet afin d'en proposer une interprétation plus détaillée. Nous examinons, dans les lignes qui suivent, les vers d'Ovide dans le contexte de la *Première Pontique* et dans le cadre plus global des œuvres poétiques de sa période en prenant en compte le dossier des inscriptions isiaques qui a été considérablement enrichi et systématisé durant ces dernières années.

Ovide à Tomes, la *Première Pontique* et le passage relatif à Isis

Les raisons de la relégation d'Ovide à Tomes ne sont pas entièrement claires. À en croire les paroles du poète, elle serait faite sur ordre d'Auguste lui-même et serait due à deux "crimes" (*duo crimina*) : le premier, ce serait un poème (*carmen*) qu'il a composé ; le second, une erreur (*error*), dont il ne précise pas le caractère (Ov., *Tr.*, 2. 207). Si le poème en question a été bien identifié comme étant l'*Art d'aimer* (Ov., *Tr.*, 2. 211-212 ; 2. 240), publié quelques années plus tôt, comme s'accordent à le penser la plupart des chercheurs, l'erreur commise par le poète latin, dont on peut présumer qu'elle était plus récente que la publication de ce dernier poème, demeure un mystère. Le poète y fait référence en termes voilés, en insistant sur le fait qu'il ne lui appartient pas de révéler la cause de sa relégation (Ov. *Tr.* 2. 207-208 ; 4. 10). Il se contente d'indiquer que le péché qu'on lui reprochait, était d'avoir eu des yeux (*occulos habuisse*, Ov. *Tr.* 3. 50), c'est-à-dire d'avoir été témoin oculaire de faits (Ov. *Tr.* 2. 103-104). Les faits en question sont l'objet d'hypothèses variées touchant à des fautes de caractère politique, intime ou religieux qu'on a attribuées à Ovide à l'époque moderne pour tenter d'expliquer les raisons ayant motivé l'ordre d'Auguste (Thibault 1964 ; Goold 1983). Pour certains, le crime de la violation d'un culte, comme celui de la déesse Bona dea ou encore celui d'Isis, n'est pas à exclure (Hermann 1938). Quel qu'eût été le caractère de son erreur, le poète resta en relégation, nous livrant des témoignages sur sa vie à Tomes, jusqu'à sa mort vers l'an 17/18 p.C.

Avant d'examiner les données sur les cultes isiaques de cette ville, arrêtons-nous pour un moment sur les vers 51-54 de la *Première Pontique* et sur leur contexte. Le passage qui nous intéresse apparaît au premier poème du Livre I, dans un cadre qui s'apparente fortement à un préambule. Le texte sert à présenter l'ouvrage, le replaçant entre les autres œuvres d'Ovide (Gaertner 2005, 93) mais aussi à inciter le lecteur à y prêter attention. Le poète y développe par ailleurs les thèmes de la faute qui a causé sa relégation et de la souffrance résultant de son destin. La *Première Pontique* se caractérise aussi par sa forte résonance religieuse perceptible à travers les références aux divinités et au *princeps*, qualifié de "dieu" (48), à des pratiques des cultes de Cybèle et d'Isis (37-45), au motif de la punition divine et du pardon accordé par les immortels (55-58) et au statut du poète qui déclare être un prophète divinement inspiré (47).

Le poème s'ouvre sur les encouragements adressés par Ovide à Brutus, son destinataire. Ce dernier est invité à accepter les vers sans inquiétudes, même s'ils sont à lire en privé (*sub lare privato*, 10) et qu'ils ne peuvent pas entrer dans les bibliothèques publiques (*publica monimenta*, 5) en raison du statut du poète après son départ de Rome (1-14). Plus loin dans le texte, Ovide explique quels sont les sentiments qui l'animent et parle de ceux qui pourraient se produire chez Brutus : l'ouvrage qu'il envoie est triste (*triste*, 15), tout comme celui qu'il a composé auparavant, c'est-à-dire les *Tristes*. Contrairement à ce dernier, les *Pontiques* révèlent les noms de leurs destinataires mais ces poèmes peuvent être acceptés sans crainte, car les œuvres d'autres personnages s'étant opposées, dans le passé, à la famille d'Auguste sont encore lus et trouvent leur place dans les bibliothèques (16-24). Précisant ensuite qu'il est loin de se comparer à ces personnages, Ovide note que ses vers ne sont nullement dirigés contre les dieux et ne manquent pas de rendre honneur (*honore*, 28) au césar. Son poème (*carmen*, 30) chante des éloges des dieux (*laudes deorum*, 29) (15-30) mais vante aussi Auguste, car, dans les lignes qui suivent, l'auteur incite à penser aux origines mythiques de la famille des Jules. Il insiste d'ailleurs sur le fait que toutes les voies devraient être ouvertes devant son ouvrage qui porte le nom du père de la patrie (*patriae pater*, 36), tout comme les feux de Troie s'ouvraient devant Énée qui transportait son père (31-36).

Ovide dépeint ensuite une série d'images relatives aux cultes de deux divinités féminines d'origine étrangère, Isis et Cybèle (37-44). À ces deux déesses, selon la leçon transmise par une partie des manuscrits, il faut ajouter le nom de Diane (41), dont la présence ici fait discussion. Cette lecture, acceptée par certains éditeurs comme A. L. Wheeler (*Dianae* dans Wheeler 1939 mais *dearum* dans Wheeler 1988) et J. F. Gaertner (Gaertner 2005), peut être comprise par référence à Hécate/Cybèle ou encore à la famille des Jules, par rapprochement avec Dione/Vénus (Gaertner 2005, 115-116). Poursuivant sur l'idée que son poème porte le nom d'Auguste et de la *gens* Julia, le poète demande s'il est justifié de refuser les gestes faits en respect des dieux et inspirés par leur volonté (*numina superorum*, 43) et déclare qu'il prophétise et instruit sous l'effet de l'inspiration divine (*vaticinor moneoque*, 47). Il réclame ainsi qu'on attribue à son ouvrage la place qu'il mérite puisqu'il porte des noms sacrés. Comparant Auguste à un dieu, le poète ajoute que, s'il a bien mérité ou ressenti la colère du *princeps*, il continuera à l'honorer (49-50).

Le début du poème possède donc une résonance fort personnelle, tout en étant riche en images et en terminologie religieuse. Ovide y caractérise sa poésie de prophétique et insiste sur le statut divin du *princeps*, introduisant par ailleurs le motif des cultes d'Isis et de Cybèle. Ces détails préparent l'auditoire aux vers suivants articulés, quant à eux, autour du thème de la confession et de la punition divine.

Les vers 51-54 développent les motifs de la punition divine et de la confession à travers une scène qu'Ovide rattache au culte d'Isis. Sans donner des précisions sur les circonstances décrites, le poète dépeint cette scène qu'il dit avoir vue (*vidi*, 51) : un personnage avouant avoir outragé la volonté d'Isis à la tenue en lin (*linigerae numen violasse fatentem / Isidis*, 51-52) assis devant un autel isiaque (*Isiacos ante sedere focos*, 52) et un autre, privé de vue (*privatus lumine*, 53) pour une faute similaire à celle-ci (*ob huic similem culpam*, 53) qui criait au milieu de la rue qu'il l'avait bien mérité (*clamabat media se meruisse via*, 54).

Le poète précise immédiatement que les dieux se réjouissent souvent de ce type de proclamations publiques (*praeconia*, 55) qui témoignent de leurs pouvoirs. Les divinités sont, affirme-t-il, souvent capables de lever les châtiments (*levant poenas*, 57) qu'elles ont infligés aux hommes et de rendre la vue enlevée (*eraptaque lumina reddunt*, 57) lorsqu'elles voient que les pécheurs se sont repentis réellement (*bene penituisse*, 58).

Revenant sur son propre destin, Ovide déclare se repentir de son acte et sentir la terreur qu'il provoque (59-60), sa souffrance étant double puisqu'elle résulte de son exil mais aussi de sa faute (*culpa*, 61). La pensée du poète se porte donc vers un motif qu'il exploite souvent dans ses œuvres de Tomes : celui de la faute qui a causé sa relégation et de la possibilité d'obtenir la grâce du *princeps*. C'est dans ce sens qu'il affirme que, même s'il se voyait pardonné par les dieux, qui sont eux-mêmes dépassés par la présence d'Auguste, il souffrirait toujours et jusqu'à sa mort (63-66). Le poème se termine sur une série de comparaisons relatives à la souffrance (67-76), l'auteur prétendant que, si les dieux pouvaient peut-être le croire, il pourrait espérer changer de lieu d'exil (77-80).

Conçu comme ouverture de la collection des *Pontiques*, ce texte a pour objectif d'attirer l'attention de l'audience et, comme le suggèrent ses vers, de favoriser la réception de cette collection de poèmes. Il insiste par ailleurs sur les sujets qui semblent avoir préoccupé Ovide durant une grande partie de sa relégation à Tomes : sa souffrance et le regret de son erreur ainsi que la grâce qu'il espérait obtenir.

Pour développer ces sujets, l'auteur des *Métamorphoses* choisit d'évoquer des pratiques religieuses rattachés à Cybèle et à Isis. À cette dernière divinité, il fait référence une première fois au vers 37-38, au moyen de l'adjectif *Pharia*, qui rappelle les origines égyptiennes de la déesse et qui était couramment utilisé comme épithète d'Isis. Son culte est ensuite cité une deuxième fois aux vers 51-54 où sont mentionnées la scène de confession publique et la punition par aveuglement apportée par la déesse. Dans les lignes suivantes, Ovide s'attarde sur le motif de la confession prononcée à voix haute et de la punition divine. Il reste néanmoins plus vague sur les noms des divinités, ce qui lui permet de faire allusion à Auguste. Celui-ci est, rappelons-le, assimilé à un dieu à plusieurs reprises dans le poème, et, de ce fait, la relégation d'Ovide à Tomes pourrait être regardée comme une punition divine. Expliquant que les dieux peuvent être sensibles aux confessions publiques et lever leurs punitions, le poète ajoute qu'il se repent lui-même de son erreur, établissant un parallèle entre le développement plus général relatif aux dieux et son propre cas. Il apparaît ainsi que ce passage possède un double sens : d'une part, les vers font référence au culte d'Isis et aux croyances associées à cette déesse ; d'autre part, ils exploitent les motifs de la confession et de la punition divine pour les adapter à la situation du poète.

La présence des cultes isiaques à Tomes

À l'époque de la composition des *Pontiques*, les cultes isiaques étaient, semble-t-il, bien établis dans les régions du pourtour du Pont Euxin, où ils étaient présents, selon les données que nous possédons, à partir d'une période plus ancienne. La ville de Tomes, en particulier, était un des centres où ces cultes étaient pratiqués dans la période s'étalant du Ier s. a.C. au IIIe s. p.C. (Dunand 1973, 201-204 ; Atanassova dans le présent volume), comme en témoigne le dossier d'inscriptions de sa région.

La présence de cultes des divinités égyptiennes dans la ville est établie à partir de la période hellénistique grâce à une série de monuments répertoriés par M. Tacheva-Hitova (Tacheva-Hitova 1983). Plus récemment, L. Bricault a revu ces données pour les inclure dans son importante collection de *testimonia* concernant les cultes isiaques en les complétant de traductions que nous reprenons ci-dessous (Bricault 2005). Parmi ces témoignages, on trouve une inscription sur une stèle en pierre faisant mention de la fête de Charmosyna, qui était déjà connue par Hérodote et qui était célébrée, à date ancienne, en l'honneur de la déesse Isis. Cette même inscription, datée vers la période du Ier s. a.C.-Ier s. p.C., révèle l'existence d'un temple de Sarapis (τὸ ἱερὸν τοῦ Σαράπιδος) dans la ville (Tacheva-Hitova 1983, I, 13 ; Bricault 2005, 618/1001). De cette période, nous possédons aussi une plaque en marbre dont le texte suggère la consécration d'un monument à Sarapis, Isis, Anubis et à tous les dieux (κατεσκεύασεν ... καὶ Σαράπιδι καὶ Εἴσιδι καὶ Ἀνούβιδι καὶ θεοῖς πᾶσιν, Tacheva-Hitova 1983, I, 14 ; Bricault 2005, 618/1002). Une dédicace consacrée à Sarapis et datée du Ier s. a.C., aujourd'hui perdue, fait allusion à la pratique de l'incubation à travers la formule "à la suite d'un songe" (κατὰ ὄναρ, Tacheva-Hitova 1983, I, 15 ; Bricault 2005, 618/1003).

Ces données sont complétées par une série d'inscriptions qui mentionnent, ensemble ou séparément, les noms d'Isis, de Sarapis et d'Anubis et qui sont datées entre le Ier et le IIIe s. p.C. La première inscription de cette série figure sur un fragment de table en marbre, son texte étant consacré à Agrippine, la mère de Néron, et mentionnant un prêtre de Sarapis et d'Isis (ἱερέως Σαράπιδος καὶ Ἴσιδος, Tacheva-Hitova 1983, I, 16 ; Bricault 2005, 618/1004). La deuxième inscription a été découverte sur un autel en marbre qui a été transporté au milieu du XIXe s. à Paris. Son texte, qu'on pouvait encore lire dans la cour d'un hôtel de la rue de Hambourg au temps de M. Brillant (Brillant 1912) et qui se trouve aujourd'hui à l'université de Caen, en Normandie, est relatif à la consécration de l'autel en question en l'an 160 (Tacheva-Hitova 1983, I, 17 ; Bricault 2005, 618/1005 ; Avram 2006). Elle s'ouvre sur les noms de "Zeus Soleil grand Sarapis" et les "dieux qui partagent le même temple" (Διὶ Ἡλίῳ μεγάλῳ Σαράπιδι καὶ τοῖς συννάοις θεοῖς) auxquels sont associés l'empereur Antonin le Pieux et le césar Marc Aurèle, indiquant, comme le texte précédent, une relation avec le pouvoir impérial. À côté de ce premier autel, nous avons conservé aussi un autel en marbre de datation incertaine, comportant une représentation dont l'assimilation à Osiris fait discussion (Tacheva-Hitova 1983, I, 31).

Ce dossier est complété par deux bustes, dont l'un représente Isis et l'autre cette même déesse ou une de ses prêtresses ainsi que par une porte ornée de personnages assimilés à Isis, Harpocrate, Aphrodite et Éros, ces trois objets pouvant être datés de la seconde moitié du Ier s. à la période du règne de Constantin (Tacheva-Hitova 1983, 13-14).

À l'époque d'Ovide, les cultes isiaques étaient donc pratiqués dans la ville de Tomes comme dans d'autres régions côtières de la Mésie et de la Thrace. Isis y faisait partie d'une dyade divine avec Sarapis. Ce dernier est resté une divinité importante dans la ville au cours de la période impériale, comme le confirme une représentation assimilée à ce dernier, datée du IIIe s., qui a été retrouvée sur le site de la ville (Tacheva-Hitova 1983, I, 28) et une inscription datée de la même période et portant le nom de ce dieu (Bricault

2005, 618/1006). Quant à Isis, cette déesse était vénérée comme divinité guérisseuse mais aussi comme déesse protectrice de la navigation, ce dernier rôle ayant sans doute contribué à l'expansion de son culte (Bricault 2006, 251-254). Les échanges avec l'Égypte ont favorisé, semble-t-il, l'expansion des cultes isiaques dans les contrées où les voyages par voie maritime étaient fréquents, c'est-à-dire dans les zones du littoral. Tomes, ville côtière du Pont Euxin, s'inscrit bien dans cette catégorie (Atanassova 2020, 37-38). La ville a d'ailleurs possédé, à une date plus récente, un lieu de réunion du collège des armateurs ou des pilotes de navires de Tomes (ὁ οἶκος τῶν ἐν Τόμει ναυκλήρων), comme l'indique une inscription de la période impériale (Cagnat *et al.* 1901, I, 610). Des négociants alexandrins y avaient également leur lieu de réunion (Bricault 2005, 618/1005). Isis, protectrice des marins et de la navigation, y était vénérée également comme divinité guérisseuse, aux côtés de Sarapis et d'Harpocrate (Bricault 2006, 266).

Le dossier examiné plus haut permet d'affirmer que les cultes isiaques étaient bien établis à Tomes au temps d'Ovide. Le poète a-t-il pu s'inspirer de cette présence ? En raison de son caractère abstrait, le passage de la *Première Pontique* n'autorise pas à trancher cette question avec certitude. Le point qui semble avoir préoccupé le poète davantage touche aux motifs de la punition par aveuglement et de la confession. Il convient donc d'examiner de plus près ces deux motifs pour mieux comprendre ce passage et son rapport avec le culte d'Isis.

Isis, déesse qui punit et qui guérit

Avant de se pencher sur ces deux motifs, attardons-nous sur l'attitude officielle à l'égard des cultes isiaques à Rome. La pertinence de ce point pour notre propos tient au fait qu'Ovide vint s'installer à Tomes après avoir quitté l'*Urbs* et que les poèmes de son exil étaient donc forcément marqués par le souvenir de son passé dans la capitale de l'Empire. Les vers composés durant son séjour sur la côte du Pont Euxin étaient certes adressés à des proches mais leur publication en faisait des textes publics (McGowan 2009, 23). Le poète choisissait donc ses paroles avec précaution. Étant donné la situation d'Ovide et les allusions à Auguste dans la *Première Pontique*, on peut soupçonner que ce texte tienne compte, du moins en partie, de l'attitude envers les cultes isiaques qui était de mise à Rome.

À l'époque d'Auguste, le culte d'Isis ne manquait pas d'attirer des critiques à Rome. Une série de témoignages de la période nous informe de la méfiance des Romains à l'égard des pratiques associées à cette déesse et à ses lieux de vénération (Thibault 1964, 98-100 ; Bricault 2011). Au milieu du Ier s. a.C., en réaction aux cultes isiaques, le Sénat enjoignait la destruction d'autels et de statues consacrés à Isis et Sarapis. Les événements politiques durant les années suivantes ont probablement motivé la décision d'Auguste de bannir les cultes isiaques au sein du *pomoerium* romain en l'an 28 a.C. L'interdiction de leur pratique a été rapidement étalée à la région autour de l'*Urbs* en 21 a.C. (Turcan 2000, 121). Cette position officielle correspondrait à l'attitude générale du *princeps* à l'égard des cultes étrangers telle qu'elle est décrite par Suétone (Tacheva-Hitova 1983, 46 ; Thibault 1964). Souhaitant encourager les valeurs et la religion traditionnelle romaine, celui-ci se montrait respectueux à l'égard d'une partie des cultes étrangers qui avaient étaient fondés à date ancienne. Il exprimait sa tolérance de ceux-ci sur leurs lieux d'origine tout en se gardant de certaines pratiques religieuses et en refusant parfois de visiter des temples de divinités étrangères (Suet., *Aug.* 91). Ovide lui-même semble avoir adopté une attitude similaire en affirmant, plusieurs années avant de quitter Rome, que les temples d'Isis offraient des plaisirs comparables à ceux que Io avait jadis procurés à Jupiter (Ov., *Ars amat.* 1. 77-78). À l'époque d'Auguste, la position du pouvoir public était plus nuancée envers la pratique des cultes dans le domaine privé ainsi qu'envers l'utilisation de motifs d'inspiration égyptienne (Takačs 1995, 75-80). Cette façon nuancée de regarder les cultes étrangers était probablement connue par Ovide qui a donc pu en tenir compte au moment de la composition de notre texte. Les vers relatifs à Isis dans la *Première Pontique* ont une résonnance fort différente par comparaison aux ouvrages ovidiens du passé, le ton du poème ayant un caractère plus privé et personnel. Les motifs de l'aveuglement et de la confession s'inscrivent bien dans un tel développement, car ils touchent à l'aspect personnel du culte d'Isis, lequel présente cette déesse comme une divinité omnipotente, capable de punir et de guérir les mortels.

Si l'on se tourne à présent vers la poésie grecque et latine, on peut explorer cet aspect du culte de la déesse dont nous avons conservé des témoignages datant des premiers siècles de l'Empire. Les poètes de cette période font état des pouvoirs d'Isis sur la vue humaine en indiquant que la divinité est capable de châtier les hommes par l'aveuglement. Le poète latin Juvénal, contemporain d'Ovide, remarque à ce propos que la déesse pouvait aveugler ceux qui avaient commis un parjure (Juv., *Sat.*, 13. 85-119). D'une manière similaire, l'*Anthologie palatine* cite Isis et Harpocrate parmi les dieux pouvant ôter la vue des hommes (*AP*, 11. 115). Ce type de punition divine est un motif présent dans la mythologie où elle intervient en cas de transgression d'un interdit, dont le parjure (Husquin 2018 ; Godwin 2020, 147). On peut donc soupçonner qu'il s'agit d'un motif plus ancien qui a été repris dans certains textes relatifs à Isis. D'autre part, parmi les déesses du panthéon gréco-romain capables d'infliger une telle punition, on trouve Artémis-Diane, qui a été assimilée à Isis. Ces données laissent à penser que la scène décrite dans la *Première Pontique* reprend un motif connu par les poètes de l'époque.

Pour les Anciens, les yeux étaient un organe qui pouvait souffrir et guérir de façon miraculeuse. Selon les Évangiles, la guérison d'un homme aveugle est, rappelons-le, un des miracles effectués par Jésus dans la ville de Bethsaïde, en Galilée. En nous éloignant de Judée, on constate que la popularisation progressive des cultes isiaques était, semble-t-il, associée aux pouvoirs guérisseurs de Sarapis et d'Isis et que ce fut le cas également parmi les Romains (Bricault 2011, 13). Des récits rapportés par Suétone et par Tacite suggèrent que ce furent des guérisons faites par Sarapis à Alexandrie qui auraient poussé Vespasien à s'intéresser au culte du dieu, celui-ci ayant aidé un homme à retrouver la vue (Suet., *Vesp.*, 7 ; Tac., *Hist.*, 4. 81-82). La liste des patients de Sarapis comptait d'ailleurs des personnages célèbres dans l'Antiquité, dont Démétrios de Phalère. Celui-ci aurait retrouvé la vue grâce à la divinité, comme le rapporte Diogène Laërce (D. L. 5. 5. 76).

Quant à Isis, sa capacité de remédier à l'ophtalmie est d'abord perceptible à travers son image de divinité guérisseuse. Les origines des pouvoirs guérisseurs de la déesse peuvent être retracées jusqu'en Égypte ancienne. Dans ce pays, Isis était vénérée pour l'aide qu'elle apportait aux souffrants de maladies variées (Pettazzoni 1937, 1-2 ; Bryan, 1974 [1930], 41). Ailleurs aussi, la déesse bénéficiait d'un statut similaire, au côté de son époux Sarapis. À ce couple, parfois accompagné d'Anubis, qui vint s'adjoindre aux deux divinités déjà citées dans le contexte gréco-romain (Bricault 2006, 248), on attribuait en particulier la capacité de remédier aux problèmes de vue, comme en témoigne le nombre important d'objets votifs en forme d'yeux en or et en argent découverts à Délos (Roussel 1916, 290-291 ; Tallet 2021, 326).

Sur ce point, il convient de préciser encore que les Anciens ne se contentaient pas d'attacher à Isis un pouvoir guérisseur général. La déesse égyptienne était concrètement vénérée par des individus ayant souffert de problèmes des yeux. À cet égard, un petit dossier de deux inscriptions relatives à des guérisons effectuées par Isis nous semble pertinent pour notre propos. Le premier document est connu sous le nom d'Arétalogie d'Isis de Maronée et date de la période hellénistique (IIe s.-Ier s. a.C.). Ce texte, qui mentionne aussi Sarapis au cours de son développement, s'ouvre sur des remerciements adressés à Isis ; cette dernière est louée par son auteur pour avoir exaucé les prières concernant ses yeux (Grandjean 1975 ; Tacheva-Hitova 1983, I, 50 ; Bricault 2005, 114/0202). Le second document, issu de la région de la ville Luni en Italie, est une inscription, aujourd'hui perdue et de date inconnue, dont le contenu est conservé dans un manuscrit de Santo Varni. Son texte énumère des offrandes à Isis parmi lesquelles figuraient des yeux en or (Bricault 2005, 511/0701). Ce type d'objets était présenté en remerciement de guérisons des yeux, comme en témoigne la collection de Délos. Confronté aux passages d'Ovide et des poètes qui font référence au châtiment par aveuglement, ce petit dossier d'inscriptions met en évidence deux aspects du pouvoir d'Isis sur la vue humaine. Cette déesse possédait, selon les Anciens, un pouvoir sur la vue des hommes et ce pouvoir était double : il avait un aspect négatif exprimé à travers l'aveuglement et un aspect positif manifesté par la guérison des yeux.

Revenant vers le texte d'Ovide, il convient à présent d'examiner les informations relatives au motif de la confession. Comme nous l'avons vu, la *Première Pontique* évoque ce motif à deux reprises. Celui-ci est introduit d'abord au vers 51-54 où l'un des individus punis par Isis déclare à voix haute qu'il a bien mérité son châtiment. Ovide reprend la même idée quelques vers plus loin, en indiquant que les divinités célestes (*caelestes*) se réjouissent des confessions prononcées à voix haute (*praeconia*) et que celles-ci constituent une preuve de leurs pouvoirs. Au sujet de la confession encore, le poète précise que la reconnaissance des erreurs peut inciter les dieux à lever les peines infligées aux hommes (v. 58-59).

Les recherches menées sur le motif de la confession ont permis d'établir qu'il est caractéristique des cultes d'origine étrangère et, en particulier, des cultes orientaux, comme ceux de Lydie et de Phrygie (Chaniotis 1995 ; Ricl 1995 ; Belayche 2008). Sa présence est en effet attestée dans un certain nombre de cultes de ce type, y compris ceux de Cybèle et d'Isis. Tout comme le thème de la punition divine, celui de la reconnaissance des erreurs a été exploré par la poésie latine qui témoigne de rites de repentir et de confession (Pettazzoni 1937). Parmi les poètes ayant exploité ce thème, on trouve Ovide lui-même qui s'en sert dans les *Fastes* à propos du culte de Magna Mater (Ov., *Fast.*, 4.305-327). Juvénal, déjà cité plus haut, apporte un témoignage intéressant relatif à la confession publique (Juv. 6.526-530), une pratique similaire est aussi attestée par Apulée dans les *Métamorphoses* (*Met.* 8.28). D'ailleurs, d'après des témoignages épigraphiques, des pratiques de confession auraient existé en Égypte ancienne dès le IIe millénaire a.C. (Pettazzoni 1937, 1).

Sur le plan pratique, la confession était un rite religieux constitué d'actes et de paroles. Un tel rite impliquait une invocation à la divinité accompagnée d'un geste des mains dirigées vers le ciel et une confession des erreurs commises, suivie de la demande adressée au dieu et d'une purification par l'eau. Cette séquence des actes et des paroles est attestée par Ovide lui-même dans les *Métamorphoses* (Ov. *Met.* 11.131-142 ; v. aussi la structure des stèles de confession chez Petzl & Malay 1987, 459-460 ; Belayche 2008). La confession publique n'excluait pas, aux yeux des anciens, une forme d'expérience religieuse personnelle, dans le culte d'Isis, une telle expérience pouvait coexister avec le statut universel et exigeant de cette déesse (Turcan 2000, 122). La confession était un moyen d'honorer la divinité et d'obtenir la levée de sa punition. Le rite effectué par les mortels invitait la divinité à montrer sa puissance (de Hoz 2017, 40) ; si elle levait sa punition, elle manifestait un des deux extrêmes de son pouvoir. Isis, qui pouvait punir par l'aveuglement, avait aussi le pouvoir de guérir les yeux des mortels. On comprend alors pourquoi, selon Ovide, la confession serait une preuve des pouvoirs divins. Un tel rite mettait en évidence de façon pratique le genre d'omnipotence divine dont nous avons la description dans les arétalogies d'Isis (Versnel 1998, 66-67 ; sur le rapport entre confession écrite et arétalogie, v. aussi Belayche 2008, cf. Nock 1972, 427, n. 77 ; de Hoz 2009 ; Belayche 2013, 261, 269, 272).

Parole poétique et vision prophétique

La poésie issue de la période de la relégation d'Ovide à Tomes se caractérise par un autre aspect qu'il est nécessaire, pensons-nous, de prendre en compte afin de compléter l'interprétation de notre passage. Cet aspect concerne le statut du poète et touche directement à la scène décrite au vers 51-54.

La lecture de la *Première Pontique* permet de dégager la position de notre auteur au sujet du statut de poète : celui-ci revendique un statut spécifique, supérieur à celui des autres mortels, d'après une tradition qui remonte à Homère. Cette conception se conjugue, chez Ovide, à ses connaissances en matière de rhétorique. Notre auteur fut formé, dans sa jeunesse, à l'art oratoire, ce qui était une étape préparant les Romains aux affaires publiques et à l'exercice de la parole dans le cadre juridique. À ce titre, Ovide maîtrisait parfaitement la parole, comme cela est visible par l'emploi de la terminologie juridique dans ses poèmes. En bon orateur, il utilisait, à toutes les périodes de son œuvre, des notions du domaine de la loi dans ses poèmes, y compris dans les *Pontiques* (McGowan 2009, 41-55). Il pouvait donc, s'il le souhaitait, s'exprimer de façon à donner un double sens à ses vers ou à rester élusif sur certains détails. Cette maîtrise de la parole lui permettait de jouer sur la signification des mots mais aussi sur les images qu'il décrivait dans ses poèmes.

Sur le plan de la philosophie et de la religion, le statut du poète fait l'objet d'une réflexion qui remonte aux présocratiques. La pensée présocratique établissait une relation entre les dieux et la figure du poète, cette relation étant illustrée par Homère. Selon cette conception, l'aède aveugle avait un statut supérieur à celui des mortels grâce à la volonté divine, ses connaissances sur le passé et sur l'avenir dépassaient ce qui était accessible au reste des hommes. En ce sens, son statut était similaire à celui d'un prophète, c'est-à-dire d'un maître de vérité (Detienne 1979) et ce statut revenait aussi à ses héritiers. La poésie latine, qui a hérité de cette conception, exprimait la relation entre la poésie et la prophétie à travers le terme *vates*, qui pouvait désigner à la fois le prophète et le poète inspiré par les dieux. Les mots issus de la racine de *vates*, comme les verbes *vaticino* et le substantif *vaticinator*, avaient ainsi une signification qui renvoyait à la prophétie et à la parole prononcée au nom des dieux. Le latin rattachait une signification similaire au terme *carmen* qui pouvait désigner à la fois un poème et la réponse d'un oracle ; la même polysémie s'appliquait au verbe correspondant à ce substantif, *cano*, signifiant "chanter" et "prophétiser" depuis la plus haute Antiquité (Guittard 2004).

Dans la *Première Pontique*, Ovide insiste sur cet aspect de la poésie et sur son statut de poète inspiré à travers les termes *carmen* (30) et *vaticinator* (42, 47). Il fait par ailleurs allusion à Homère en rappelant la sortie d'Énée de Troie (33-34). Notre auteur indique ainsi, d'une manière subtile, que, tout comme l'aède aveugle, le poète latin qu'il était pouvait voir et exprimer ses visions à travers la parole divinement inspirée. Pour relayer ce message, il joue sur la signification des mots mais aussi sur les images. Dans le passage qui nous intéresse, Ovide emploie le verbe *video* (51) afin d'introduire la scène au vers 51-54. Ce verbe, qui signifiait couramment "voir", avait aussi une signification plus nuancée renvoyant non à la faculté de percevoir par les yeux mais aux images qu'on pouvait percevoir dans son esprit, c'est-à-dire aux visions dans son imagination. Ces nuances de la langue latine permettent de présenter notre scène relative à Isis comme une vision et Ovide un comme un *vates*. La scène devant l'autel de la déesse revêt donc la valeur d'une image inspirée que le poète était capable de décrire en détail, tout comme Homère chantait la guerre de Troie malgré sa cécité. En réclamant le statut de poète inspiré, Ovide couvre d'un voile de mystère ses vers relatifs à Isis : à son auditoire de juger s'il décrivait des faits réels ou des images de son esprit.

Quant au *princeps*, assimilé aux immortels dans le poème, il pouvait, s'il le souhaitait, accorder son pardon à celui qui le demandait et qui confessait ses erreurs. Au divin Auguste donc de montrer les deux extrêmes de sa puissance. On a remarqué à juste titre que l'interprétation ovidienne du statut du *princeps* va plus loin que les traitements proposés par les poètes de la même période (McGowan 2009, 83-84 ; 120). Si cette interprétation s'inspirait de l'omnipotence des dieux égyptiens, elle serait une sorte d'anticipation du rôle de ces dieux au cours de l'histoire de l'Empire.

Les dates de la relégation d'Ovide à Tomes et de la composition de la *Première Pontique* correspondent à une période à laquelle les cultes isiaques étaient bien établis dans cette ville sur la côte du Pont Euxin. Les informations que nous possédons à date actuelle ne permettent pas de conclure avec certitude que le passage d'Ovide s'inspire de pratiques que le poète a réellement rencontrées à Tomes. Les vers 51-54 et suivants s'inscrivent, pensons-nous, dans un développement auquel l'auteur a consciemment donné un double sens et qui est motivé tant par la situation personnelle du poète que par ses connaissances du culte d'Isis et de sa pratique au début de l'Empire. Ce texte reste néanmoins intéressant pour l'étude du culte de la déesse à cette époque, notamment parce qu'il permet d'explorer les conceptions qui ont existé au temps d'Ovide des pouvoirs d'Isis sur la vue humaine et du rôle de la confession dans son culte.

Isis and Sarapis in the context of the civic religion (3rd century CE). Case study - Moesia Inferior (Tomis)

Ştefana Cristea

Изида и Сарапис в контекста на гражданската религия (3 век). Примерът на Долна Мизия (Томи)

Стефана Кристеа

В статията се изследват основните характеристики на гражданската религия и до каква степен в нея настъпват промени през 3 век, като се набляга на навлизането на боговете от египетски произход (Сарапис и Изида). Времевата рамка на изследването е дефинирана с Едикта на Каракала и управлението на Диоклециан (212 – 285 г.). Използваният пример е град Томи в провинция Долна Мизия и присъщата му действителност. Първата част на статията дефинира най-важните термини. Във втората част се очертават някои характеристики на гражданската религия като публична религиозна проява на императора и неговото семейство в централна позиция, наблюдавайки тяхното съществуване в споменатата провинция и използвайки информация от други провинции (като Галиция) от 2 век. Използвани са както археологически, епиграфски и нумизматични източници, така и писмени сведения.

Introduction

In the last fifteen years, studies related to different aspects of Roman civic religion as part of public religious manifestation have multiplied considerably. And although the directions already established are continuated, such as the one regarding the legislation and the expression of imperial power, they focus in particular on the relationship of the emperor with the provinces or the army, the involvement of women in civic religion, the relevance and contextualization of using terms such as "civic identity", "urban religion" etc. The environment is the one of the city, and the research direction is increasingly interested in the individual and his personal way of living religious manifestations, shaping or being shaped by them. These research directions are also valid for the 3rd century CE, although the particular situation of this century makes the exploration of civic religion much more demanding.

In general, in the scientific literature, when referring to the military anarchy, the 3rd century CE is defined as starting in 235 with Maximinus Thrax and ending in 285 with Diocletian. However, it may be appropriate to include also the Severan dynasty (193-235 CE) in the discussion for several reasons: on the one hand, due to the relevance regarding the changes that take place in the definition of citizenship with the *Constitutio Antoniniana* and the implicit consequences in the civic identity of the inhabitants of the empire; on the other hand, because Septimius Severus was acclaimed emperor by the Pannonian legions represents a relevant step in what will become a common practice particularly after Maximinus Thrax, when being a good soldier is no longer a desirable quality to be an emperor, but the principal necessary quality.

At the very core of the imperial Roman civic religion was the emperor and the imperial house, and this type of institutionalized Roman religious manifestation is one of the essential elements that give coherence and cohesion to the empire as a whole. Considering that, we believe it is meaningful to understand how it is perpetuated in the 3rd century CE in the conditions of large-scale disruption of the imperial power. Defining the term "civic religion" from both ancient and modern perspectives helps us dismantle this religious manifestation into its component elements in pursuance of their dynamics in the period of crisis that we are dealing with. If other researchers discussed the role of some institutions (e.g., *Augustales*), the army, local elites, and different types of archaeological materials in the dynamics of the civic religion (e.g., coins, inscriptions), we wanted to capture the involvement of the gods of Egyptian origin in it.

Of course, the archaeological elements that we rely on in this study represent only the hitherto archaeological research and probably reflect the existing situation in the 2nd or 3rd centuries CE only to a certain extent. These artifacts mostly belonged to citizens who were part of the elite of the Roman Empire and therefore reflect their position inside the civic religious expressions and not one of all citizens. With all these limitations, the study of civic religion as it manifests in the 3rd century CE in the border provinces of the empire, such as Moesia Inferior, should be pursued for a better understanding of the role of this province within the empire. At the same time, such studies will bring clarifications on the dissemination of the deities of Egyptian origin and how they adapt to their role within the civic religion and urban communities. Unfortunately, these studies are still far too small in number.

It is well known that starting from the 2nd century CE, and especially in the 3rd century CE, religion changes in the Roman Empire. This study pursues one aspect of these internal changes of the civic religion under the influence of the rapid succession of the emperors. The presence in the context of the civic religion of Isis and Sarapis is traced in a clear urban context: Tomis (Moesia Inferior), a Greek colony on the Black Sea.

Civic religion, civic identity, polis and urban religion

To be as transparent as possible, we believe it is necessary to start the article with a theoretical approach of terms such as civic religion, civic identity, and the polis/urban religion.

The term civic religion, as we understand it today, was coined for the first time in a theoretical manner by Jean-Jacques Rousseau. Even for the most trained minds capable of moving away from the modern content of some terms or expressions, the repeated exercise of their use in the contemporary context remains imprinted in the subconscious. That is why we will start by defining civic religion, as is found in chapter 8, book 4 of *The Social Contract* (1762).

Rousseau believed that the state needed a religion that would help people to be good citizens, to ensure social unity, a religion that would bring together high moral values inspired by a divine force and a love for lows. To be, at the same time, a religion in which the divine authority and the source of political power are intertwined in such a way that for the citizens "to serve the state means to serve the tutelary deity" and "to violate the laws means impiety"[1]. The civil religion it was not to be just another religion, but "a religion who makes citizens to love their duties", "a civil profession of faith whose articles are set by the sovereign as feelings of sociability" (Beiner 2011, 11-16). The role of the sovereign is crucial within the civil religion because this type of faith was to be

[1] I would like to thank dr. Vessela Atanasova for the opportunity to participate in the conference *Egyptian Cults on the Black Sea Coast* and for the incredible memories from Varna and Sofia. My thanks also go to dr. Ștefan Georgescu for the photo of the statue of the citizen from Tomis. This article was written during the "Vasile Pârvan" postdoctoral fellowship at Rome granted by the Romanian Academy, the Ministry of National Education and Scientific Research, and the Ministry of Foreign Affairs to the author through the Scholarships and Credits Agency. I thank all these institutions, as well as the Accademia di Romania in Rome which became my second home. I thank the British School in Rome and the American Academy in Rome, who generously offered access to their libraries and workspace. I must especially thank my colleague and friend dr. Călin Timoc, for the endless discussions, for his patience in reading several versions of the article, and for his support and friendship. I also thank dr. Cristina Codarcea for her valuable comments and suggestions. Last but not least, I want to thank the editors of this volume for including the present article, and for their patience and understanding.
For Romans, the notions of *pietas* and *impietas* are only partially related to actions that involve the gods, rather than having a legal, social, civic, or political dimension (when it refers to the person of the emperor) : Potter 1999, 125-128.

constructed, imposed, and controlled from the top down. He ratifies and maintains: the belief in a deity, the belief in an afterlife in which the righteous are rewarded and the wicked punished, and the belief in religious tolerance. For Rousseau, religion represents the core of the social agreement, and he pointed out the inseparability of governance and religion. It is important to note that, unlike the civic religion defined by Rousseau, which has among its principal goals the concept of "good citizens" who were to resemble their virtuous leader, the Roman imperial civil religion of the 3rd century CE, when it refers to the qualities of the emperor, instead seeks to legitimize his power, no matter how short the period in which he exercises it.

In the political context of the assassination of Caesar, Marcus Tullius Cicero (106-43 BCE) writes in October-November 44 BCE the treatise in three books, *De Officiis*. The first book employs honorable conduct (*honestum* considered synonymously with the Stoic *virtus*), the second book with what is useful (*utile*), and the third one with the conflicts between the two. The four key virtues described by Plato were wisdom, justice, courage and temperance, but Cicero is going further distinguishing between *sapientia* and *prudentia* (the practical wisdom which is considered very important in the implication in public life). For Cicero, behind knowledge, it must be a practical, civic justification, as the service to the community, and beneficence and good faith (*fides*) are a meaningful part of justice. In what concerns courage, Cicero "outset that this virtue looks to the welfare of the community rather than the prestige of the individuals" because "the desire for glory often leads to acts of injustice" (Walsh 2000, xx). Regarding the members of the Roman administration, "they must protect the interests of the citizens in such a way that all they do should be directed towards that end without thought of personal advantage" and also to be impartial "so that they not protect one section at the expense of the rest" (Cic. I, 85). In *De Officiis*, modesty, temperance, and moderation, made possible "the fitting" (*decorum*) which is interlinked with honorable (Cic. I, 93-96) (Walsh 2000, 33-34). The influence exerted by Cicero's treatise was felt immediately after his death and persisted in antiquity (in the books of Valerius Maximus in the reign of Tiberius, Pliny the Elder in the reign of Vespasian, Lactantius in the 3rd-4th centuries CE, Nonius Marcellus in the 4th century CE) and further in the Middle Ages (e.g. "*Moralis philosophia de honesto et utili*" of Hildebert of Lavardin in the 12th century, "*Summa Theologiae*" by Thomas Aquinas) and in the modern writings (e.g. John Milton, John Locke, Montesquieu) (Walsh 2000, xxxiv-xlvii).

The divine is present in the religious practice from the Roman society through rituals performed in a specific space and with a clear visual, social and political consequence. For the Roman poet Publius Terentius Varro (82-35 BCE) (Potter 1999, 115-117), the theology could be seen from three perspectives: natural (philosophical), mythical (poetical), and civic (civil) (Rüpke 2012, 173; Latham 2016, 45-48). Varro is not referring to an actual theological system, a system created consciously by priests in order to represent the theoretical guiding lines of the religious manifestation, but more like three concrete aspects of the religious life of the Romans, three points of view of the same reality. His "theology" was "conceived not as a policing measure but as a meta-term for distinct types of thinking about religion" (Rüpke 2007, 119). Varro's civic or civil "theology" refers to the practical aspects of performing the public religious act for the benefit of all the citizens as an extended "political community". If the gods will be worshiped in the correct way, the most pleasing way for the gods, then the gods will bestow their generosity to the community. As A. Wallace-Hadrill underline "Varro's *Antiquities* offered a map of the city: its topography was synonymous with the specificities of its ritual practice" (Wallace-Hadrill 2008, 259). Varro's writings are known in the period immediately following his death and therefore exert a decisive influence on the mentality of the beginning of the imperial period.

Velleius Paterculus (19 BCE – 31 CE) connected the moral values of the emperor to the moral values of the citizens for whom the emperor was supposed to represent a legitimate model. He believed that the emperor's authority is increasing through personal example (Gordon 1990b, 209). The same personal example, in favor of civic religion, is also provided by the images found in the art of the Principate, especially during the time of Augustus and rarely after him, which has the emperor as the main sacrificer. But, as R. Gordon underlines, the sacrificial role of the princeps is closely connected to the moral values that he embodies in an ideal manner as *pietas augusti* (that can be found on the coins until the end of the Principate), *philanthropia* (benevolence), and *liberalitas* (generosity) (Gordon 1990b, 210-219). The best-known example is the one offered by Augustus who received from the Senate on 16 January 27 BCE the *clipeus virtutis* on which are mentioned his most prominent moral qualities who recommend him for this honor: *virtus*, *clementia*, *iustitia*, *pietas* (Christodoulou 2015, 187-188). These are qualities that will be associated with him throughout his life and which will also be desired by the emperors who follow him.

What characterizes the 3rd century CE is the physical absence of the emperors from Rome, which becomes less and less important as the center of the Roman world, but also the rapid change of the emperors, that local, provincial communities risking to make dedications to the wrong emperor. This leads to a more meaningful local identity, but as well as placing sometimes at the center of the civic religion the empire as a whole, at the expense of the emperor as the source of civic identity (Manders & Hekster 2011). Although some scholars considered that the Severan era represents the peak of the presence of gods from the Isiac family on coins, it is still evident that their popularity did not decrease even in the following years (Bricault 2015, 94-95). The coins illustrate the struggle of the provincial cities to express allegiance to the right emperor. Despite his precarious position, the emperor remains in the 3rd century CE the central figure of the empire, the last resort in resolving local petitions (Manders & Hekster 2011). However, the way the emperors wanted to be perceived changes in the 3rd century CE, this being especially evident in the way they choose to represent their power on centrally minted coins. E. Manders and O. Hekster (Manders & Hekster 2011) concludes that 22,5% from these coins are "referring to the armies, victories, or depicting the emperor in a military role", 21,8% from them "associate imperial power with the divine" and 19,2% "emphasis on imperial virtues or the message that the Golden Age was coming about"[2].

In the 3rd century CE, the number of coins which stresses the emperor's military qualities such as *virtus* and *providentia* increased, and the number of those on which *aequitas* is depicted decreased, simultaneously increasing the number of coins on which the emperor is depicted as a soldier. The emphasis is therefore placed in this period of instability and war on promoting the image of the emperor as a character capable of fighting, winning in battle, and bringing peace (Manders & Hekster 2011). An intriguing and relevant aspect of imperial propaganda through coins is the increased number of associations with the divine realm coin types. As Manders and Hekster underline (Manders & Hekster 2011), the emperor in his form of *sacerdos* is represented especially on the coins of the first half of the 3rd century CE, a phenomenon also supported by the increasingly rare expression of the status of *pontifex maximus* on this type of artifacts. And certainly, there was a connection between the emperors' distancing from Rome and the need to legitimize their actions and status and their increasing proximity to the divine (Manders & Hekster 2011). In this context, the civic religion in the second half of the 3rd century CE, is no longer exercised by the emperors but for the emperors.

If, during the Republic and at the beginning of the 1st century CE, citizenship had an elitist approach, progressively, Roman citizenship became more common as a less special status. At the beginning of the 3rd century CE "the Roman government worked to maximize the number of persons to whom Roman *ius civile,* the low of Roman citizens, applied" (Mathisen 2006, 1013), culminating with the Antonine Constitution in 212 in which the emperor Caracalla (211-217 CE) granted citizenship to almost all free *peregrini* in the Roman Empire, maybe with the exception of *dediticii* (Crawford 2015) (stigmatized freedman who had been branded or tortured, or who had fought in the arena (Mathisen 2006, 1020)): "The safeguarding of the city was inseparably tied to that of the empire. This was the very justification used officially for Caracalla's edict of 212, which extended Roman citizenship to all free men of the empire: "I believe that I can serve the glory of the immortal gods (the Greek gods and the gods of Rome) by making all those who are part of my people participate in the cult of the gods with me. This is why I grant Roman citizenship to all the *peregrini* of the earth." Rome had become the common homeland of all (*Digesta* 50.1.33)" (Van Andringa 2007, 92). The concept of citizenship was forced to evolve in a very modern way by including the barbarians, immigrants, foreigners in general (Mathisen 2006, 1015).

---

[2] For the discussion about the understanding of the coins iconographic messages on imperial power and their changes, and for a more in depth analysis of the 3rd century coins see Manders 2012, 33-62.

The provincial and municipal citizenship was deeply connected to the civic identity, especially in the 3rd century CE when to be a citizen to a particular city was more meaningful than ever (in the 4th century, Ammianus Marcellinus use the term *cives Romani* for the citizens of Rome as a particular case of the citizens of the Roman Empire (Mathisen 2006, 1016)). The polis religion could embody the local versions of myths, be celebrated in civic festivals and reflected in local civic coinage as expression of civic identity. For J. Rüpke, to be part of a polis represent the most relevant membership and an important aspect, if not the most important one, of the social identity because the polis provide for its citizens the privileges and also the legal status (Rüpke 2007, 18).

The civic identity is a complex one: a religious one (joining a specific group characterized by the participation of a religious cult in the civic life or active involvement in festivals dedicated to particular deities), a social one as the legacy of belonging to a specific community (city, tribe), but it is also a legal and political one. Civic identity can be looked at from a double perspective: the civic identity of a city/region/province and a civic identity of a person. The civic identity of a city was closely connected with the coins minted by the city, in which the flavor of the civic religion and imperial propaganda can be included in multiple ways along with iconographic elements relevant only at the local level.[3] The coins minted in the Roman Empire reflect a confrontation between elements of the local/provincial identity and those designed for the entire empire, having in the background the imperial ideology (Howgego 2005, 2). The imagery on the coinage is that of a polis religion, defining the view of those who controlled the polis and less the vast majority of the inhabitants who assume the identity offered by the community in which they live (Howgego 2005, 2). For all the provinces, the most visible social group from an archaeological point of view was the elite (even a rural elite) who were also the negotiators of the local identity. The personal identity as citizens of the Roman empire is a mixture of more types of identity that coexist[4] (as citizens of the empire, a regional identity, or an ethnical identity[5]) and could be connected to "patterns of behaviour" (Mattingly 2011, 208).

The relationship of the Roman imperial house with the gods of Egyptian origin fluctuates over time, from rejection to acceptance, to initiation into the Isiac mysteries or identification with Sarapis in official representations. There were emperors from the 2nd century CE known to have developed a strong bond with the gods from the Isiac family: Hadrian, who founded numerous temples dedicated to these gods, and Commodus, during the reign of which Sarapis became "conservator Augusti" on coins, and it was mentioned that

[3] "What coinage most obviously provides is an enormous range of self-defined and explicit representations of public/official/communal identities, principally civic in nature." (Howgego 2005, 1).

[4] J. Nederveen Pieterse to exemplify multiple identities uses King Herod who was "by birth an Idumean (i.e. Edomite), by profession a Jew, by necessity a Roman, by culture and by choice a Greek." (Nederveen Pieterse 2015, 232.)

[5] Jones 1997, 56-83; Wells 1999, 99-121. We use ethnicity as a self-categorized group by the dedicants of the inscriptions or as they are present in Latin written sources.

the emperor would have participated in Isiac processions (Christodoulou 2015, 189). The emperors of the 3rd century CE only continued this already existing tradition, and it is well known that the Severan emperors had a positive attitude towards the gods of Egyptian origin (Fishwick 1973, 643-645; Podvin 2014), particularly Caracalla, who build or repair their temples, including within the *pomerium*, and during whose reign the god Sarapis often appears on coins (Christodoulou 2015, 189). During the Severan period, the number of representations of Sarapis with sun rays increased. The concept of "partnership" between the emperor and the god is taken to another level by the emperors Gordian III (238-244) and Philip II (247-249). The presence of the gods of Egyptian origin can also be observed after the "3rd century crisis" in the tetrarchic period[6] and even further[7]. Most of the archaeological evidence belonged to noble families therefore most of the references will be made to them.

Case Study

The chosen case study of Tomis in the province of Moesia Inferior, allows us to apply the already described concepts. We appoint it for several reasons. First of all, by selecting a city of Greek tradition we can illustrate the enduring of the previous manifestation and materiality of civic religion in the 3rd century CE, the progressive integration of the Roman emperor and the imperial family in this phenomenon, and the involvement of gods of Egyptian origin in this context. We will observe how Isis and Sarapis are assimilated into the urban structures of the Greek religious tradition, as well as the complex civic identity of the citizens who make dedications to these gods.

Tomis – Moesia Inferior

For advertising the presence of Sarapis and Isis in the 3rd century CE civic religion of Tomis, are employed a few categories of archaeological items: inscriptions, coins, and iconographical representations. The inscriptions discovered in Tomis (Tacheva-Hitova 1983, 8-15) until now, connected to the gods of Egyptian origin, are dated from the 2nd century BCE[8] until the 3rd century CE, and it is a process that involved different catego-

[6] The presence of the gods Isis and Sarapis on the so-called arch of Galerius in Thessaloniki, together with the two emperors (Diocletian and Maximian) and the two Caesars (Galerius and Constantius Chlorus) and deities who embody the imperial power over the entire universe (Caelus, Tellus and Gaia, Oceanos and Tethis, the personifications of the provinces), the moral values that the leaders of the empire represent and the ability to emerge victorious regardless of the circumstances (Virtus, Victoria, Jupiter, Dioskouroi, Mars/Honos, Fortuna/Tyche) show the privileged place that the gods of Egyptian origin occupy in the tetrarchic political program. The proof of the position of these gods is also emphasized by their representation on coins that commemorate *vota publica* and the fact that temples for both of them were built in Rome (Christodoulou 2015, 190-192).

[7] For the end of the 4th century CE see Bricault 2014.

[8] [T]ῆι βασιλ[ί] / [σ]ση(ι) Ἴσιδ[ι] / [Ἀ]ρτέμ[ιδι]- / [.]ΥΣ- - - - - (Avram 2014, 452-454; see also RICIS 618/1009).

ries of citizens of the city (Bricault 2001, 31). In the 1st century BCE - 1st century CE an inscription (*ISM* II,7; *RICIS* 618/1001) referred to an Isiac public festival that takes place in the city, *Charmosyna*; also mentioned a priest of Isis and the existence of the temple of Sarapis (Covacef 2006, 166-167) in which other gods from the Isiac family could probably be found. The festival involved the members of an Isiac association, and there was a celebration in which the image of Isis was carried through the streets in a procession. Another inscription dated in the same period (1st century BCE – 1st century CE) is dedicated not only to Sarapis but also to Isis, Anubis, and other gods (*ISM* II, 154(39); *RICIS* 618/1002), probably referring to the healing powers of Sarapis manifested through dreams and to a specialist in the interpretation of the dreams. The practice of incubation at Tomis, probably in a temple of Sarapis, is also mentioned in another inscription dated by L. Bricault at the beginning of the 1st century BCE (*ISM* II, 152(37); *RICIS* 618/1003). The devotee, the son of Polydoros, claims his origin from Sinope, allowing us to see a double civic identity: the one linked to Tomis, the city where the god expresses his desire through a dream, and the one linked to Sinope, his city of origin. There are no manifestations of the Roman civic religion, but rather individual or group activities, which involved only a limited number of the city's inhabitants and no association with the emperor, the imperial house, or with priests who served the Roman civic religion. However, festivals such as *Charmosyna* can be considered part of the civic religious manifestations specific to Greek cities.

In an inscription dated to the middle of the 1st century CE, a priest of the gods Isis and Sarapis is involved in the cult of *diva Agrippina*, the deified mother of Nero, and is also mentioned his gesture of civic patronage represented by building a monument or construction for the benefit of the community from his own money[9]. In a recent paper (Avram & Hălmagi 2019) which recapitulates especially the epigraphic evidence of the presence of Isiac cults in Tomis, A. Avram and D. Hălmagi give the inscription another reading and a slightly different interpretation[10]. The authors consider the possibility that "l'*honorandus* soit un étranger, peut-être un Alexandrin." We are already witnessing the association of gods of Egyptian origin with the Roman civic religion, which has the

[9] *ISM* II, 37(3); *RICIS* 618/1004. P. Christodoulou gives another reading of the inscription. Translation: To Good Fortune. [...] of goddess Agrippina, [...] on the sixth of (name of the month) [...] under the care of [name, son of ...]onios, [... priest (?)] of Sarapis and Isis [...] showing [...] love for the fatherland [...] to the gods [...] (demos?) of the citizens of Tomis [...]. He considers that the honouree was a priestess of diva Agrippina, and he believes that Agrippina Major is the best option, her connection with Isiac cults being known from other inscriptions. If his reading is correct, then the inscription does not directly mention Agrippina but a priestess of hers, which does not affect the association between the empress and the deities of Egyptian origin (Christodoulou 2015, 179-183)

[10] "Sous la prêtrise de la divine Agrippine Auguste, le sixième jour du mois Apaturéôn (?), [...] Untel fils de [Poseid?]onios étant président de l'assemblée d'élection des magistrats, les archontes ont fait la proposition: attendu que le prêtre de Sarapis et d'Isis, Untel fils d'Untel, éprouvant une disposition, d'une part, pieuse à l'égard de la divinité, d'autre part, bienveillante envers (notre) patrie ..." (Avram & Hălmagi 2019, 65-70).

emperor and the imperial family at the center and also the political and economic importance of Tomis on the western shore of the Black Sea. L. Buzoianu and M. Bărbulescu emphasizes that between the reign of Claudius and that of Domitian (41-96 CE), the inscriptions show Tomis' interest in the imperial house, a phenomenon that was enhanced during the reign of the Antonines (e.g., Traian) (Buzoianu & Bărbulescu 2008, 14).

Proof of the involvement of the god Sarapis as Zeus Helios Sarapis[11] in the civic religion at Tomis in the 2nd century CE is an inscription discovered in Sinope dedicated to Zeus Helios Sarapis and Isis *myrionyma*. The devotee, Stratoneikos, son of Euarestos, declares himself a citizen of both cities - Tios and Tomis, both ports on the Black Sea in two different provinces. Sarapis is not the only one who benefits from this dedication, as he is associated with the most complex version of the goddess Isis, Isis *myrionyma*, the one with countless names. It is a concept explicitly stated in the Isiac aretalogies in which all other female divinities are included, a concept that represents a level of complete authority reached by Sarapis as Zeus Helios Sarapis / Jupiter Sol Sarapis. Avram and Hălmagi highlights the fact that in an inscription possibly from Tomis and preserved in the National Museum of Antiquities (Institute of Archeology "Vasile Pârvan" in Bucharest, inv. L 871), the name of the god Serapis could be accompanied by the same epithet, [θεῷ μεγάλῳ Σ]αράπ[ιδι] (Avram & Hălmagi 2019, 70).

An inscription from Tomis[12] (*ISM* II, 153(38); *RICIS* 618/1005; Avram 2006; Christodoulou 2015, 173, 183) from the second half of the 2nd century CE (March 29, 160 CE) is dedicated to the great Zeus Helios Sarapis and the other gods with whom he shares the temple. The inscription is important because associates explicitly the Isiac gods, their temple, and their priests with a Roman emperor and the imperial family (Antoninus Pius and Marcus Aurelius). The inscription mentions, at the same time, an association of merchants from Alexandria[13]. Antoninus Pius' sympathy for Helios is well known, the god's images being encountered during his reign, from colossal statues to coins, and the association with Sarapis is also frequent. The addition of Zeus to this amalgamation only

---

[11] The association of the three gods was known since the Hellenistic period, and it was completed in the imperial era, even in Egypt, with an evident political and social role (Bricault 2013, 467-469) and is frequently mentioned in inscriptions of the 3rd century CE.

[12] About the change of the location of the inscription see Avram 2006, 277-278.

[13] "Le rôle des Alexandrins dans cette véritable contagion cultuelle se révèle tout aussi important que celui des Égyptiens et des Rhodiens, car plus durable. (...) Ce lien avec des activités commerciales impliquant des Alexandrins se retrouve, plus de deux siècles plus tard, dans une autre dédicace découverte, cette fois, à Tomi en Mésie Inférieure, sur les rives du Pont Euxin. En 160 apr. J.-C., un collège de négociants alexandrins consacre un autel associant les divinités isiaques et les empereurs dans un sanctuaire au sein duquel ils possèdent leur propre lieu de réunion (*oikos*)."(Bricault 2013, 145.) It also the case of few dedications from Portus Ostiae in which Alexandrian shipowners are implicated in *pro salute* dedications to the emperors - dated at the end of the 2nd century CE and beginning of the 3rd century CE: *RICIS* 503/1204, *RICIS* 503/1217; *RICIS* 503/1207; *RICIS* 503/1215; *RICIS* 503/1216 and *RICIS* 503/1211.

increases the civic dimension of the resulting divinity[14]. If we look at other information provided by the inscription, we will notice a triple civic identity. The devotee, Karpion, who has a father with an Egyptian theophoric name - Anubion, consecrates an altar probably in the already mentioned temple, for the benefit of this association: he is a resident of Tomis, probably a member of the association of Alexandrians, and although he does not explicitly declare Alexandria as his place of origin, the inscription might suggest it. Besides the civic identity, this also expresses an ethnic identity. The Alexandrians association is a religious, ethnic, and professional one. By dedicating the inscription of a version of Sarapis in syncretism with the great Zeus, the official god by excellence, and to the emperor and his son, he also recognizes himself as a citizen of the Empire. Two priests are mentioned in the text of the inscription, one of them with an Isiac theophoric name, Sarapion. As P. Christodoulou pointed out, "It is tempting to see in this attitude a continuation of the Hellenistic habit of presenting offerings to Sarapis, Isis and Anubis in favour of the Ptolemies" (Christodoulou 2015, 173).

L. Buzoianu and M. Bărbulescu mention the importance of the reign of the emperor Antoninus Pius (138-161 CE) in the existence of Tomis, from his time dating the first epigraphic document in which the city is called the metropolis of the Left Pontus (μητρόπολις τοῦ Εὐωνύμον Πόντου) (*ISM* II, 54), title which appears since that moment also on coins. Public buildings were built during his reign when the governors were L. Minicius Natalis Quadronius Verus, Q. Fuficius Cornutus and Titus Flavius Turbo (Buzoianu & Bărbulescu 2008, 16-17).

Another inscription dated to the second half of the 2nd century CE was discovered on a limestone column in the Turkish cemetery on the left side of the Constanta-Cumpăna road. Unfortunately, the inscription, only partially read it due to its advanced deterioration, is no longer preserved. Some authors read in the text the name of Sarapis and the city of Tomis, assuming that it is a monument dedicated to the god of Egyptian origin (*ISM* II, 398(7); *RICIS* 618/1006).

Among the inscriptions discovered at Tomis in connection with the Isiac gods, the one dated in the 3rd century CE is also one of the most interesting. The *hieronautai* and the association of *pastophores* are mentioned in this inscription[15] (*ISM* II, 98(64); *RICIS* 618/1007). As Bricault underlines, this association is found in Egypt serving Isis, but also other divinities and is involved in celebrations that take place in spring (*Navigium Isidis* when the sailing season opens) and autumn (*Isia* and *Inventio Osiridis*), festivals that engage a consistent

[14] For Zeus Helios Sarapis see Bricault 2021.

[15] The version suggested by A. Avram is the following: - - - - - - - - - - - - - - - - - - / [- - - - - - - - -]φιλ[- -] / [- - - - - - - - κ]ράτου[ς] / [μητέρα π]αστοφόρω[ν] / γυναῖκα δὲ Α[- - - - - -] / [ἱ]εροναῦται /ἀν[έθηκαν] / ἐκ τῶν ἰδίων [- - - - - -] / [π]ροστατοῦντος [(δὲ) -] / [- -]τάρχου Ἰ[- - - - -] / - - - - - - - - - - - - - - - - - - (Avram 2018).

number of devotees, and images of the gods from the Isiac family[16]. It is Bricault who also mentions, concerning this inscription the fact that, if the *hieronautes* could represent that group of devotees that carries the boat consecrated to the goddess Isis in the procession of the *Navigium Isidis* festival, then the *pastophores* could be the ones that carry the sails with the image of the goddess (Bricault 2020, 223). The lecture of the inscription, as suggested by Avram, implies a female figure presiding over this association of pastophores from Tomis (Avram 2018). It is clear that we are in the presence of a Greek tradition, civic religious manifestation as aspect of the urban religion, the start of the sailing season on March 5th being a very important moment for the prosperity and development of the entire city. As W. Van Andringa pointed out "religious activities were not limited to cults which focused on politics or identity: expatriate groups, as well as the other communities, created their own religious systems, systems which took into account the activity exercised just as much as the local context" (Van Andringa 2007, 91). As could be seen from the previous inscriptions, the Isiac gods become part of the civic pantheon of the city, reality also preserved in the imperial period, including in the 3rd century CE (Van Andringa 2007, 85). The celebration of this local civic festival of Egyptian essence does not exclude the association with the Roman emperors, as can be seen in the mural painting discovered in Ostia, probably representing the *Navigium Isidis* and the busts of the emperor Septimius Severus and his two sons (Podvin 2014, 320). Such local celebrations in which a large number of citizens participate can give them the necessary feeling of belonging to a community, make them feel safer in periods of instability, and shapes the urban civic identity. The presence of Isiac gods and of the merchants from Alexandria (*ISM* II 463) in Tomis doesn't end with Diocletian but continues in the 4th century CE, yet we did not intend to continue our analysis beyond the year 285. Nevertheless, worth mentioning the representation of the gods Isis and Harpocrates together with Aphrodite and Eros on a false stone door that also represents a Nilotic landscape found in a tomb together with a coin from Constantine (Bordenache 1969, no. 310, pl. CXXXVIII-CXXXIX; Tacheva-Hitova 1983, 15; Bricault 2001, 31).

Connected maybe to the popularity of Isiac gods in Tomis, we should also mention the use of theophoric names inspired by these gods, such as Sarapion, Isidorus, or Anubion. Some of these citizens were priests or hold leadership positions in Tomis, and the inscriptions sometimes emphasize the role played by them in various aspects of civic life. There is a reasonably high number of inscriptions in this sense dated in the 1st century BCE - 1st CE, but also at the end of the 2nd century CE - the beginning of the 3rd century CE (*ISM* II, 17, 83(49), 96 (62), 125(10), 153 (38), 154 (39), 298(134), 314(150)). For example, a decree (*ISM* II, 2; Covacef 2006, 160; Buzoianu & Bărbulescu 2008, 9) of the archons of the city, for which has been proposed an early dating, the end of the 2nd century BCE, and

16 "À la toute fin du roman d'Apulée, Lucius intègre à Rome un collège, celui des pastophores, personnages dont les attributions et la fonction principale ont longtemps fait débat. On les trouve mentionnés aussi bien dans le monde hellénophone, en Égypte sourtout, mais également à Tomi (*RICIS* 618/1007), que dans le monde latin, à Rome (...)" (Bricault 2013, 315).

which establishes an additional city guard caused by an external threat, mentions the priest Sarapion, the son of Dioscurides.

The leading figure in relation to the Roman imperial power is Sarapis, also represented on the coins minted in Tomis, including a temple image. And, as we already underlined, the local coins, speak for the way the cities are manifesting their civic identity and, at the same time, for the way the emperor wants to be perceived[17]. The fact that Tomis became at one point the residence of the governor of Moesia Inferior probably influenced the great variety of coins on which gods of Egyptian origin are depicted. The same phenomenon can also be observed in Perinth, which became the residence of the governor (of province Thrace) during the Roman imperial period, but unlike Perinth, Tomis' coins with representations of the gods Sarapis or Isis were minted only in the Roman imperial period, starting from Commodus until Philip II. Meanwhile, communities of Alexandrian merchants are documented in both cities, an important phenomenon for the expression of the civic identity of the cities (Bricault 2008, 206-207).

Except for one type of coin on which Isis is associated with Fulvia Plautilla, Caracalla's wife (Bricault 2008, 207), Sarapis is the one who creates the connection between the city and the imperial house, being represented as a bust, on a throne or standing. An intriguing version of these coins minted during the time of Severus Alexander and Gordian III, U. Peter considers could have been appropriated from Alexandrian coins - the frontal representation of Sarapis' bust sitting above the imperial eagle with open wings (Bricault 2008, 207, Tomis 11). The latest coins from Tomis that depict the god are those from the reign of Philip II or Philip the Younger (238-249 CE), in which the god and the emperor are depicted facing each other (Bricault 2008, 207, 247). It is a type of coin issued during the reigns of Gordian III and Philip II in Moesia Inferior (Dionysopolis, Marcianopolis, Odessos, and Tomis) and Thrace (Mesambria), where the emperor maybe considers himself an equal of the god sharing the same divine sphere as partners, "making a real *comes Augusti* out of Sarapis" (Christodoulou 2015, 189). D. Boteva believes that this image is connected with the young age of the two: Gordian III as a sole a*ugustus* at 12 or 13 years old and Philip II *caesar* at 6 or 7 years old (Boteva 2017, 331), and that god Sarapis substitutes the father figure (Boteva 2017, 332). She also advances the hypothesis according to which the five cities minting the coin with this iconographic model were part of a league with political and economic implications (Boteva 2017, 335). This type of coin shows not only a way of disseminating the imperial propaganda but also a divine justification of the emperor's actions as the equal of the god and mediator between him and humankind, and also the expression of the city's civic identity as part of the relationship with the emperor and the empire. "Sarapis thus is a genuine *comes Augusti*, the companion of the young Emperor, and at the same time the prince becomes something of a partner of the god", as Bricault points out (Bricault 2015, 96).

[17] "minting coins would have been one of the first acts of a new emperor seeking to assert his power and legitimacy" (Haegemans 2003, 472).

The discovery of the busts of Isis and Sarapis and other artifacts connected to the Isiac cults (Tacheva-Hitova 1983, 14-15; Bricault 2001, 28-29, 31), reinforce these conclusions. From the Flavian era dates a small marble bust of the goddess with a height of only 0.23 m (Bordenache 1969, no. 170, pl. LXXIV; Tacheva-Hitova 1983, no. 19). The goddess has the characteristic knot on the chest, the hair is represented on her shoulders as long Libyan locks, and over her forehead there is a crescent moon and a lotus bud. In 1962, the so-called "thesaurus of sculptures from Tomis" was discovered, which consists of 24 artifacts, including one bust representing the goddess Isis (Tacheva-Hitova 1983, no. 20; Covacef 2011). The bust of the goddess Isis, part of this thesaurus, made of white marble with large crystals, 0.75 m high, with a 0.20 m plinth, is dated to the first half of the 3rd century CE. Over the chiton she wears a himation tied in the typical knot of Isis and a new moon over her forehead. A small fragmentary marble tablet (Bordenache 1969, no. 171, pl. LXXV; Tacheva-Hitova 1983, no. 24) that represented Isis, Harpocrates, and Serapis, preserved only the lower part where Harpocrates can be recognized making the gesture of putting his finger to his mouth and the feet of the other two gods. It was probably used as an *ex voto*, just like the previously mentioned small bust of Isis, and was dated to the middle of the 3rd century CE or in the second half of this century. A significant artifact is the head of a Sarapis (Bordenache 1969, no. 165, pl. LXXI; Tacheva-Hitova 1983, no. 25) of translucid marmor, 0.195 m high, fragment of a statue or bust of the god from Severan era. The *modius* is missing, yet the area where it should have been placed is still visible. The features are those of a mature man with rich hair and beard and a severe expression. Four other small artifacts from Tomis, from which three do not have some unequivocal iconographical element to consider that represents Sarapis, are analyzed by G. Bordenache (Bordenache 1969, no. 166-169, pl. LXXII-LXXIII; Tacheva-Hitova 1983, no. 28) and were dated to the middle of the 2nd century and the beginning of the 3rd century CE. As far as Osiris is concerned, he may be represented under its mummiform appearance on a marble altar with a height of 0.90 m and a width of 0.42 m, discovered in 1913 following some works in the port of Constanța (Bordenache 1969, no. 172, pl. LXXV; Tacheva-Hitova 1983, no. 31). On the same altar is also represented an eagle in its classic Roman form, thus realizing a connection with Jupiter and the symbol of the Roman imperial power. Unfortunately, only a modest fragment of the inscription was preserved (...ΟΣΤΟ), the appearance of the letters helps, however, to date the altar to the 2nd century CE.

Conclusions

For the civic religion of the 3rd century CE, regardless of whether we refer to the Roman or Greek cities, an important role is played by the traditions established in the previous centuries. We can address this aspect from the perspective of habitus as defined by the French sociologist P. Bourdieu (Asimaki & Koustourakis 2014) or from the perspective of religious memory by Ph. Borgeaud (Borgeaud 1988, 7-20). However it may be, it is clear that this learned way of life gives to those who live it "le sentiment d'une intégrité"

(Borgeaud 1988, 7) and that forgetting these traditions can create identity issues both at the individual and at the collective level. "C'est par la pratique et l'imitation, la répétition machinale de gestes et de paroles transmis dans le cadre d'une tradition maintenue par un groupe social auquel il a le sentiment d'appartenir, que l'individu mémorise, sans s'en rendre compte, le plus grand nombre des informations nécessaire à son juste comportement social et religieux" (Borgeaud 1988, 10). The religious life of Roman or Greek cities benefits from intentional memorization by establishing a religious calendar of the city displayed in the public space, but also from mechanical memorization achieved by repeating the rituals, processions, and saying specific formulas, all this happening in the public space. Because if writing can convey technical aspects of religious activities (a precise time of the year when they take place, the name of certain functions), what really attracts the inhabitants of antiquity, just like today, to one or another of the cults are the images, the gestures, the attitudes, the feelings they have when they participate in these religious activities. And as Apuleius described these rituals and festivals of the gods of Egyptian origin, their staging was as convincing as possible. The importance of this religious behavior in shaping individual and collective identity is evident, an aspect observed archaeologically in the inscriptions. The members of religious associations identify themselves in the inscriptions they dedicated individually, and they are also recognized by the community they belong to, with the help of the position they hold within the association at a given time. The transformations of religious practices over time show the adaptability of the Isiac gods to the audience and the demands of the moment, an adaptability that makes them capable of surviving (Borgeaud 1988, 13-14). It is enough to think about how the gods of Egyptian origin transform themselves from Sarapis, to Zeus Helios Sarapis / Jupiter Sol Sarapis, from Isis to Isis myrionima. Van Andringa[18] rightly observes that one of the consequences of the *Constitutio Antoniniana* is the fact that *peregrini,* who have now become citizens, will no longer identify themselves with the social category of the conquered but of the conquerors, adopting their gods in the dedications or remodeling their own gods so that they resemble up to identity with the gods of the conquerors[19].

The article aims to illustrate the complexity of the process, and not the final product, that represents the civic religion in the Roman Empire and its fluidity. This process knows a continuous transformation[20], and the delimitation of time and space is vital. The discus-

[18] "as a result of the political integration of the various population, the place of provincial communities became less and less distinct from that of truly Roman groups in the provinces – military units and the associations of Roman citizens settle in foreign lands." (Van Andringa 2007, 91).

[19] "The people of the provinces progressively emerged from submission to become conquerors, sharing this with the local gods." (Van Andringa 2007, 95).

[20] "In Asia Minor, Greece, or in the Greek cities of Egypt, the gods already wore togas and were conversant with civic life; in the west, the gods changed and adapted in response to the changes imposed by the spread of the civic system". (Van Andringa 2007, 86).

sion about civic religion will involve the use of imperfect terms, and defining them as precisely as possible helps to eliminate some of the ambiguity they can create. Some of the previous places of worship in both Greek and Roman cities from the east are utilised by religious manifestations centered on the emperor and the imperial family that dominates the local religion, a phenomenon different from the west of the empire, connecting imperial power and civic local manifestations (Van Andringa 2007, 85).

As Urcioli and Rüpke pointed out, in order to define civic religion it is very important to take into account "that city-space engineered the major changes that revolutionised Mediterranean religions, where this space is understood as the array of urban spatial and structural forms, forces, processes, and agents" (Urcioli & Rüpke 2018). And although "the relationships of religion and space, in general, and between religion and urban space, in particular, are still under-researched" as it is pointed out by the same researchers, we believe that a big progress has being already made. Probably we would understand the religious phenomenon if we look at the ancient religions as "the outcome of specific effects and uses of space and their social and cognitive bases rather than as inherent characteristics of a specific 'religion'" (Urcioli & Rüpke 2018), especially in the Late Antiquity.

As for the gods from the Isiac family and the civic religion of the 3rd century, it is impossible to look at it without considering what is happening in the previous centuries and without acknowledging the fact that we are not dealing with a single civic identity. The chosen example showed that depending on the social agents that interact with these gods, we will encounter diverse situations. For the cities of Greek tradition, their incorporation into the Roman Empire means adaptation to a new reality, which does not imply the complete disappearance of the previous way of organizing society. The civic religion at Tomis continues to preserve the previous characteristics in which the gods of Egyptian origin are present through the celebration of annual festivals for the benefit of the entire community, and at the same time, begins to manifest the type of civic religion specific to the Roman Empire, which has the emperor at its center as the keeper of exemplary civic virtues. The representations of deities belonging to the Isiac family on the coins show us their involvement in the civic identity of the city, accepting at the same time the fact that there was an influence of the religious preferences of the emperors and the imperial propaganda on these monetary issues.[21] Although Tomis is not immune to the unrest and changes that characterize the period of military anarchy, nevertheless, the army does not get to have the importance here that it has in the not-so-far Troesmis, or almost all the cities of Dacia. However, we must not forget the role played by the commercial relations between Alexandria and Tomis in the reputation of the Isiac cults.

---

[21] For an overview over the presence of the Isiac gods on coins see Bricault 2015.

Orpheus in Egypt

Vanya Lozanova-Stancheva

Орфей в Египет

Ваня Лозанова-Станчева

Статията предлага кратка систематизация на изворовите нива, на които функционират орфическите идеи и текстове в Египет и най-вече в Александрия. Втората четвърт на 3. в. пр. Хр. е време, когато присъствието на орфическите религиозни идеи в Египет вече е осезателно доловимо на много духовни нива: от мистериозните култове и магията до фантастичната литература и философия.

На едно първо ниво са анализирани гръцки писмени източници, каквито са гръцките папируси, открити в Египет и свидетелстващи за практикуването на орфическите ритуали (Птолемейският кралски едикт BGU VI 1211; гръцкия папирус от Гуроб; папирус PSI VII 850; P. Argent. 1313), както и много от магическите папируси, включващи елементи от орфически обреди. На същото ниво трябва да се постави информацията на античните автори – особено на Диодор Сицилийски, Плутарх и Филодемус, Климент Александрийски и др. Специфична група писмени източници представляват магическите формули в египетските магически текстове от 3. и 4. в. сл.Хр., които съхраняват редица орфически елементи, както следва:

- клетвите, дадени от посветените преди ритуала, обещавайки да пазят тайна, обикновено придружени от магически заклинания;
- магически заклинания – обръщане към определени (орфически) божества;
- текстове, показващи смесица между мистерии, катабаза, космология и магически заклинания с призиви към хтоничните богове.

На едно второ ниво са анализирани орфическите идеи и идеите, функционирали в еврейската общност в Александрия (от началото на 2. в. пр.Хр. нататък): Аристобул (в средата на 2. в. пр.Хр.), Псевдо-Орфей, Артапан от Александрия.

Хронологически най-късната група източници оформят орфическите и гностическите текстове. Внимателният сравнителен анализ на тези текстове демонстрира подчертаното сходство между гностическите представи и орфическите теогонични, космогонични и антропологични митове; идеята за двуполовия първичен бог; идеята за пътуването на душата след смъртта; образът на тялото като затвор и гроб на душата и др. Чрез този анализ са доловими процесите на взаимодействие и синкретизъм, които ще кулминират в християнството. Някои ранни форми на херметизма също възприемат орфически ритуални и митологични елементи, но за съжаление запазват само оскъдни фрагменти от този аспект на традицията, който е подхранвал алхимията и магията в рамките на херметичната традиция.

Систематизацията на писмените източници очертава интелектуално пространство на интензивно взаимодействие между елинските религиозни и литературни идеи и тези на различни културни и религиозни общности на египетския свят – източник на религиозна и духовна мъдрост.

From ancient times Egypt has had the halo of a source of wisdom – sacralized and ritualized. As early as the second half of the 5th cent. BCE, Herodotus speaks of Egypt as a cradle of religious wisdom and put forward some arguments in favor of the belief that the Hellenic religion derives its origins from the Egyptian one. He (Hdt. 2.81) reports the ancient Hellenic tradition that Orphic and Bacchic mysteries originated in Egypt. Some even claimed, according to him, that Osiris was Dionysus (Hdt. 2.42). Herodotus often conceals details of the mystery cult, referring to some ἱερὸς λόγος (2.48; cf. 2.47; 2.171) (Hernández 2013, 250-260) – most likely it is about the mysteries of Dionysus in a funerary context closest to or identical with Orphic mysteries (Hernández 2013, 255 with bibliography).

Diodorus of Sicily (4.25.1-4), who wrote between 60 and 30 BCE, claims that Orpheus brought the mysteries to Hellas from Egypt, following Hecataeus of Abdera (Diod. Sic. 1.96.3; 4.43.1; 5.49.6; 5.64.4; 5.75.4; 5.77.3; cf. Linforth 1941, 27, 204-205). According to *Orphic Argonautica* (§§ 43-45) (Kern 1922, Frg. 40), the Thracian singer visited Memphis and the sacred city of Apis on Nile, composing his *Sacred Logos* during his stay in Egypt:

> Then I described the sacred test of the Egyptians in Memphis that is used to convey prophesy, and I described the sacred city of Apis, which is surrounded by the river Nile (Colavito 2011).

> ἠδ’ ὅσον Αἰγυπτίων ἱερὸν λόγον ἐξελόχευσα,
> Μέμφιν ἐς ἠγαθέην περάσας, ἱεράς τε πόληας
> Ἄπιδος ἃς πέρι Νεῖλος ἀγάρροος ἐστεφάνωται

The ancient tradition invariably connects the figure of Orpheus and his sacraments with Egypt (**Fig. 1**). The Orphic *Testimonia* (99a, 100, 103, 165, 216, 225) and *Fragmenta* (247, 293 and 301) sheds additional light on the "sacred Egyptian history", collected and systematized by Otto Kern (Kern 1922; cf. Bernabé 2004; cf. also de Landaluce 2011).

On the one hand, Orpheus' journey to the land of wisdom follows the model of a clear socio-political positioning beyond the Hellenic, i.e. the *polis* world, resp. the Hellenic *paidea*; on the other hand, it is a model of mytho-geographical behavior beyond the borders of the civilized, *resp.* of the inhabited world, which constructs both the basic liminality of the singer-musician and the unique perspective of a mystical journey Beyond, where he acquired extraordinary knowledge. It is a specific means of constructing the figure, crossing but also uniting the boundaries between Hellenism and Others, between civilized and wild, between human and inhuman, between human and divine world, which gives it supernatural powers. The model of this variant rationalizes and replaces the mythologem of the journey of Orpheus Beyond, from where he returns with the mysterious knowledge, thanks to which he established the sacred rituals and sacrifices of the gods (Diodor. 1.96.4). The figures of the Hellenic sages who traveled to Egypt such as Orpheus, Homer, Plato, Solon, Pythagoras, etc. (Diodor. 1.69.1-4; 1.96.1) follow this rationalized paradigm.

But along with the theme of Orpheus' journey to Egypt and the cult of his figure, the problem of the spread of Orphic ideas and the influence of Orphic texts in the Egyptian space is more important.

The second quarter of the 3rd century BCE is the sure chronological boundary from which the presence of Orphic religious ideas in Egypt is now perceptible. The religious policy of the Ptolemaic dynasty made Alexandria an important center of Dionysian mysteries. Remarkable is the description of Callixenus of Rhodes of the glamorous procession of the city stadium in Alexandria, relayed by Athenaeus (Calixenus in FGrH 627 F 2 – Athenaeus, 5.196a-203b; Dunand 1986), in the center of which were Dionysus and Dionysian mythological characters. It was organized by Ptolemy II Philadelphus and dated between 280/75 and 270 BCE.

This particular emphasis seems to have been largely intended to highlight the royal family's relationship with Alexander the Great and his religious policy. The association of the royal dynasty with Dionysus is sometimes explained by the ancient Egyptian connection of the pharaoh with Horus / Osiris and the Hellenic identification of Osiris with Dionysus, which experts of Antiquity do not always accept (Tondriau 1946, 149-171). The initiatives of Ptolemy IV Philopator place new emphasis on this policy. According to Eratosthenes, he "created festivals and competitions of all kinds in honor of Dionysus" (Eratosth. in Athen. 7.276 a-c). He publicly introduced himself as Dionysian *telestēs* and even called himself "New Dionysus" (Plutarch, *Cleomenes*, 33; Plutarch, *Moralia*, 60a; Clem. Alex., *Protr.*, 48). In this context is his efforts to impose control over the Dionysian communities and cults in Egypt, which some scholars consider reform.

◂

Fig. 1.

Statuette of *Orpheus* with a lyre from *Ahnassia in Egypt*.

I. Orphism is present on many religious levels in Egypt: from mystery cults and magic to fiction and philosophy

I.1. At first, perhaps the earliest level of distribution of Orphic ideas and rituals in Egypt could be registered through the texts preserved on papyri. There are at least four papyri of great importance found in Egypt, testifying to Orphic rituals in honor of Dionysus, as well as a series of magical papyri, including elements of Orphic rituals.

One of the earliest and most significant evidence in this regard is the famous edict of Ptolemy IV Philopator (221-205 BCE), preserved in 16 lines on papyrus, dated c. 215/214 BCE[1], although some scholars still support the older dating between 220 and 205 BCE. The decree is an attempt to impose control over the private religious communities organized into "families" that performed the initiation rituals of Dionysian mystery in the country, being included in the official register in Alexandria. They had to declare from whom they inherited the sacred objects (τὰ ἱερά) perhaps in the sense of ἱερὰ μυστικά, *cista mystica* (Zunz, 1963, 228-239; cf. Jahn 1869, 317-334) at least three generations ago (ἕως γενεῶν τριῶν, i.e. on the principle of "father to son"), thus proving legitimacy through their hereditary rights to the priests of Dionysus (τελοῦντες τῷ Διονύσῳ), and to hand over the sacred books (ἱερὸς λόγος) to the royal office in Alexandria, each stamped with his name[2].

In this way, the rulers of Alexandria must have ensured that they received information about δεικνύμενα, λεγόμενα and δρώμενα, about their authenticity, as well as about the legitimacy of the performers τελεῖν τῷ Διονύσῳ and the quality of their sacraments. In any case, this decree is just one of the many religious acts of Ptolemy IV Philopator, affirming the Dionysian mystery cult on Egyptian soil.

Three other notable papyri integrate clear elements from the Orphic *teletai*: Greek Papyri from Gurob (**Fig. 2**)[3], dated shortly before the decree of Ptolemy IV Philopator (c. 275 BCE); and two other highly fragmented papyri from the 2nd and 3rd centuries CE, which to some extent complement the text of Gurob Papyri. They mark a considerable historical space between the 3rd century BCE – 3rd century CE, in which the Orphic traditions are perceptible in texts of a ritual nature.

Josiah Gilbart Smyly, who published the first part of the Gurob Papyrus, dates it around the middle of the 3rd century BCE. It contains an interesting mixture of invocations and prayers (possibly in hexameter?), ritually based around Orphic-Dionysian sacraments, which is why O. Kern published it with a critical apparatus in his Orficorum fragmenta

1 *BGU* VI 1211; Turner 1983, 148-152; for dating see Schubart 1917, 189-198; see the text on the site http://ww2.smb.museum/berlpap/index.php/03310/.

2 Burkert 2004, 78; 1990; http://hermetic.com/pgm/pgm-I54.html; Herrero 2010, 52-53.

3 Smyly 1921; publication of the full text see in Hordern 2000, 131-140.

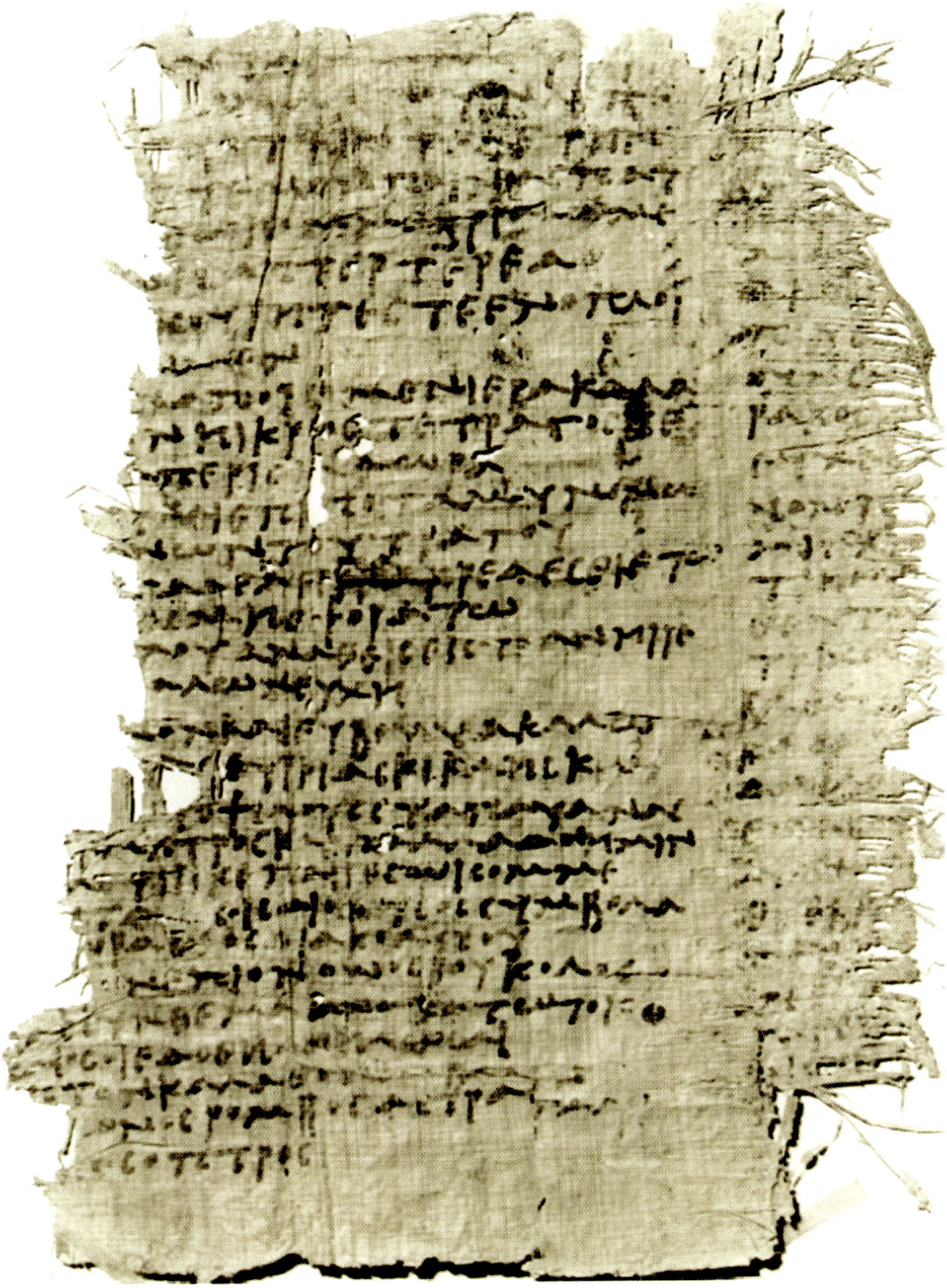

Fig. 2.
Gurôb I
(J. Hordern, Tafel III).

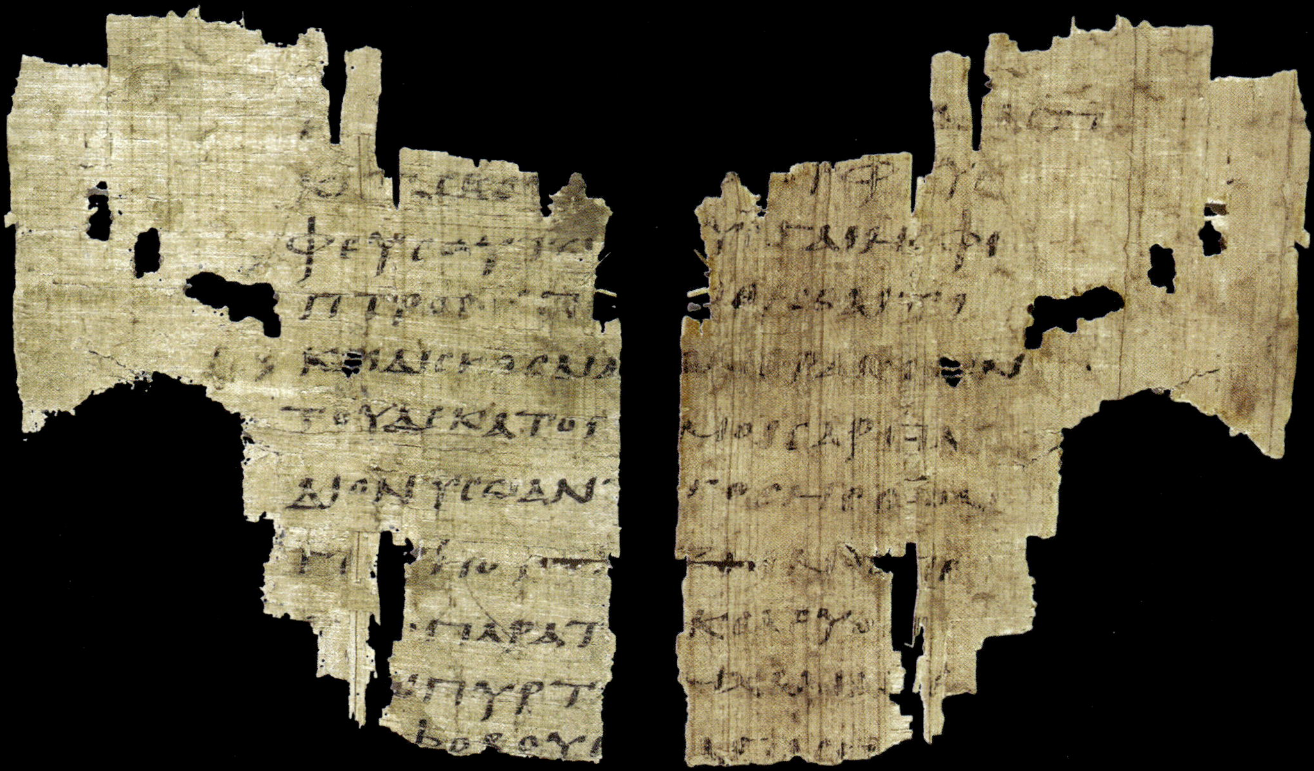

Fig. 3.
Papyrus PSI VII 850 r and PSI VII 850 v.

(Kern 1922, 101-104, fragmenta veteriora: frg. 31). The prosaic parts contain instructions for ritual actions and perhaps replicas of the initiate or the hierophant. Walter Burkert connects the papyrus with the edict of Ptolemy IV Philopator (221-204 BCE), which suggests the existence of a collection of "sacred books" of the Orphic-Dionysian mysteries (Burkert 1987, 70ff.; Hordern 2000, 131-140).

Traces of this tradition can be found in the other two papyri from the 2nd and 3rd centuries CE:

Papyrus PSI VII 850[4] has preserved about 20 verses, giving clear allusions to the myth of the tearing of Dionysus by the Titans (**Fig. 3**). The appearance of the name Orpheus suggests that it is a text attributed to the Thracian singer – possibly a mythographic treatise and realities of events: fire, mirror, possibly – raw meat – sacral elements similar to those in Papyrus from Gurôb.

Papyrus Argent. 1313 also shows associations with myths about the Titans, reminiscent of the Orphic Hymn and suggests some invocations made in the Orphic community (Herrero 2010, 56).

I.2. On the background of these texts appears – albeit scarce – information of a literary nature, such as that of Jewish (late 3rd and early 2nd century BCE) and early Christian authors such as Clement of Alexandria (*Protrepticus*, 2.17.2 – the second half of the 2nd – beginning of the 3rd century), which suggest a common poetic source at least with Papyrus from Gurôb (Herrero 2007, 19-50). Miguel Herrero examines the relationship between the two texts and does not rule out the possibility that these texts and their original sources belong to the collection of *sacred logoi* in the royal office of Alexandria (Wilamowitz-Möllendorff 1931, 378; Burkert 1987, 70f.; Hordern 2000, 131-140.; Herrero 2010, 54, n. 58) mentioned in the Edict of Ptolemy IV Philopator.

To this literary situation must be added the information of Diodorus Siculus, Plutarch, Philodemus. Also noteworthy is an interesting episode inserted by Lolianus (c. 2nd CE) in his novel *Phoinikika*, which describes a group of bandits inhabiting the most remote, inaccessible regions of Egypt. They performed a strange ritual with unambiguous features of Orphic mystery: they killed a child, tore him apart, ate his heart, and then the initiates swore to keep secret what they saw, heard and experienced (Henrichs 1972). Most likely, these are mimic acts of an imitative nature, in which the story of Zagreus' death and his mystical resurrection was presented. Dio Cassius (72.4), Heliodorus and Achilles Tatius (who lived and worked in Alexandria in the early 2nd century CE) also describe similar bandits, reflecting the features of closed ritual societies reduced to marginalized groups.

---

4 http://www.psi-online.it/documents/psi;7;850; Körte 1927, 270; Turner 1977, 121, no. 398.

Although scarce and highly fragmented, the source picture suggests a stable and long-lasting (3rd century BCE – 3rd century CE) tradition of following and preserving Orphic rituals on Egyptian soil maintained by small closed communities.

I.3. A third group of Greek written sources outline another aspect of functioning and retelling, rather the influence of Orphic rituals and texts. These are the mysterious formulas in **the Egyptian magical texts** from the 3rd and 4th centuries CE, which have preserved a number of Orphic relics. A special place among them occupy:

- the preserved and fragmentarily interpolated oaths uttered by the initiated neophytes before the ritual, by which they promise to keep the secret of what they have experienced, heard and seen. Two 3rd century CE papyri (PSI X 1162 and 1290) contain an oath of silence with cosmogonic elements in a Gnostic tone. Miguel Herrero believes that they offer two complementary texts, which gives reason to assume that they ascend to a well-known poem, later edited in a ritual hymn (Herrero 2010, 58-59). Different oaths contain a papyrus from the 4th century CE with verses in which traces of Gnostic cosmogony also creep in: P. Mag. XIII P-H (Dieterich 1990-1994). The oath formulas usually are accompanied by magical spells;
- magic spells with invocation to certain deities;
- texts demonstrating a mixture of mysteries, catabasis, cosmology and magical spells, in which invocations to chthonic gods are intertwined[5].

II. Orphic doctrinal ideas have been well known since at least the beginning of the 2nd century BC of the Jewish community in Alexandria (Stroumsa 2012, 141-157, 143)

Aristobulus (quoted in Eusebius' *Praeparatio Evangelica*), the first known Jewish philosopher to live in Alexandria in the middle of the 2nd century BCE, reports that both Orpheus and Pythagoras studied the law of Moses (Walter 1964, 10-13; Charlesworth 1976, 81-82). They, like Socrates and Plato, were introduced by Moses to monotheism (Walter 1975; Walter 1980; Holladay 1996a). Even the Hellenic poets Homer and Hesiod had borrowed much from him.

Aristobulus was one of the most famous and influential Jews in Egypt in the middle of the 2nd century BCE. Fragments of his work, called *Commentaries on the Law of Moses*, are preserved by Clement of Alexandria (*Strom.*, 1.15), who first mentions it only in the 2nd century CE. A little later we find quotes from him in Eusebius (*Praeparatio*

[5] Jordan 1988, 245-259; cf. Faraone 1994, 81-85; see Preisendanz 1973/74; Betz 1986; Merkelbach 1990/91; review of recent research in Stroumsa 2012, 141-157; cf. Herrero 2010.

Evangelica, 8, 9, 13, 12; *Historia Ecclesiastica*, 7.32). The *Second Book of Maccabees*, also known as *Second Maccabees* (1:10), mentions a prominent Alexandrian Aristobulus, who came from the family of anointed priests and teacher of King Ptolemy (possibly Philometor VI – 181-145 BCE) (Clem. Al., *Strom.*, I. 22, 150; Euseb., *Chron. ad. Olymp.*, 151; *Chronicon Paschal.*, I, p. 337 Dindorf; Schürer 2014, 579-586).

[10] In the year one hundred and eighty-eight, the people that is at Jerusalem, and in Judea, and the senate, and Judas, to Aristobulus, the preceptor of king Ptolemee, who is of the stock of the anointed priests, and to the Jews that are in Egypt, health and welfare[6].

This mention fueled the speculations of Hellenistic authors – especially Clement of Alexandria and Eusebius (Clem. Al., *Strom.*, 5.14.97; Eusebius, *Praep. Ev.*, 8.9), who identified him with the Jewish philosopher and writer, and relating him to the time of Ptolemy IV the Philopator; Anatolius in Eusebius' *Church History* (7.32.16) dates him to the time of Ptolemy II Philadelphus. Written in the form of a dialogue, the work of Aristobulus was addressed to King Ptolemy VI Philometor and dates between 175 and 170 BCE. His dominant claim is that Moses is the father of Greek philosophy and culture, the ultimate source of Hellenic culture. The text of Aristobulus is at the beginning of a stable pseudepigraphical tradition, attributing to Orpheus works created in Jewish intellectual circles during the Hellenistic period[7]. In this tradition the Thracian singer adopted monotheism (Walter 1983). In the figure of Orpheus Jewish authors apparently sought ambivalent associations with esotericism.

According to many Jews and later – Christian apologists, Orpheus traveled in his youth to Egypt, where he received philosophy training not from anyone else but from Moses himself. He became acquainted with monotheism, preserved it, and in his old age left his *Testament* to his son Musaeus, advising him to renounce the pagan gods and believe in the only true god, that of Moses. Fragments of this Pseudo Orpheus poem, composed in Greek in hexameter, have been preserved and are dated between the end of the 3rd century BCE and c.150 BCE and even in the 1st century BCE. Verses from it have been quoted by various authors between the 2nd century BCE and the beginning of the 5th century CE: Clement of Alexandria, Aristobulus, Pseudo Justin, Theophilus, Cyril of Alexandria, Theodoret (Aristobulus, frg. 4 in Eusebius, *Praep. Evang.*, 13.12.4-5; Pseudo-Justin, *De Monarchia*, 2.4; Theophilus, *Autolycum.*, 3.2; Clem. Al., *Prot.*, 4.3-5; and *Strom.*, 5.78.4-5; 123.1-124.1; 126,5; 127.2; 133.2; Pseudo-Justin, *Cohortatio ad Graecos*, 15.1; Cyril Alex., *Contra Julianum*, 1.35; Theodoret, *Graecorum Affectionum Curatio*, 2.30-31; *Theosophia Tubingensis*, 55.56).

---

6 https://www.biblegateway.com/passage/?search=2%20Maccabees%201%3A10&version=DRA .

7 See below for the Jewish poem of Pseudo-Orpheus.

Different researchers indicate different numbers of possible retransmissions. Christoph Riedweg believes that the poem functioned in the Jewish literary tradition in two versions – a shorter pra-version of 21 verses, dating back perhaps even to the end of the 3rd century BCE; and a longer version of 41 verses whose roots go back to Aristobulus, i.e. c. 150 BCE or more generally, in the words of Emil Schürer (Schürer 2014, 584), to the early Hellenistic era. According to Nikolaus Walter and Carl R. Holladay, the poem has worked in at least four versions (Walter 1983, 135-276; Holladay 1998, 192-220; cf. Holladay 1996).

According to the text, Orpheus invokes Musaeus to abandon his former (polytheistic) faith and turn to the one and only God. The poem begins with the Orphic mystery formula to close the door to the uninitiated. It is more reminiscent of ἱερὸς λόγος, which introduces the *myst* into true teaching, and its language follows the model of initiating esoteric religious-philosophical instruction. An interesting circumstance is that the text has been preserved and retransmitted mainly by early Christian authors.

The Jewish historian Artapanus, who also wrote in the 2nd century, transformed the Hecataeus of Abdera tradition that Egyptian wisdom and knowledge were passed on to the Greeks from Orpheus: ὑπὸ δὲ τῶν Ἑλλήνων αὐτὸν {ἀνδρωθέντα} Μουσαῖον προαγορευθῆναι. γενέσθαι δὲ τὸν Μώυσον τοῦτον Ὀρφέως διδάσκαλον (Euseb., *Praep. Evang.*, 9.27.3 = Artapanus in FGrHist 726 F 3a, 3 = OF 942 Bernabé). He identified speculatively Musaeus with Moses, turning him into a teacher of Orpheus, to suggest that Greek philosophy was of Jewish origin. Moses was considered by the priests to be worthy of divine reverence and was called, according to Artapanus, also Hermes, "because of his ability to interpret the scriptures" (*Praep. Evang.*, 9.27.1-6). In this interpretation the Jewish author seems to follow the Egyptian mythology of Hermes as a universal teacher and especially of the goddess Isis (Diod., 1.17.3; 1.27.4).

An alternative direction of research on the issue follows the hypothesis of the possible reverse influence of Jewish authors on Orphic ideas and texts, which is acceptable but difficult to prove (Gruen 1998). Such is the much-criticized theory of the syncretic Jewish mysteries in Hellenistic Egypt and the existence of "Orphic Judaism" (Goodenough 1935; cf. Liebes 1993).

III. At the next level, texts characterized as Gnostic can be systematized

whatever that means[8]: from "sharp Hellenization of Christianity" and a mixture of Christianity and Greek philosophy (Harnack 1893) to a grand synthesis between the Hellenic world and the Orient (Reitzenstein 1904). Gnosticism included many different dualistic teachings and mysterious sects that flourished in the 2nd and 3rd centuries before

---

8 For the development of the terms γνῶσις and γνωστικός in this context, see Casey 1935, 45-60.

settling in the 4th century and spilling over into other movements. According to Tertulian (Tertul., *Adv. Valentinianos*, 39), this was originally the name of the members of only one heretical sect, while Irenaeus (Irenaeus, *Adv. Haeres.*, 1.5.1; 1.28.8) claims that the Valentinians came from the Gnostics (γνωστικός), i.e. from the Ophites, and that Valentinus was the first offshoot of the so-called gnostic heresy, describing his doctrine about the original dyad and the demiurge.

The subject of the influence of Orphism on Gnosticism or of the affinity between them has long been the subject of extensive research (Wobbermin 1896; cf. Burkert 1977, 1-8). Many researchers are convinced that the ideas of the Gnostics were preceded by Orphism, and Francis Legge even identified, albeit greatly exaggerated, Orphism as the earliest Gnosticism, finding many features of Orphic doctrine, especially in the so-called post-Christian Gnosticism (Legge 1915, 121-148).

Direct relations and connections between the two religious movements could hardly be identified (Thomassen 2010, 463-474). However, through the comparative analysis of Gnostic and Orphic texts, the processes of interaction and syncretism (Edwards 1991, 25-40 with litt) that will culminate in Christianity could be discerned. To what extent this interaction was mediated or not by Platonic and Neoplatonic reinterpretations of Orphism, as well as by other philosophers such as Empedocles, remains naturally always hypothetical (Herrero 2010, 106; Crahay 1967, 323-339).

From the first edition of Hans Leisegang's *Die Gnosis*, there is no doubt that there are significant parallels between the doctrinal ideas of the Gnostics and those of the Orphics. He admits the Orphic origin of the doctrine of reincarnation in Basilides and Carpocrates; he deciphered in the teachings of Valentinians traces of Orphic influence. In this regard, he even sees a "revival" of Orphism and Pythagoreanism during the early Roman Empire.

At the heart of the theme of Gnosticism is the work, attributed to the most important theologian of the third century Hippolytus of Rome (170-235 CE) *Philosophumena sive Refutatio omnium haeresium* (*Refutation of All Heresies*) (Cosentino 2018, 218-237), possibly compiled around 230 CE. Hippolytus constructed his heresiological treatise around the explicit claim that heretics were a direct continuation of the ideas of the ancient Hellenic philosophers in the "new skin".

It is well known that the whole system of Sethian doctrine was "sewn" (συνεκάττυσαν) "by the ancient theologians Musaeus, Lynus, Orpheus, who made rituals and mysteries especially famous" (Hippol., *Haer.*, 5.20.4-5; cf. Irenaeus, *Adv. Haer.*, 2.14.1; Aristoph., *Av.* 693-702; Marcovich 1986; Marcovich 1974, 447-451). Simon Magus and Marcion borrowed from Empedocles (6.11.1; 7.29.2), Basilides – from Arisoteles (7.14.1),

Valentinus and his followers – from Pythagoras and Plato (6.21.1; 6.29.1), and so on. It has long been noticed that the Sethian ideas about the serpent demiurge have parallels in Orphic myths: from water and heavier materials was born the serpent demiurge Chronos – Hercles.

Phanes, the son of Chronos – Hercles – also has a serpentine image (Damascius, *De princ.*, 123 – OF 54; Athenagoras, *Leg.* 18 = OF 57; cf. Hippol., *Haer.*, 5.19.13, 19). The Setians are thought to have used Orphic cosmogony for the Phanes (Marcovich 1974, 447-451; cf. Rasimus 2005, 235-263; Rasimus 2009). Ophites (Ophians), one of the earliest known Gnostics put the serpent at the center of their cult (Irenaeus, *Adv. Haer.*, 1.30.5; Origen, *Contra Celsum*, 6. 24ff). The Naassenes according to Hippolytus (Hippol., *Haer.*, 5.9.11-12) were so named from the Hebrew word for serpent "naas" (νάας), which gives reason to some researchers to identify them with Ophites (Edwards 1996, 74-80; cf. Casey 1926, 374-387). Mark J. Edwards even finds confirmation of this information of Hippolytus (Hippol., *Haer.*, 5.20.40) in the famous cup of Orphic verses, whose umbo at the bottom represents a dragon surrounded by naked adorants (Delbrueck 1934, 129-139).

▲

Fig. 4.

The Orphic cup whit ritual scene.

The cosmic egg from which heaven and earth emerge is guarded by this serpentine creature (**Fig. 4**) (Damascius, *De princ.*, 123 = OF 54; Hermias, *Plat. Phaedr.*, 246 c = OF 78; Hippol., *Haer.*, 5.19.19). Even a skeptic like Einar Thomassen (Thomassen 2010, 470) can't deny that Orphic myth about Phanes is perceived in the Gnostic texts, texts, although retransmitted by sources who have given a philosophical interpretation of the myth – possibly Neo-Pythagorean and Neoplatonic. Careful comparative analysis cannot overlook the marked similarity of Gnostic notions with Orphic theological, cosmogonic, and anthropological myths; the bisexual primordial god; the journey of the dead after death; the image of the body as a prison and a grave of the soul, etc. While Jewish Hellenistic literature was mainly marked by the figure of Orpheus, Gnostic texts ignored it and mainly demonstrated structural parallels with Orphic mythology, soterology, and rituals (Stroumsa 2012, 153).

Some early forms of Hermetism also adopted Orphic Dionysism, but unfortunately only sparse fragments of this aspect of the tradition that nurtured the alchemy and magic within the Hermetism have survived. It is no coincidence that Orphic images and symbols were attributed to the alchemy, integrating Dionysian /Zagrean themes.

Although highly summary, the current brief systematization of the levels at which Orphic ideas and texts functioned in Egypt, and especially in Alexandria during the Hellenistic and Roman periods, clearly outlines an intellectual space of intense interaction between Hellenic religious and literary ideas and those of different cultural and religious communities of the Egyptian worl – the source of religious and spiritual wisdom.

The Egyptian Veil of the Hellenistic Olbia

Viktoriia Kotenko

Египетското влияние над елинистична Олбия

Виктория Котенко

Понтийска Олбия има тесни икономически и културни връзки с древноегипетските центрове през елинистичната епоха. Вносът от Александрия оказва културно влияние върху полисите от Северното Черноморие. Сред артефактите преобладават предметите на лукса и такива с култово предназначение. Специално внимание трябва да се обърне на керамиката в стил Хадра. Семантиката на флоралната живопис върху урните може да бъде свързана с духовната сфера. Като цяло можем да говорим за адаптиране на вносните стоки към местната култура.

The polis of Olbia is located on the right bank of the Dnipro and South Buh estuary and culturally belongs to the ancient centers of the Northern Black Sea region. Various categories of goods were imported here at Hellenistic times. Among them, some artefacts from Egypt, especially from Alexandria, are poorly researched and therefore controversial. Written sources describe Pontic poleis' contacts with Alexandria rather cursorily. They mostly concern the Bosporan Kingdom (e.g. about the diplomatic mission of Paerisades II to Ptolemy II Philadelphus) (P.Lond. VII 1973, SB III 7263, TM 1536) and are not very informative (Litvinenko 1991, 13-15). So the paper will pay special attention to archaeological material if we are talking about Olbia (**Fig. 1**). Geopolitical changes on the map of Ancient Greece were quite noticeably reflected in the remote poleis of the Northern Black Sea region. New trade routes and relocation of craft and trade centers caused significant changes. Poleis of Taurica, Lower Buh and Transnistria (the cities of Bosporus, Olbia, Tauric Chersonesos, Tyras, Niconium) acutely felt the change of economic and cultural hegemons, and this is indicated by a series of objects of Eastern ori-

gin. With the formation of new Hellenistic monarchies, there was a rapid growth of the cities of the East, which became the main suppliers not only of exotic goods, but also of new ideas in the cultural and religious life of the Pontic Hellenes. Among these cities, for obvious reasons, Alexandria played a special role.

The Egyptian collection of antiquities from Olbia is small, but a number of great finds indicate the existence of certain economic and cultural contacts between the regions at this time. A characteristic feature of these things is their cult context. The small number of finds may be due to the fact that the Hellenistic horizons in Olbia have not been enough explored, and some of the discovered materials need a new interpretation based on new data.

▲

Fig. 1.
Polis of Olbia (2021).

The interest of researchers in eastern imports in the ancient centers of the Northern Black Sea region has been recorded since the turn of the 19th and 20th centuries. At this time, on the wave of popularity of antiques in society, private collections of specific finds began to create. This is partly due to the fact that artifacts of Egyptian origin were considered extremely rare and unusual. They differed in style from most Greek materials, which were already well known in society and among art connoisseurs.

In historiography we find information that expensive fabrics, aromatic substances, and spices were imported from Egypt to poleis of the Northern Black Sea region (Shurgaya 1965, 139-140; Bondar 1957, 37). Unfortunately, it is impossible to record this import archaeologically and the ways of this importation remain debatable (Litvinenko 1991, 14-15), so special attention should be paid to other categories of things. Probably the most famous category of Egyptian things in the Northern Black Sea region are the rings of the Ptolemaic type (*see here M. Treister*). This topic is well covered in historiography (Litvinenko 1991, 15-24; Olszta-Bloch 2011, 139-154; Zelinskyi 2020), so we're going to consider the less-known finds. Among the categories of Alexandrian finds from Olbia, we can mention sculpture. For example, two stone male heads and one female head, which were made in the same style, come from the excavations of 1902-1903 (remains of a Hellenistic house under a mound with a *crepidus*). In the publication of 1906, according to the characteristic features of an artistic image, they were interpreted as the deities Asclepius, Hygieia, and Eros. These statuette fragments were attributed to Alexandrian production and dated to the end of the 3rd cent. BCE (Farmakovsky 1906, 191-213). Two fragments of female statuettes made of Pentelic marble also belong to this category of finds. Only the torso survived from the first figurine. The statuette represented a standing woman in a dynamic pose, dressed in a *chiton* and a *himation*. From the second statuette, only part of the bust was preserved. These finds were also dated to the Hellenistic period, probably the 3rd cent. BCE (Farmakovsky 1906, 177-178, fig. 127). B.V. Farmakovsky also mentions a marble head of Serapis, probably belonged to the "Alexandrian school" (Farmakovsky 1918, 49-50, fig. 78). They are recorded in the list of things bought from peasants near Olbia at the beginning of the 20th cent. and most likely comes from the necropolis. At the same time, it was assumed that such things came to Olbia through the mediating role of Rhodes (end of the 3rd - beginning of the 2nd cent. BCE), although today we do not have direct evidence of exactly such economic contacts.

Another category of artefacts is represented by amulets or scarabs (*see here V. Atanassova*). For example, one amulet made of light green paste in the form of the god Ptah come from Olbia (Bondar 1957, 36). Representative series of "faience" of the Late Classical and Hellenistic period with zoomorphic images discovered in Olbia and Borysthenes (Ostroverkhov 2014, 43-51, fig. 5). This category of finds also includes a scaraboid with an image of Eye of Horus (?) on the shield, which was found during the clearing of the crypt in the Olbian necropolis (**Fig. 2**).

Fig. 2. 1, 2
Scaraboid from Olbia (2005).

The Alexandrian production in Olbia also includes some items made of precious metals. In particular, there are a silver medallion with the image of Athena, a gold ring, a silver cup. But information about these finds is extremely limited (Bondar 1957, 37).

But the most Alexandrian imports in the Northern Black Sea region are represented by clay products. Very interesting are the artifacts of Egyptian production, founded at the beginning of the 20th cent. In particular, we are talking about a clay figurine of Silenus with an amphora, a pyxide with images of Erotes (Farmakovsky 1909, 130-131, fig. 56-58). We should also mention the find of a lamp with a paired image of Bes (Touraieff 1912, 71-75, tab. II).

A significant phenomenon is the presence of Hadra style pottery in Olbia, which was an important element of the material culture of the Hellenistic world. It should be noted that among the Olbian ceramics of the 4th-2nd centuries BCE Alexandrian products occupy a rather small part. Such vessels are known for single fragments. The largest collection of Hellenistic painted vases was obtained during looting excavations at the end of the 19th cent. and maybe they came from the necropolis. Now it can be argued that the Alexandrian import of painted vases provoked the development of similar ceramics of local production in the poleis of the Northern Black Sea region. Therefore, it is also worth making a short essay about the history of the study of vases (urns) of the Hadra style, especially in the context of finds from Olbia.

Active research into the Hellenistic ceramics of Alexandria began with the discovery of the Hadra necropolis on the eastern outskirts of the city in 1883-1884. The burial urns from here became not only a valuable source of ancient Greek epigraphy, but also gave the name to a peculiar style of vase painting. The first batches of such ceramics should be dated to the end of the 3rd cent. BCE and attributed to the reign of Ptolemy I Soter, i.e. to the beginning of the Ptolemaic era in Egypt. The peculiarity of these urns was the presence of inscriptions with information about the deceased. For the first time, a series of such burial urns was published in 1885 in an article by A. Ch. Merriam, R. Pagestecher, B. Cook (Merriam 1885, Pagestecher 1909, Cook 1966) also made an important contribution to the study of Hadra vases; the controversy about their origin is developed in the papers of L. Guerrini, P. J. Callaghan (Guerrini 1965, Callaghan 1980). Apart from Alexandria, such ceramics were later found in various ancient centers. In the Northern Black Sea region, Hadra vases and their reminiscences are known in Histria and Callatis (Lungu 2003; Lungu 2007; Lungu & Dupont 2014).

The historiography of ceramic imports from Alexandria to the poleis of the Northern Black Sea region is extremely limited. The article by E.R. von Stern in 1910 was the first comprehensive paper on this topic. He published Hellenistic painted ceramics from Olbia and mistakenly attributed local products to Alexandrian imports (Stern 1910).

Also, the author was inclined to the opinion that painted *hydriae* were used in burial practice, like to the eastern necropolis of Alexandria. However, archaeological research studies have shown different results in Olbia. At least one of the *hydria* Hadra here was found in the Hellenistic house. E. R. von Stern also concluded that in the middle of the 3rd cent. BCE, probably during the reign of the Ptolemy II Philadelphus and Ptolemy III Euergetes, there were close economic relations between Olbia and Alexandria (Stern 1910, 174). Accordingly, the cultural influence of Alexandria in the Northern Black Sea region was significant (Stern 1910, 173). T. M. Knipovich in her paper of 1941 described the history of painted ceramics of the Black Sea centers (Knipovich 1941). Based mainly on the materials of Olbia, she argued the issue of local production of painted ceramics in the Hellenistic period. Modern developments will prove the significant influence of Alexandrian ceramics and the appearance of a new local style (pseudo-Hadra). Tauric Chersonesos was one of the centers where such pottery was made (Kotenko 2019). In her conclusions T.M. Knipovich noted that such cultural influence from Hellenistic Egypt was possible and based on close ties with the Northern Black Sea region (Knipovich 1941, 149). Later, Alexandrian ceramics were considered in publications as one of the attributes of imports from Ptolemaic Egypt to remote centers of the Northern Black Sea region (Blavatsky 1953, 244-246).

Import of Alexandria to the Northern Black Sea region, including in Olbia, was considered in the paper of I. G. Shurgaya in 1965, who studied the issue of Egyptian and Pontic contacts (Shurgaya 1965). The author confirmed observations of E. R. von Stern that Hadra urns are mostly known from the Olbia necropolis. He also supported the conclusions about their Alexandrian origin with the technological features of such products. Gypsum primer, as a traditional element of Egyptian ceramic production, was reliable indicator in this question (Shurgaya 1965, 133). He identified Olbia among the main exporters of Egyptian goods in the Northern Black Sea region. The chronology of Hadra vases, proposed by the author, still relevant (3rd cent. BCE).

Modern archaeological studies make it possible to distinguish a series of Hadra *hydriae* that were most typical for different center or region (Buora & Lafli 2016). This type is represented in Olbia by "narrow" biconical forms with characteristic monochrome (black) painting. For example, such hydria comes from the territory of the Lower City of Olbia (**Fig. 3**). It was found in the basement of a living room in a complex of Hellenistic objects (ceramics, transport amphorae and roof tiles).

All structural parts of the *hydria* were painted. According to the morphology, this vessel belongs to the Dropped Floor Class. Despite the fact that this *hydria* represents the type of Hadra in general characteristics, it has a number of features. For example, *hydriae* from Alexandria and other centers have larger dimensions and spherical body. The closest analogy is known from the Corpus Vasorum Antiquorum catalog (T.496) and also

2

▲

Fig. 3. 1, 2
Hydria of Hadra style from Olbia.

comes from Olbia. A similar painting with a palmette complements the image of a cock-fight, and the morphology is similar to the described vessel. Vases from Olbia have a narrow oval body and biconical shoulder. The production of such *hydria* probably belongs to Alexandria: such forms were recorded during the excavations of the Mustafa Pasha necropolis in the 1930s (Shurgaya 1965, 131).

The chronology of the *hydria* from the residential complex is important, because the context of the finds from the Olbia necropolis, unfortunately, still unknown. Usually, such products with a narrow body date back to the period no earlier than the second half of the 3rd cent. BCE. In this period, Egypt was under the rule of the Lagidae. The first rulers of the Ptolemaic dynasty controlled large territories, including the eastern coast of the Aegean Sea and the road to Pontus was opened (*see here V. Atanassova*). However, the complex of other things from Olbian house with *hydria* indicates its dating at the end of the 2nd cent. BCE. It is known that Alexandria lost its position as a hegemon in the Mediterranean at this time. Therefore, such products can represent late imports. Historical development of Olbia also shows such situation in the Hellenistic period. An abandonment of this Olbian house with the find may be connected with the systemic crisis of the polis in the 2nd cent. BCE, when a number of signs indicate its symptomatic weakening (Lawall et al. 2014, 42-43). The presence of such pottery may indicate the pre-crisis standard of living in the Lower City.

Why was painted pottery from Alexandria interesting to the local population of Olbia and functionally integrated into the cultural life of the Pontic Hellenes? First of all, it is worth noting that, unlike Alexandria, the ceramics of the Hadra style were not directly associated with funerary rites in Olbia. There is no epigraphic information on the vases, and the find of 2005 does not come from the necropolis. In our opinion, the value of such vessels was precisely in the painting, which stylistically was close to the culture of the local population and was possibly connected with cults. Its known, that floral motifs were organically included in the mythological plots of the Hellenes. Their deep semantics are well researched, and the symbolism of these images can be transferred to the practical of ceramics studies.

Based on the fact that original examples of Hadra vases aren't well known, it is also worth to pay attention on local imitations. They demonstrate the direct influence of Egyptian ceramics on local production.

The image of the *ampelos* (**Fig. 4: 1, 2**) was the most popular floral ornament (a grape or curls of young grapes). Viticulture was a strategically important industry in the economy of the ancient world. It is known that grapes were associated with the god Dionysus in Greek mythology, who gave people the first vine and showed them winemaking. Mythological stories about the transformation of Ampelos, the companion of Dionysus, and

Fig. 4. 1, 2
Fragment of pseudo-Hadra jugs from Olbia:
1, 2 – neck with painted *ampelos* and laurel;
3 – body with painted branch of olive and graffiti.

Ambrosia, one of his maenads, into a vine are also connected with grapes. Ampelos (grape vine) was also one of the Hamadryad nymphs. Despite this, the cult of Hercules probably also associated with winemaking, which was widespread in the Northern Black Sea region (Shevchenko 2011, c. 74-75). Thus, the painting of a grape vine (*ampelos*) on jugs from Olbia, especially with the specific graffiti (Kotenko 2022, 440-441, fig. 3.1), (probably of Chersonese production) is thematically combined with the cults of Dionysus and Hercules, popular in Hellenistic times.

Another motif is visually close to the image of a laurel branch (**Fig. 4: 1, 2**) in bloom. Thin, paired leaves, symmetrically placed relative to the central shoot, were painted on table jugs mainly on the neck. Laurel, or Daphne, is also closely related to the cult sphere of the Hellenic life. From myths, for example, it is known that Apollo's beloved Daphne was transformed into a laurel tree. Since then, the laurel wreath is an attribute of Apollo, which was awarded to the winner of the Pythian Games. The cult of Apollo was extremely important in the polis religion of the Pontic Greeks. This issue has been considered in historiography, and therefore the image of a laurel on locally produced tableware does not cause conflicting opinions. The laurel tree is also semantically connected with the goddess Artemis, the owner of laurel groves, and Daphne was one of her companions.

Some floral ornaments on the jugs can be identified with an olive branch (**Fig. 4: 3**). Considering the economic significance of the cultivation of this plant, of course it was important in the cult sphere of the Hellenes. It is mentioned in the myth of Athena's victory in the dispute over the patronage of Athens and in the story of the metamorphosis of the nymph Moria, Athena's companion. Therefore, olive is most often associated with Athena, whose cult was popular in the Northern Black Sea region (Rusiaeva 2005, 493; Solomonik 1984, 7-12).

In many cases, we can talk about a combined ornament. Stripes and floral images were often combined on the surface of one vessel, creating a beautiful ornamental composition. Conventionally, the central place in the composition was often assigned to the Ampelos, the curls of which were painted on the shoulders and in the central part of the body. Schematically, the stripes and branches of the plants represented a closed circle, which can be symbolically associated with a wreath as an indispensable attribute of sacred beings and an element of the Hellenic festive clothes. Perhaps the color of the painting was also important: dark red, ocher was popular because such a color scheme used on painted terracotta.

Given the fact that floral painting is less popular than "striped" painting, it can be assumed that these were ceremonial vessels used along with black-glazed ware. Also it should be mentioned some graffiti (monograms) on the pseudo-Hadra jugs (**Fig. 4: 3**), which are traditionally associated with Hercules. This can be an additional argument about the cult purpose of the vessel.

There are several opinions regarding the style of such painting. From the point of view of art history, the ornaments of the Hellenistic period do not belong to any of the stages of the development of ancient Greek vase painting, because it was a period of degradation and trivial images. And maybe local craftsmen painted such ceramics to their taste, based on ceramics of the Hadra style, which were popular at that time.

Some researchers of the Northern Black Sea region see in such motifs the deep origins of archaic motifs that were organically combined with Hellenistic elements. Therefore, it is necessary to take into account the specifics of the cultural development of the polis of the Northern Black Sea region, where Panhellenic plots could be adapted to local characteristics. In general, we have a situation where the local population of Olbia adapted the meaning of burial urns from Egypt to their own cultural needs, perceiving some cult component in the floral painting. It is too early to talk about religious syncretism on the basis of such ornamentation, although such a moment should not be ignored.

Thus, the import from Alexandria to Olbia is closely intertwined with the study of ceramic art at the Hellenistic period. In the 3rd cent. BCE, and probably somewhat later, there were close economic contacts between these centers, which are recorded by certain categories of things. In exchange for Black Sea goods, the capital of Ptolemaic Egypt supplied here not only famous textiles and glass products, but also specific ceramics, which were a kind of exclusive and influenced on the cultural development of the Pontic centers. In general, Egyptian imports to Olbia have distinctive features.

First, according to the materials, the Egyptian imports to Olbia are dominated by things related to the cult sphere of life if the Hellenistic period (household items and common ware pottery are practically unknown). Among such artifacts, exclusive things are most represented, so it can be assumed that they were expensive. This, in turn, outlines the material culture of the wealthy stratum of Olbia's population. Therefore, we can say that Alexandria, in relation to the centers of the Northern Black Sea region, and Olbia in particular, dictated the demand for refined objects and taste preferences. And this is particularly confirmed by local reminiscences of ceramics. It is possible that other categories of things were also imitated. From this it follows that Hellenistic Egypt definitely influenced on the cultural life of the Pontic Hellenes, especially on the religious life. Imported items were adapted to the local worldview. In general, the Egyptian veil of Hellenistic Olbia, according to known things, can be characterized by a specific category of finds. Items of exquisite of the 3rd-2nd centuries BCE dominated among them. This demonstrates the inclusion of the Black Sea region in the cultural orbit of the state of Alexander the Great.

Bibliography

Abbreviations

AJA: *American Journal of Archaeology.*

Arch. Anz.: *Archäologischer Anzeiger in Jahrbuch des [kaiserlichen] deutschen archäologischen Instituts (JDAI).*

BCH: *Bulletin de Correspondance Hellénique.*

BGU: *Aegyptische Urkunden aus den Königlichen Staatlichen Museen zu Berlin, Griechische Urkunden*, 15 vol., Berlin, 1895-1983.

BIFAO: *Bulletin de l'Institut français d'archéologie orientale.*

Cat. Amsterdam (2010): Trofimova 2010.

Cat. Kerch (2017): *Mirovoe nasledie Evropeyskogo Bospora. Kollektsii Vostochno-Krymskogo istoriko-kul'turnogo muzeya-zapovednika. Katalog*, Kerch & Simferopol.

Cat. London (2001): Walker & Higgs 2001.

Cat. Maikop (2014): Erlikh 2014.

Cat. Milan (1985): De Juliis 1985.

Cat. Moscow (2017): Kuznetsov & Tolstikov 2017.

Cat. Moscow (2019): Nikulin, Sadekova & Tugusheva 2019.

Cat. New York (2016): Picón & Hemingway 2016.

Cat. St. Peterburg (2007): Trofimova 2007.

ÉPRO: Études préliminaires aux religions orientales dans l'Empire romain.

JSHRZ-NF: Lichtenberger & Oegema 2005.

ISM II: Stoian, I. and Suceveanu, Al., *Inscripțiile din Scythia Minor. Grecești și latine, vol. II (Tomis și teritoriul său).* București (1987).

LIMC: *Lexicon Iconographicum Mythologiae Classicae.*

OLA: *Orientalia Lovaniensia Analecta.*

RICIS: Bricault 2005.

RGRW: *Religions in the Graeco-Roman World.*

SNRIS: Bricault 2008.

VDI: *Vestnik drevney istorii (Journal of Ancient History).*

ZPE: *Zeitschrift für Papyrologie und Epigraphik.*

Bibliography

Abramzon, M. G. (2015): "Ekonomika Fanagorii v pozdneellinisticheskiy period po numizmaticheskim dannym", in: Abramzon & Kuznetsov 2015, 9-30.

Abramzon, M. G., Kuznecov, V.D., eds. (2015): *Monetnye klady vremeni Mitridata VI Evpatora s khory Fanagorii*, Fanagoriya. Rezul'taty arheologicheskih issledovanij 3, Moscow.

Ackermann, G., Krapf, T., Pop, L., eds (2020): *ἀποβάτης Mélanges eubéens offerts à Karl Reber par ses étudiant·e·s à l'occasion de son 65ème anniversaire / Euböische Schriften für Karl Reber von seinen Student /-innen aus Anlass seines 65. Geburtstags*, Lausanne.

Alföldy-Rosenbaum, E. (1980): "Ruler Portraits on Roman Game Counters from Alexandria", in: Jucker & Stucky 1980, 29-39.

Apakidze, A. (1947): "Gvianantikuri khanis arkeologiuri dzeglebi urekidan [Archaeological Sites of Late Antiquity from Ureki]", *Bulletin du Musée de Géorgie* XIV B., 94-125.

Archibald, Z. H. (2007): "Contacts between the Ptolemaic Egypt and the Black Sea in the Early Hellenistic Age", in: Gabrielsen & Lund 2007, 253-272.

Arsent'eva, E. I., Gorskaya, O. V. (2019): *Antichnye yuvelirnye izdeliya iz chastnykh sobraniy. Kol'tsa i perstni. Katalog kollektsii*, Saint Petersburg.

Asimaki, A., Koustourakis, G. (2014): "Habitus: An Attempt at a Thorough Analysis of a Controversial Concept in Pierre Bourdieu's Theory of Practice", *Social Sciences* Vol. 3, No. 4, 121-131.

Atanassova, V. (2020): "Les cultes isiaques: de l'Égypte à Serdica", in: Atanassova & Bricault 2020, 36-59.

Atanassova, V., Bricault, L., eds. (2020): *Les cultes isiaques à Serdica*, Sofia.

Atanassova, V. (2023): "Lampa s izobrajenie na grako-egipetskiya bog Sarapis ot Deultum" *Nauchni izvestiya*. Bulletin "Nasledstvo BG" 4, 5-13.

Avram, A. (2003): "Antiochos II Théos, Ptolémée II Philadelphe et la mer Noire", *Comptes rendus des séances de l'Académie des Inscriptions et Belles-Lettres,* 147.3, 1181-1213.

Avram, A. (2006): "Une inscription de Tomis redécouverte à Caen", in: Mihailescu-Bîrliba & Bounegru 2006, 277-283.

Avram, A. (2007): "L'Égypte lagide et la Mer Noire: approche prosopographique", in: Laronde & Leclant 2007, 127-153.

Avram, A. (2014): "Notes épigraphiques (IV)", *Pontica* 47, 451-463.

Avram, A. (2018): "Sur les pastophores de Tomis", in: Popescu, Achim & Matei-Popescu 2018, 121-126.

Avram, A., Hălmagi, D. (2019): "Nouveaux documents sur les cultes égyptiens a Tomis", *Greci e romani sur le sponde del Mar Nero. Aristonothos. Scritti per il Mediteraneo antico* 15, 61-76.

Bailey, D. M. (2008): *Catalogue of the Terracottas in the British Museum 4: Ptolemaic and Roman Terracottas from Egypt*, London.

Basch, L. (1985): "The Isis of Ptolemy II. Philadelphus", *The Mariner's Mirror*, 71:2, 129-151.

Beard, M., North, J., eds. (1990): *Pagan priests. Religion and Power in the Ancient World*, London.

Beglova, J. (2002): "Kopflos und gefesselt – Bestattungen der ganz anderen Art. Ein Ritualkomplex mit menschlichen Opfergaben aus der Grabstätte von Tenginskaja", *Antike Welt* 3, 297-304.

Beglova, E. A. (2010): "Gosudarstvennyj muzej narodov Vostoka. Pozdneellinisticheskij i rimskij periody", in: Bongard-Levin & Kuznetov 2010b, 410-422.

Beglova, E. A., Erlikh, V. A. (2018): *Meoty Zakuban'ya v sarmatskoe vremya. Po materialam Tenginskogo gruntovogo mogil'nika*, Moscow.

Beiner, R. (2011): *Civil Religion. A Dialogue in the History of Political Philosophy*, New York.

Belayche, N. (2008): "Du texte à l'image: les reliefs sur les stèles « de confession » d'Anatolie", in: Estienne, Jaillard & Pouzadoux 2008, 181-194.

Belayche, N. (2013): "Fonctions de l'écriture dans les inscriptions religieuses de l'Anatolie romaine : du *monumentum* à l'ériture efficace", *Revue de l'histoire des religions*, 230, 2, 253-272.

Benoist, S., Daguet-Gagey, A., Hoët-Van Cauwenberghe, C., eds. (2011): *Figures d'empire, fragments de mémoire: Pouvoirs et identités dans le monde romain impérial (IIe s. av. n. è.–VIe s. de. n. è.)*, Villeneuve d'Ascq.

Berger, C., Clerc G., Grimal N., eds. (1994), *Hommage à Jean Leclant*, vol.3. Le Caire.

Berges, D. (1997): "Die Tonsiegel aus dem karthagischen Tempelarchiv", in: Rakob 1997, 10-214.

Bernabé, A., ed. (2004): *Orphicorum et Orphicis similium testimonia et fragmenta. Poetae Epici Graeci*. Pars II. Fasc. 1. München, Leipzig [OF Bernabé].

Bernabé, A., M. Herrero de Jáuregui, J. S. Cristóbal, A. Isabel, R. M. Hernández, eds. (2013): *Redefining Dionysos*, Berlin/Boston.

Bespalyj, G. E. (2016): "Otchet o provedenii arkheologicheskih raskopok na uchastkakh stroitel'stva muzeynogo zdaniya, ob'ektov infrastruktury i ekspozitsionnogo pokaza v granitsakh ob'ekta kul'turnogo naslediya federal'nogo znacheniya «Arkheologicheskiy muzey-zapovednik "Tanais" v khut. Nedvigovka Myasnikovskogo rayona Rostovskoy oblasti v 2012 g. V 14 tomah. Archive AMZ «Tanais», without no.

Betz, H. D., ed. (1986): *The Greek magical papyri in translation, including the Demotic spells*, Vol. 1: *Texts*, Chicago, London.

Bianchi, U. (1967): *Le origini dello gnosticismo*, Leiden.

Bilde, P. G., Petersen J.H., eds. (2008): *Meetings of cultures in the Black Sea region: Between Conflict and Coexistence*, *Black Sea Studies* 8, Aarhus.

Bilde, P. G., Lawall, M. L., eds. (2014): *Pottery, People and Places. Black Sea Studies* 16, Aarhus.

Bitch, O. (1959): "Premières fouilles de la nécropole de Panticapée", *MIA* 69, Moscow-Leningrad.

Blavatsky, V. D. (1953): *Istoriya antichnoj raspisnoj keramiki*, Moscow.

Boardman, J. (2001): *Greek Gems and Finger Rings. Early Bronze Age to Late Classical*, London.

Boardman, J., Vollenweider, M.-L. (1978): *Ashmolean Museum. Oxford. Catalogue of the Engraved Gems and Finger Rings. I. Greek and Etruscan*, Oxford.

Bokeria, M. et al. (2009): "Archaeobotanical evidence from West Georgia (South Caucasus)". *Bulletin of the Georgian National Museum, Natural Sciences and Prehistory Section*, N 1, 140-150.

Bondar, M. M. (1957): "Torhivlya Ol'viyi z hrets'kymy mistamy v ellinistychnyy chas", *Arkheolohiya*, XI, 35-44.

Bongard-Levin, G. M., Kuznetsov, V. D., eds. (2010a): *Antichnoe nasledie Kubani* II, Moscow.

Bongard-Levin, G. M., Kuznetsov, V. D., eds. (2010b): *Antichnoe nasledie Kubani* III, Moscow.

Bonacasa, N., Di Vita, A., eds. (1984): *Alesandria e il mondi ellenistico-romano, Studi in onore di Achille Adriani,* III, Rome.

Bonnet, C. Ribichini, S., Steuernagel, D., eds. (2008): *Religioni in contatto nel Mediterraneo antico. Modalità di di usione e processi di interferenza, Atti del 3 colloquio su "Le religioni orientali nel mondo greco e romano", Loveno di Menaggio (Como), 26-28 maggio 2006*, Mediterranea IV, Pise.

Bonnet, C., ed. (2021), *Noms de dieux. Portraits de divinités antiques*, Toulouse.

Bordenache, G. (1969): *Sculture greche e romane del Museo Nazionale di Antichità di Bucarest. I – Statue e relievi di culto, elementi architettonici e decorativi*, Bucarest.

Borgeaud, Ph. (1988): "Pour une approche anthropologique de la mémoire religieuse", in: Borgeaud 1988, 7-20.

Borgeaud, Ph., ed. (1988): *La mémoire des religions*, Genève.

Boteva, D. (2017): "Gordian III and Philip II on coin obverses with two face-to-face busts depicting Sarapis/Theos Megas", in: Boteva 2017, 327-338.

Boteva, D. ed. (2017), *Ex nummis lux. Studies in ancient numismatics in honour of Dimitar Draganov*, Sofia.

Bounni, A. (1979): "La quatrième campagne de fouilles (1978) à Ras Ibn Hani. Lumières nouvelles sur le royaume d'Ugarit, les Peuples de la Mer et la ville hellénistique", *Comptes rendus des séances de l'Académie des Inscriptions et Belles-Lettres,* 123/2, 277-294.

Boussac, M.-Fr., Invernizzi, A., eds. (1996): *Archives et Sceaux du monde hellénistique, BCH Suppl.* 29, Paris.

Boussac, M.-F., Starakis, P. (1998): "La collection de bagues, intailles et camées gréco-romains du Musée d'Alexandrie", in: Empereur 1998, 159-164.

Braund, D. (2018): *Greek Religion and Cults in the Black Sea Region. Goddesses in the Bosporan Kingdom from the Archaic Period to the Byzantine Era*, Cambridge.

Bresson, A., Ivanchik, A., Ferrary, J.-L., eds. (2007): *Une koinè pontique. Cités grecques, sociétés indigènes et empires mondiaux sur le littoral nord de la Mer Noire (viie s. a.C. – iiie s. p.C.)* Bordeaux.

Bricault, L. (1994): "Isis myrionyme", in: Berger, Clerc & Grimal 1994, 67-86.

Bricault, L. ed. (2000): *De Memphis à Rome. Actes du Ier Colloque international sur les études isiaques, Poitiers–Futuroscope, 8-10 avril 1999, RGRW* 140, Leiden-Boston-Köln.

Bricault, L. (2001): *Atlas de la diffusion des cultes isiaques, Mémoires de l'Académie des Inscriptions et Belles-Lettres* XXIII, Paris.

Bricault, L. (2005): *Recueil des Inscriptions concernant les cultes isiaques (RICIS)*, Mémoires de l'Académie des Inscriptions et Belles-Lettres XXXI, 3 vols., Paris.

Bricault, L. (2006): *Isis, Dame des flots. Aegyptiaca Leodiensia* 7, Liège.

Bricault, L. (2007): "La diffusion isiaque en Mésie Inférieure et en Thrace: Politique, commerce et religion", in: Bricault, Versluys & Meyboom 2007, 245-266.

Bricault, L., ed. (2008a): *Sylloge Nummorum Religionis Isiacae et Sarapiacae*, Mémoires de l'Académie des Inscriptions et Belles-Lettres XXXVIII, Paris.

Bricault, L. (2008b): "Fonder un lieu de culte", in: Bonnet, Ribichini & Steuernagel 2008, 49-64.

Bricault, L. (2011): "Isis à Rome", in: Montesino, J.-P. *De Cybèle à Isis*, Paris, 137-151.

Bricault, L. (2013): *Les cultes isiaques dans le monde gréco-romain*, Paris.

Bricault, L. (2014): "Gens isiaca et identité polythéiste à Rome à la fin du IVe s. apr. J.-C.", in: Bricault &Versluys 2014, 326-359.

Bricault, L. (2015): "The *Gens Isiaca* in Graeco-Roman Coinage", *The Numismatic Chronicle* 175, 83-102.

Bricault, L. (2017): "Sarapis au droit des monnaies provinciales romaines d'Asie Mineure et de Thrace", *The Numismatic Chronicle* 177, 213-244.

Bricault, L. (2020): *Isis Pelagia: Images, Names and Cults of a Goddess of the Seas, Religions in the Graeco-Roman World* 190, Leiden & Boston.

Bricault, L. (2021): "Le glaive et la patère: Zeus Hélios grand Sarapis", in: Bonnet 2021, 176-212.

Bricault, L. (2023): "Jean Leclant et la genèse des études isiaques", *Anabases* 38, 231-243.

Bricault, L., Delrieux, F., Leschhorn, W. (2008): "Troade, Mysie, Bithyne, Paphlagonie", in: SNRIS, p. 97-111.

Bricault, L., S. Müskens, M. J. Versluys (2015): "Epilogue: Eastern Provinces with Oriental Gods?", in: Müskens & Nikoloska 2015, 427-435.

Bricault, L., Pantalacci, L. (2024): "Parthénios & Cie : une famille de notables de Coptos au Ier s. apr. J.-C., entrepreneurs commerciaux et intendants d'Isis", *Bibliotheca Isiaca* V (forthcoming).

Bricault, L., Podvin, J.-L. (2011): "Statuettes d'Isis en argent et en bronze", in: Bricault 2008c, 7-21.

Bricault, L., M.J. Versluys, P. G. P. Meyboom (2007): *Nile into Tiber: Egypt in the Roman World. Proceedings of the IIIrd International Conference of Isis Studies, Leiden, May 11-14 2005, Religions in the Graeco-Roman World*, 159, Leiden–Boston.

Bricault, L., Versluys M.J., eds. (2012): *Egyptian Gods in the Hellenistic and Roman Mediterranean: Image and Reality between Local and Global, Mythos Suppl.* 3, Palermo.

Bricault, L., Versluys M.J., eds. (2014): *Power, politics and the cult of Isis. Proceedings of the Vth International Conference of Isis Studies, Boulogne-sur-Mer, October 13-15, 2011*, Leiden.

Bricault, L., Veymiers, R. (2012): "Quinze ans après", in: Bricault & Versluys 2012, 1-24.

Bricault, L., Veymiers, R., eds. (2011): *Bibliotheca Isiaca* II, Bordeaux.

Bricault, L., Veymiers, R., eds. (2014): *Bibliotheca Isiaca* III, Bordeaux.

Bricault, L., Veymiers, R., eds. (2020): *Bibliotheca Isiaca* IV, Bordeaux.

Bru, H., Lebreton, St., Kirbihler, Fr., eds. (2009): *L'Asie Mineure dans l'Antiquité. Échanges, populations et territoires*, Rennes.

Brillant, M. (1912): "Inscription de Tomes", *Revue de philologie, de littérature et d'histoire anciennes* 36, 284-296.

Bruneau, Ph. (1975): *Le sanctuaire et le culte des divinités égyptiennes à Érétrie, ÉPRO* 45, Leiden.

Bryan, C. P. (1974): *Ancient Egyptian Medicine. The Papyrus Ebers*, Chicago (1re éd. London 1930).

Budde, L. (1987): *St. Pantaleon von Aphrodisias in Kilikien*, Recklinghausen.

Buora, M., Lafli, E. (2016): "Hadra Vases from Rough Cilicia", in: Japp & Kögler 2016, 317-328.

Burkert, W. (1977): *Orphism and Bacchic Mysteries : New Evidence and Old Problems of Interpretation*, Berkeley, CA. (Center for Hermeneutical Studies in Hellenistic and Modern Culture, Protocol of the 28 Colloquy, 13 march 1977), 1-8.

Burkert, W. (1987): *Ancient Mystery Cults*, Cambridge, Mass.–London.

Burkert, W. (2004): *Babylon, Memphis, Persepolis: Eastern Contexts of Greek Culture*, Cambridge–London.

Burton, A. (1972): *Diodorus Siculus, Book I. A Commentary, ÉPRO* 29, Leiden.

Butz, P. A. (2017): "The Bronze Head of Arsinoë III in Mantua and the Typology of Ptolemaic Divinization on the Archelaos Relief", in: Spinelli et al. 2017, 46-56.

Buzoianu, L., Bărbulescu, M. (2008): "Tomis în epoca romană timpurie (sec. I-III p. CHR.)", *Revista Romana de Studii Eurasiatice* 4, 7-48.

Cagnat, R., Toutain, J., Lafaye, G., Henry, V. (1901): *Inscriptiones graecae ad res romanas pertinentes*, I, Paris.

Calinescu, A., ed. (1996): *Ancient Jewelry and Archaeology,* Bloomington–Indianapolis.

Callaghan, P. J. (1980): "The Trefoil Style and Second-Century Hadra Vases", *The Annual of the British School at Athens* 75, 33-47.

Cancik, H., H. Lichtenberger, P. Schäfer, eds. (1996): *Geschichte - Tradition -Reflexion. Festschift fur Martin Hengel zum 70. Geburt stag.* Band 3: *Frühes Christentum*, Tübingen.

Cannavò, A., Thély, L., eds. (2018): *Les royaumes de Chypre à l'épreuve de l'histoire. Transitions et ruptures de la fin de l'âge du Bronze au début de l'époque hellénistique, BCH Suppl.* 60, Athens.

Casey, R. P. (1926): "Naassenes and Ophites", *The Journal of Theological Studies*, Vol. 27, No. 108, 374-387.

Casey, R. P. (1935): "The Study of Gnosticism", *The Journal of Theological Studies*, Vol. 36, No. 141, 45-60.

Chacheva, M. (2021): "Aegyptiaca Pontica: Old and New Evidence from the West Pontic Coast", in: Manoledakis 2021, 95-103.

Chaniotis, A. (1995): "Illness and cures in the Greek propitiatory inscriptions and dedications of Lydia and Phrygia", in: Horstmanshoff, van der Eijk & Schrijvers 1995, 323-344.

Charbonneaux, J. (1958): "Sur la signification et la date de la Tasse Farnèse", *Monuments et mémoires de la Fondation Eugène Piot* 50, 85-103.

Charlesworth, J. H. (1976) : "The pseudepigrapha and modern research", in: *Society of Biblical Literature : Septuagint and Cognate Studies* 7, 81-82.

Chernenko, V. G. (2013): "Perstni s portretnymi izobrazheniyami ptolemeevskogo tipa iz Tanaisa", in: *8-ya Mezhdunarodnaya arheologicheskaya konferenciya studentov i aspirantov «Problemy arheologii Vostochnoj Evropy»*, Rostov-on-Don, 126-129.

Chernenko, V. G. (2015): "Perstni s portretnymi izobrazheniyami ptolemeevskogo tipa iz Tanaisa", in: *Konferentsiya Lomonosov 2015.*

Christodoulou, P. (2015): "Sarapis, Isis and the Emperor", in: Müskens & Nikoloska 2015, 166-214.

Chrzanovski, L., ed. (2012): *Le luminaire antique, Lychnological Acts 3. Actes du 3e congrès international de l'ILA (Université d'Heidelberg, 21-26 IX 2009), Monographies instrumentum* 44, Montagnac.

Chrzanovski, L., Zhuravlev, D. (1998): *Lamps from Chersonesos in the State Historical Museum-Moscow*, Rome.

Clerc, G., Leclant, J. (1994): "Sérapis", in: *LIMC* VII.1, 666-692; VII.2, 504-518.

Colavito, J. (2011): *The Orphic Argonautica. An English Translation.*

Cook, B. F. (1966): *Inscribed Hadra Vases in The Metropolitan Museum of Art, The Metropolitan Museum of Art Papers* 12.

Cosentino, A. (2018): "The Authorship of the Refutatio omnium haeresium", *Zeitschrift für Antikes Christentum* 22 (2), 218-237.

Covacef, Z. (2006): "Templele Tomisului", *Peuce* S.N. III-IV, 159-172.

Covacef, Z. (2011): *Sculptura antică din expoziția de bază a Muzeului de Istorie Națională și Arheologie Constanța (Ancient sculpture in the permanent exhibition of the Museum of National History and Anchaeology Constanța)*, Cluj-Napoca.

CR *St. Pétersbourg* (1873): *Compte rendu de la Commission Impériale Archéologique: pour l'année* 1873, *St. Pétersbourg*, 1876.

Crahay, R. (1967): "Eléments d'une mythopée gnostique dans la Grèce classique", in: Bianchi 1967, 323-339.

Crawford, M. (2019): "Dediticii", *Oxford Classical Dictionary*, online.

Cullin-Mingaud, M., Doncheva, M., Landes, Ch., eds. (2007): *Des Thraces aux Ottomans: la Bulgarie à travers les collections des musées de Varna,* Paris.

Cumont, Fr. (1929[4]): *Les Religions orientales dans le paganisme romain*, Paris.

Cuvigny, H. (2021): *Rome in Egypt's Eastern Desert*, ed. by R. S. Bagnall, 2 vols., New York.

Dan, A. (2009): "Sinope 'capitale' pontique dans la géographie antique", in: Bru, Lebreton & Kirbihler 2009, 67-131.

Dan, A. (2011): "La Mer Noire et le Levant ancien : quelques domaines d'enquête", *Rivista di Studi Fenici* XXXI, 2, 211-258.

De Blois, L., Erdkamp, P., Hekster, O., de Kleijn, G., Mols, S., eds. (2003): *The representation and perception of Roman imperial power. Proceedings of the third workshop of the International Network Impact of Empire (Roman Empire, c. 200 B.C. – A.D. 476) Netherlands Institute in Rome, March 20-23, 2002*, Amsterdam.

De Hoz, M. P. (2009): "The Aretalogical Character of the Maionian "Confession" Inscriptions", in: Martínez Fernández 2009, 357-368.

De Hoz, M. P. (2017): "Religious discourse in Hellenistic and Roman times: content topoi in Greek epigraphic cult foundations and sacred norms", *Kernos* 30, 187-220.

De Juliis, E.H., ed. (1985): *Gli ori di Taranto in età ellenistica,* Milan.

De Landaluce, M. S. Or. (2011): "Αἰγυπτίων ἱερός λόγος (OF 40-63)", in: Herrero de Jáuregui et al. 2011, 55-60.

Delbrueck, R., Vollgraff, W. (1934): "An Orphic Bowl", *The Journal of Hellenic Studies*, Vol. 54, Part 2, 129-139.

Delev, P. (2004): *Lisimach* (Лизимах), Sofia.

Demargne, P. (1958): *Xanthos. Fouilles de Xanthos. I. Les piliers funéraires*, Paris.

Denis, P. (1996): "Recent Acquisitions of Ancient Jewelry by the Royal Ontario Museum", in: Calinescu 1996, 207-214.

Derksen, J.J., Vermaseren, M.J. (1984): "Isis kosmokrateira", in: Bonacasa & Di Vita 1984, 430-432.

De Ridder, A. (1924): *Musée du Louvre. Département des antiquités grecques et romaines. Catalogue sommaire des bijoux antiques*, Paris.

Depauw, M., Coussement, S., eds. (2041): *Dentifiers and Identification Methods in the Ancient World, Legal Documents in Ancient Societies* III, *OLA* 229.

Detienne, M. (1979): *Les maîtres de vérité dans la Grèce archaïque*, Paris (1re éd. 1967).

Dieterich, A. (1891): *Abraxas*, Leipzig.

Dijkstra, J., Kroesen, J., Kuiper, Y., eds. (2010): *Myths, Martyrs, and Modernity. Studies in the History of Religions in Honour of Jan N. Bremmer*, Leiden-Boston.

Dimitrov et al. eds. (2022): "Polzata ot istoriya ot Antichnostta do nashi dni (Ползата от история от Античността до наши дни)", vol. I, Plovdiv.

Draganov, B. (2022): "Carskiyat Hermes" I svedenieto na Herotod (5.7.1) (Realnost ili sluh) („Царският Хермес " и сведението на Херодот (5.7.1.) (Реалност или слух)", in: Dimitrov et al. 2022, 13-35.

Dunand, Fr. (1973): *Le culte d'Isis dans le bassin oriental de la Méditerranée*, *ÉPRO* 26, 3 vols., Leiden.

Dunand, Fr. (1986): "Les associations dionysiaques au service du pouvoir lagide (IIIe s. av. J.-C.)", in: *L'association dionysiaque dans les sociétés anciennes. Actes de la table ronde organisée par l'École française de Rome*, 1984, Rome, 85-104.

Dundua, G. F., Lodkipanidze, G. A. (1979): "Hellenistic Coins from the Site of Vani, in Colchis (Western Georgia)", *Numismatic Chronicle*, 1-6.

Dundua, T. (1996): "*Kolkhebis ajankeba da mitridate umtsrosi* [The Revolt of the Colchians and Mithridates the Junior", *Proceedings of Tbilisi State University (History, Archaeology, Art History, Ethnography)*, vol. 321.

Dundua, T. et al. (2013): *Catalogue of Georgian Numismatics*. Part one, Tbilisi.

Dundua, T. et al. (2015): *Catalogue of Georgian Numismatics*. Part two, Tbilisi.

Edwards, M. J. (1991): "Gnostic Eros and Orphic Themes", *ZPE* 88, 25-40.

Edwards, M. J. (1996): "The Naming of the Naassenes: Hippolytus, *Refutatio* V. 6-10 as *Hieros Logos*", *ZPE* 112, 74-80.

Empereur, J.-Y., ed. (1998): *Commerce et artisanat dans l'Alexandrie hellénistique et romaine. Actes de la Table Ronde organisée par le CNRS, le Laboratoire de Céramologie de Lyon et l'EFA, Athènes, 10-12 octobre 1988*, *BCH Suppl.* 33, Athènes.

Engovatova, A. V., ed. (2017): *Goroda, poseleniya, nekropoli. Raskopki 2016 g, Materialy spasatel'nykh arkheologicheskih issledovaniy* 19, Moscow.

Erath-Koiner, G. (2003): "Weibliche Schönheit und männlicher Siegerstolz. Berenike II. und ein Athletenbildnis aus dem hellenistischen Zypern", in: Karageorghis & Rogge 2003, 105-116.

Erim, K. T. (1967): "De Aphrodisiade", *AJA* 71.3, 233-243.

Erlikh, V. R. (2014): *Drevnosti «doliny yablon'»*, Moscow.

Erlikh, V. R. (2017): "Dva bogatykh ellinisticheskikh pogrebeniya iz mogil'nika Psenafa", *Scripta antiqua* VI, 13-44.

Estienne, S., Jaillard, D., Pouzadoux, C., eds. (2008): *Image et religion gréco-romaine*, Naples.

Faraone, Ch. A. (1994): "Notes on Three Greek Magical Texts", *ZPE* 100, 81-85.

Farmakovsky, B. V. (1906): "Raskopki v Ol'vii v 1902-1903 godah", *Izvestiya imperatorskoj arheologicheskoj komissii*, 13, 165-215.

Farmakovsky, B. V. (1918): "Hersonskaya guberniya. Raskopki v Ol'vii", *Otchet arheologicheskoj komissii za 1913-1915 gody*, 1-51.

Malherbe, A. J., Norris, R. W., Thompson, J. W., eds. (1998): *The Early Church in Its Context: Essays in Honor of Everett Ferguson*, Leiden-Boston-Köln.

Fernández, R. C. (2006): "Los Entalles de *Segobriga* y su territorio", *Archivo español de arqueología* 79, 259-270.

Finogenova, S .I. (2001): "Gruppa bronzovyh ellinisticheskih perstnej iz sobraniya GMII im. A. S. Pushkina", *VDI* 2, 164-167.

Finogenova, S .I. (2010): "Gosudarstvennyy muzey izobrazitel'nykh iskusstv imeni A.S. Pushkina. Antichnye drevnosti Tamanskogo poluostrova", in: Bongard-Levin & Kuznetsov 2010b, 356-379.

Fishwick, D. (1973): "The Severi and the provincial cult of the Three Gauls", *Historia* 22, 627-649.

Flourentzos, P. (2007): "An Unknown Graeco-Roman Temple from Lower City of Amathous", *Cahiers du Centre d'Études Chypriotes* 37, 299-306.

Fotiadi, P. (2011): "Ritual Terracotta Lamps with Representations of Sarapis and Isis from the Sanctuary of the Egyptian Gods at Marathon. The Variation of 'Isis with three Ears of Wheat'", in: Bricault & Veymiers 2011, 65-77.

Fraser, P. M. (1960): "Two Studies on the Cult of Sarapis in the Hellenistic World", *Opuscula Atheniensia* III, 1-54.

Furtwängler, A. (1900): *Die antiken Gemmen. Geschichte der Steinschneidekunst im klassischen Altertum*. I–III, Berlin-Leipzig.

Gabrielsen, V., Lund, J., eds. (2007): *The Black Sea in Antiquity: Regional and Interregional Economic Exchanges*, *Black Sea Studies* 6, Aarhus.

Gaertner, J. F. (2005): *Ovid. Epistulae ex Ponto. Book I*, Oxford.

Gaiu, C., Bodale, H., eds. (2004): *Centru și Periferie: Lucrările Colocviului Național, Bistrița 23-25 Aprilie 2004*, Bistrița.

Gajdukevitch, V. F. (1971): *Das Bosporanische Reich*, Berlin.

Galanina, L., Grač, N., Kellner, H.-J., Kossack, G., eds. (1987): *Scythika. Vorträge zur Entstehung des skytho-iranischen Tierstils und zu Denkmälern des Bosporanischen Reichs anlässlich einer Ausstellung der Leningrader Ermitage in München 1984. Bayerische Akademie der Wissenschaften. Phil.-hist. Kl. Abh. Neue Folge* 98, Munich.

Galbois, E. 2018: *Images du pouvoir et pouvoir de l'image. Les «médaillons-portraits» miniatures des Lagides, Scripta antiqua* 113, Bordeaux.

Gardner, E. A. (1888): *Naukratis*. Part II. *Sixth Memoir of the Egypt Exploration Fund*, London.

Găzdac, C. (2004): "Centre and periphery: The Roman monetary policy regarding the Lower Danube provinces at the mid 3rd century AD", in: Gaiu & Bodale 2004, 71-76.

Gerring, B. (2000): *Sphragides. Die gravierten Fingerringe des Hellenismus, British Archaeological Reports Int. Ser.* 848, Oxford.

Gkikaki, M. (2011): *Die weiblichen Frisuren auf den Münzen und in der Großplastik zur Zeit der Klassik und des Hellenismus*, Diss., Universität Würzburg, Würzburg.

Glomb, T., Mertel, A., Pospíšil, Z., Stachoň, Z. & Chalupa, A. (2018): "Ptolemaic military operations were a dominant factor in the spread of Egyptian cults across the early Hellenistic Aegean Sea", *PLoS ONE,* 13(3), e0193786. https://doi.org/10.1371/journal.pone.0193786

Gochev, Ya. (1987): "Kraymorskiyat bulevard na Varna (Крайморският булевард на Варна)", Nauchnopopulyaren almanah FAR'87, Varna, 349-353.

Godwin, J. (2020): *Juvenal. Satires. Book V*, Liverpool.

Goodenough, E. R. (1935): *By Light, Light: The Mystic Gospel of Hellenistic Judaism*, New Haven.

Goold, G. P. (1983): "The Cause of Ovid's Exile", *Illinois Classical Studies* 8, 1, 94-107.

Gordon, R. (1990): "The Veil of Power: Emperors, sacrificers and benefactors", in: Beard & North 1990, 199-231.

Gorrini, M. E. (2006): "Un ritratto di Arsione III a Palazzo te a Mantova: alcune considerazioni", *Numismatica e antichità classiche* 35, 221-237.

Grabowski, T. (2014): "The Cult of the Ptolemies in the Aegean in the 3rd Century BC", *ELECTRUM* 21, 21-41.

Grabowski, T. (2020) : "The Activity of Ptolemy II's Fleet in the Aegean Sea", *ELECTRUM* 27, 131-148.

Grach, N. L. (1984): "Otkrytie novogo istoricheskogo istochnika v Nimfee", *VDI* 1, 81-88.

Grač, N. (1987): Ein neu entdecktes Fresco aus hellenistischer Zeit in Nymphaion bei Kertsch", in: Galanina et al. 1987, 87-95.

Grandjean, Y. (1975): *Une nouvelle arétalogie d'Isis à Maronée, ÉPRO* 49, Leiden.

Grenier, J.-Cl. (1977): *Anubis alexandrin et romain, ÉPRO* 57, Leiden.

Gruen, E. S. (1998): *Heritage and Hellenism: The Reinvention of Jewish Tradition*, Berkeley-Los Angeles-London.

Grzybek, E. (1989): "Die griechische Konkubine und ihre „Mitgift" (P.Eleph. 3 und 4)", *ZPE* 76, 206-212.

Guerrini, L. (1964): *Vasi di Hadra: Tentativo di Sistemazione Cronologica di una Classe Ceramica*, Roma.

Guichard, C., Savoy, B. (2018): "Acquiring Cultures and Trading Value in a Global World", in: Savoy et al. 2018, 1-8.

Guittard, Ch. (2004): *Carmen et prophéties à Rome*, Turnhout.

Guldager Bilde, P., Lawall, M. L., eds. (2014): *Pottery, Peoples and Places. Study and Interpretation of Late Hellenistic Pottery, Black Sea Studies* 16, Aarhus.

Győry, H., ed. (2016): *Aegyptus et Pannonia* V, Budapest.

Gwyn Griffiths, J. (1970): *Plutarch's De Iside et Osiride*, Swansea.

Gwyn Griffiths, J. (1975): *Apuleius of Madauros. The Isis-Book (Metamorphoses, Book XI), ÉPRO* 39, Leiden.

Haegemans, K. (2003): "Representation and perception of imperial power in AD 238. The numismatic evidence", in: De Blois et al. 2003, 466-480.

Harder, R. (1943/4): *Karpokrates von Chalkis und die memphitische Isispropaganda*, Berlin.

Hemingway, S., Karoglou, K., eds. (2019): *Art of the Hellenistic Kingdoms: From Pergamon to Rome*, New York.

Henrichs, A. (1968): "Vespasian's Visit to Alexandria", *ZPE* 3, 51-80.

Henrichs, A. (1972): *Die 'Phoinikika' des Lollianos*, Berkeley.

Hermann, L. (1938): "La faute secrète d'Ovide", *Revue belge de philologie et d'histoire* 17, 3-4, 697-725.

Hernández, R. M. (2013): "Herodotus' Egyptian Dionysos. A Comparative Perspective", in: Bernabé et al. 2013, 250-260.

Herrero de Jáuregui, M. (2007): "Las fuentes de Clem. Alex. *Protr.* 2.12-22: un tratado sobre los misterios y una teogonía órfica", *Emerita: Revista Española de Lingüística y Filología Clásica* 75.1, 19-50.

Herrero de Jáuregui, M. (2010) : *Orphism and Christianity in Late Antiquity*, Göttingen.

Herrero de Jáuregui, M., J. S. Cristóbal, A. Isabel, E. R. Luján Martínez, E. R. Luján, H. R. Martín, S. Álvarez, M. Antonio, S. T. Tovar, eds. (2011): *Tracing Orpheus: Studies of Orphic Fragments. Sozomena: studies in the recovery of ancient text* Vol. 10, Berlin-Boston.

Hill, M. (2019): "Regarding Kallainopoioi: Notes on Hellenistic Faience", in: Hemingway & Karoglou 2019, 158-167.

Höckmann, O. (1999): "Naval and other graffiti from Nymphaion", *Ancient Civilizations from Scythia to Siberi,* 5.4, 303-356.

Höckmann, O. (2010): "Zur antiken Schifffahrt im Schwarzen Meer", *Kölner Jahrb.* 43, 345-369.

Hölbl, G. (2001): *A history of the Ptolemaic Empire*, London.

Holladay, C. R. (1996a): *Fragments from Hellenistic Jewish Authors.* Vol. 4: *Orphica*, Atlanta.

Holladay, C. R. (1996b): "The Textual Tradition of Pseudo-Orpheus: Walter or Riedweg?", in: Cancik et al. 1996, 159-180.

Holladay, C. R. (1998): "Pseudo-Orpheus: Tracking a Tradition", in: Ferguson et al. 1998, 192-220.

Hopfner, Th. (1922-1925): *Fontes historiae religionis aegyptiacae*, 5 vols., Bonn.

Hordern, J. (2000): "Notes on the Orphic Papyrus from Gurôb (P. Gurôb 1; Pack2 2464)", *ZPE* 129, 131-140.

Hornbostel, W. (1973): *Sarapis. Studien zur Überlieferungsgeschichte, den Erscheinungsformen und Wandlungen der Gestalt eines Gottes*, *ÉPRO* 32, Leiden.

Horstmanshoff, Ph. J., van der Eijk, H. F. J., Schrijvers, P. H., eds. (1995), *Ancient Medicine in its Socio-Cultural Context. Papers Read at the Congress Held at Leiden University, 13-15 April 1992*, Amsterdam-Atlanta.

Howgego, C. (2005): "Coinage and Identity in the Roman Provinces", in: Howgego, Heuchert & Burnett 2005, 1-17.

Howgego, C., Heuchert, V., Burnett, A., eds. (2005): *Coinage and Identity in the Roman Provinces*, Oxford.

Husquin, C. (2018): "Fiat Lux ! Cécité et déficiences visuelles à Rome : réalités et mythologies, des ténèbres à la lumière", *Pallas* 106, 243-256.

Ivanov, A. V., Trubnikov, V. V. (2018): "Poselenie «Psif-3» v Zapadnom Zakuban'e", *Drevnosti Bospora* 22, 72-89.

Jahn, O. (1869): "Die Cista mystica", *Hermes* 3, 317-334.

Japp, S., Kögler, P., eds. (2016): *Traditions and innovations. Tracking the development of pottery from the Late Classical to the Early Imperial periods,* Wien.

Jones, S. (1997): *The Archaeology of Ethnicity. Constructing identities in the past and present*, London-New York.

Jordan, D. R. (1988): "A Love Charm with Verses", *ZPE* 72, 245-259.

Jovanova, L. (2020): "Roman Lamps from Scupi with Representations of Serapis, Isis and Harpocrates", in: Bricault & Veymiers 2020, 95-113.

Jucker, I., Stucky, R. S., eds. (1980): *Eikones: Studien zum griechischen und römischen Bildnis. Hans Jucker zum 60. Jahrestag gewidmet, Beiheft zur Halbjahresschrift* AK 12, Bern.

Kakhidze, A. (2004): *Pichvnari*, vol. I, Tbilisi.

Kakhidze, A. et al. (2002): *Gonio-Apsarosi*, vol. III, Tbilisi.

Kamenjarin, I., Ugarković, M., eds. (2020): *Exploring the Neighborhood. The Role of Ceramics in Understanding Place in the Hellenistic World. Proceedings of the 3rd Conference of IARPotHP, Kaštela, June 2017, 1st-4th, International Association for Research on Pottery of the Hellenistic Period* 3, Vienna.

Kaukhchishvili, T. (1987): *Vanis akhladaghmochenili berdznuli tsartsera* [Recently discovered Greek Inscription from Vani], *Kartuli tskarotmtsodneoba* [Georgian Source-Studies], Tbilisi, 131-143.

Kaukhchishvili, T. (2009): *Sakartvelos berdznuli tsartserebis korpusi* [Corpus of Greek Inscriptions of Georgia], Tbilisi.

Kaukhchishvili, T. (2019): *Sakartvelos istoriis dzveli berdznuli tskaroebi* [Ancient Greek Sources of the History of Georgia], Tbilisi.

Karageorghis, V., Rogge, S., eds. (2003): *Junge zyprische Archäologie. Symposium Berlin, 6. April 2002,* Münster.

Kater-Sibbes, G.J.F. (1973): *Preliminary Catalogue of Sarapis Monuments, ÉPRO* 36, Leiden.

Kern, O. (1922): *Orphicorum fragmenta*, Berlin.

Khodza, E. N., ed. (2004): *Ellinisticheskie shtudii v Ermitazhe. Sbornik statey. K shestidesyatiletiyu Mikhaila Borisovicha Piotrovskogo*, Saint Petersburg.

Khoshtaria, N. et al. (1972): Arkeologiuri gatkhrebi Vanshi 1967 tsels [Archaeological Excavations in Vani in 1967], in: Vani. Vol. I. 175-185.

Kleibl, K. (2009): *Iseion. Raumgestaltung und Kultpraxis in den Heiligtümern gräco-ägyptischer Götter im Mittelmeerraum*, Worms.

Kleiner, G., Ohly, D. (1951): "Gemmen der Sammlung Arndt", *Münchner Jahrbuch der bildenden Kunst* 2, 7-31.

Knipovich, T. (1941): "Iz istorii hudozhestvennoj keramiki Severnogo Prichernomor'ya", *Sovetskaya arheologiya* VII, 140-151.

Kobilyna, M. M. (1976): *Divinités orientales sur le littoral nord de la Mer Noire*, avec un appendice de O. J. Névérov, *ÉPRO* 52, Leiden.

Koiner, G. (2013): "Ptolemies and Cypriots: Imitation and Distinction in Cypriote Portrait sculpture", in: Scherrer, Koiner & Ulbrich 2013, 119-158.

Korovina, A. K. (1987): "Perstni iz nekropolej Fanagorii i Tiramby", *Soobshcheniya GMII im. A.S. Pushkina* 8, 137-148.

Körte, A. (1927): "Literarische Texte mit Ausschluss der christlichen", *Archiv für Papyrusforschung und verwandte Gebiete* 8, Nr. 698, 270.

Kotenko, V. (2019): "Nasliduvannya stylyu hadra v khersones'komu vazopysi ta yoho poshyrennya v Pivnichno-Zakhidnomu Prychornomor'yi", *Ukrainian Ceramology* XIII (1), 109-118.

Kotenko, V. (2022): "Tauric Chersonesos Tableware on the Markets of the North-western Black Sea Region", in: Rembart & Waldner 2022, 437-447.

Kotina, A. V. (2021): "Bog molchaniya (Бог молчания)" iz Tiritaki", in: Zaykova, Kostromicheva & Lesnoi 2021, 118-121.

Kousoulis, P., Lazaridis, N., eds. (2015): *Proceedings of the Tenth International Congress of Egyptologists*, *OLA* 241, vol. 2, Leuven-Paris-Bristol.

Krasnodubets, E. M. (2018a): "Ellinisticheskie egipetskie perstni-pechati i ikh ottiski iz Khersonesa Tavricheskogo i ego khory", in: Zuev & Khrshanovskij 2018, 105-112.

Krasnodubets, E. M. (2018b): "O dvukh nakhodkah iz raskopok v IX kvartale", in: Yashaeva & Majko 2018, 105-109.

Kreuzer, M. (2004): *The Coinage of System of Cleopatra VII and Augustus in Cyprus,* Springfield.

Kriseleit, I. (1990): "Fragmente von Ptolemäerkannen in der Antikensammlung", *Forschungen und Berichte* 28, 61-64.

Krug, A. (1980): "Two Turquoise Gems from Iran", *Muse* 14, 36-42.

Kümmel, W. G., ed. (1983): *Jüdische Schriften aus hellenistisch-römischer Zeit*, Gütersloh.

Kuznetsov, V. D., Tolstikov, V. P., eds. (2017): *Pantikapey i Fanagoriya. Dve stolitsy bosporskogo tsarstva*, Moscow.

Ladynin, I. A. (2007): "Eshche raz o perstnyah «ptolemeevskogo tipa» iz Severnogo Prichernomor'ya: k vozmozhnoy interpretatsii v svete vneshney politiki ellinisticheskogo Egipta v III v. do n.e.", *Drevnosti Bospora* 11, 235-252.

Ladynin, I. A. (2011): "Rings for Grain: An Interpretation for the Abundant Finds of the So-called "Ptolemaic Finger Rings" of the 3rd Century B.C. in the North Black Sea Area", in: Olshausen & Sauer 2011, 245-260.

Ladynin, I., Popova, E. A. (2010): "An Egyptian Pendant from the Settlement "Chayka" (North-Western Crimea) and the Posthumous Divinization of Arsinoe II Philadelphos", *VDI* 273, 71-85.

Laronde, A., Leclant, J., eds. (2007): *La Méditerranée, d'une rive à l'autre: culture classique et cultures périphériques, Cahiers de la Villa Kérylos*, n° 18, Paris.

Lapis I.A., Matthieu, M.E. (1969): *Drevneegipetskaya skul'ptura v sobranii Gosudarstvennogo Ermitazha (Древнеегипетская скульптура в собрании Государственного Эрмитажа).* Moscow.

Laporte, J.-P., Bricault, L. (2020): *Le Serapeum de Carthage, Supplément à la Bibliotheca Isiaca* I, Bordeaux.

Latham, J. A. (2016): *Performance, memory, and processions in ancient Rome*, Cambridge.

Lawall, M. L., Guldager Bilde, P., Bjerg, L., Handberg, S., Højte, J. M. (2014): "The Lower City of Olbia Pontike Occupation and Abandonment in the 2nd Century BC", in: Guldager Bilde & Lawall 2014, 29-46.

Le Bohec, Y., Wolff, C., eds. (2000): *Les légions de Rome sous le haut-empire: actes du congrès de Lyon (17-19 septembre 1998), Collection du Centre d'Études Romaines et Gallo-Romaines Nouvelle série*, 20.

Leclant, J. (1956): "Notes sur la propagation des cultes et des monuments égyptiens en Occident à l'époque impériale", *BIFAO* LV, 173-179.

Legge, Fr. (1915): *Forerunners and Rivals of Christianity Being Studies in Religious History from 330 B.C. to 330 A.D.*, Vol. 1, Cambridge.

Lenger, M.-T. (1980): *Corpus des Ordonnances des Ptolémées*, Bruxelles.

Lenger, M.-T. (1990): *Corpus des Ordonnances des Ptolémées. Bilan des additions et corrections. Compléments à la bibliographie*, Bruxelles.

Lichtenberger, H., Oegema, G. S., eds. (2005-), *Jüdische Schriften aus hellenistisch-römischer Zeit. Neue Folge*, Gütersloh

Lichtenberger, A., Martin, K., Nieswandt, H.-H. & Salzmann, D., eds. (2012): *Das Diadem der hellenistischen Herrscher. Übernahme, Transformation oder Neuschöpfung eines Herrschaftszeichens? Kolloquium vom 30.-31. Januar 2009 in Münster. Euros – Münstersche Beiträge zu Numismatik und Ikonographie* 1, Bonn.

Lichtenberger, A., Martin, K., Nieswandt, H.-H. & Salzmann, D., eds. (2014): *Bildwelt. Nominalspezifische Kommunikationsstrategien in der Münzprägung hellenistischer Herrscher. Kolloquium vom 17.-18. Juni 2010 in Münster. Euros* 2, Bonn.

Limberis, N. Yu., Marchenko, I. I. (1997): "Antichnye pogrebeniya iz kurganov v okrestnostyakh Fanagorii", in: *Pontiyskie greki*, Krasnodar, 46-57.

Limberis, N. Yu., Marchenko, I. I. (2007): "Antichnye pogrebeniya iz kurgannogo nekropolya u poseleniya "Vinogradnoe 7" v okrestnostyakh Fanagorii", in: Zuev 2007, 229-236.

Limberis, N. Yu., Marchenko, I. I. (2010): "Novye materialy iz raskopok kurgannogo nekropolya u poseleniya Vinogradnoe-7 na Tamani", in: Maslennikov et al. 2010, 152-163.

Lindner, M. (2013): "Eyes of a Queen, a Marble Head in Frosinone", *Terra dei Volsci. Annali del Museo Archeologico di Frosinone* N.S., 1, 25-42.

Litvinenko, Y. N. (1991): "Ptolemeevskiy Egipet i Severnoe Prichernomor'e v III v. do n.e. [Ptolemaic Egypt and the Region to the North of the Black Sea in the 3rd Century BC]", *VDI* 1, 12-26.

Lloyd, A. B. (1975-1993): *Herodotus, Book II. Introduction and Commentary*, *ÉPRO* 43, 3 vols., Leiden.

Loebensstein, H. et al. (1983): *Festschrift zum 100-jährigen Bestehen der Papyrussammlung der Österreichischen Nationalbibliothek – Papyrus Erzherzog Rainer* (P. Rainer Cent.), Wien.

Lomtadze, G., Zhuravlev, D. (2020): "Fine Ware from the House of Chrysaliskos (Taman Peninsula, Black Sea Region)", in: Kamenjarin & Ugarković 2020, 533-553.

Lorber, C. (2014): "The Royal Portrait on Ptolemaic Coinage", in: Lichtenberger et al. 2014, 111-181.

Lordkipanidze, G. (2001): "Isidas simboloebiani monetebi dzveli vanidan (suriumi) [Coins with the Symbols of Isis from Ancient Vani (Surium)]", *Givi Zhordania* 90, 95-101.

Lund, J. (2014): "Pots and Politics: Reflections on the Circulation of Pottery in the Ptolemaic and Seleukid Kingdoms", in: Bilde & Lawall 2014, 297-305.

Lungu, V. (2003): "Céramique du style Hadra à Histria", *Mar Nero* 4, 43-87.

Lungu, V. (2007): "L'Égypte lagide et les cites grecques du Pont Nord", in: Bresson et al. 2007, 149-163.

Lungu, V. (2007a): "Une Hydrie du Style de Hadra à Décor Polychrome de Callatis", *Revue des études sud-est éuropeenne* XLV (1-4), 23-37. (да се добави "а" в Котенко)

Lungu, V., Dupont, P. (2014): "Imports and Local Imitations of Hellenistic Pottery in the Northwest Black Sea Area: Hadra and Pseudo-Hadra Wares" in: Guldager Bilde & Lawall 2014, 233-254.

Makalatia, S. (1938): *Jege-Misaronis kulti dzvel sakartveloshi* [The Cult of Jege-Misaroni in Ancient Georgia], Tbilisi.

Maksimova, M. I. (1958): "Fragment kostyanogo perstnya iz Ol'vii", *Sovetskaya arkheologiya* 28, 248-255.

Malaise, M. (1972): *Inventaire préliminaire des documents égyptiens découverts en Italie* and *Les conditions de pénétration et de diffusion des cultes égyptiens en Italie*, *ÉPRO* 21-22, Leiden.

Malaise, M. (2005): *Pour une terminologie et une analyse des cultes isiaques*, *Mémoire de la Classe des Lettres* XXXV, Bruxelles.

Malaise, M. (2014a): "Le calathos sur la tête d'Isis", *Studien zur Altägyptischen Kultur* 43, 223-265.

Malaise, M. (2014b): "Anubis et Hermanubis à l'époque gréco-romaine", *Bibliotheca Isiaca* III, 73-93.

Manders, E. (2012): *Coining Images of Power. Patterns in the Representation of Roman Emperors on Imperial Coinage, A.D. 193-284*, *Impact of Empire Series* no. 15, Leiden-Boston.

Manders, E., Hekster, O. (2011): "Identities of Emperor and Empire in the third century AD: Some considerations", in: Benoist, Daguet-Gagey & Hoët-Van Cauwenberghe 2011.

Manoledakis, M., ed. (2021): *Peoples in the Black Sea Region from Archaic to the Roman Period. Proceedings of the 3rd International Workshop on the Black Sea in Antiquity held in Thessaloniki, 21-23 September 2018*, Oxford.

Manolova-Voykova, M., Tenekedjiev, V. (2021): "Spasitelni razkopki na ul. „San Stefano" № 25 vav Varna (Rescue excavations on San Stefano Str, 25 in Varna]", *Arheologicheski otkritia i razkopki prez* 2020-2, Sofia, 2021, 644-648.

Manolova-Voykova, M., Tenekedjiev, V., Mircheva, E. (2018): "Spasitelni razkopki na ul. „Tsar Ivan Shishman" № 3-5, gr. Varna [Rescue excavations on Tsar Ivan Shishman Str. № 3-5, in Varna", *Arheologicheski otkritia i razkopki prez* 2017, Sofia, 2018, 221-225.

Manov, M. (2018): "The Hellenistic Big Rock Human Head from Bulgaria", *Journal of Ancient History and Archaeology* 5.2, 16-27.

Marangou, L. (1971): "Ptolemäische Fingerringe aus Bein", *Athenisch Mitteilungen* 86, 163-171.

Marchenko, I. I., Bochkovoj, V. V., Kononov, V. Yu. (2007): "Raskopki mogil'nika «Vinogradnyy-7» na Tamani v 2005-2006 gg.", *Materialy po istorii i arkheologii Kubani* 7, 151-392.

Marcovich, M. (1974): "Phanes, Phicola, and the Sethians", *Journal of Theological Studies,* New Series 25, No.2, 447-451.

Marcovich, M., ed. (1986): *Hippolytus Refutatio Omnim Haeresium*, *Patristische Texte und Studien* 25, Berlin-New York.

Martin, K. (2012): "Königin und Göttin, Zur Präsenz des Diadems auf hellenistischen Königinnen-Münzen", in: Lichtenberger et al. 2012, 395-423.

Martínez Fernández, Á., ed. (2009): *Estudios de Epigrafía Griega*, La Laguna.

Maslennikov, A. A., Gavrilyuk, N. A., Zavojkin, A. A., eds. (2010): *ΣΥΜΒΟΛΑ. Antichnyj mir Severnogo Prichernomor'ya. Noveyshie nakhodki i otkrytiya* 1, Moscow-Kiev.

Masson, A. (2018): "Scarabs, scaraboids and amulets", in: Villing et al. 2013-2019.

Masson, A. (2018) : "Seals and seal impressions", in: Villing et al. 2013-2019.

Mathisen, R. W. (2006): "Peregrini, Barbari, and Cives Romani: Concepts of Citizenship and the Legal Identity of Barbarians in the Late Roman Empire". *The American Historical Review* vol. 111, no. 4, 1011-1040.

Mattingly, D. J. (2011): *Imperialism, power, and identity. Experiencing the Roman Empire.* Princeton-Oxford.

Mazurek, L. A. (2022): *Isis in a Global Empire: Greek Identity through Egyptian Religion in Roman Greece*, Cambridge.

McCredie, J. R., et al., eds. (1992): *Samothrace: Excavations Conducted by the Institute of Fine Arts of New York University, Volume 7, Rotunda of Arsinoe II,* Princeton.

McGowan, M. M. (2009): *Ovid in Exile. Power and Poetic Redress in the Tristia and Epistulae ex Ponto*, Leiden.

Medvedev, A. P. (2009): "Novye materialy po istorii i kul'ture antichnoy Fanagorii (iz raskopok Vostochnogo nekropolya v 2005-2007 gg.)", *Nortia* VI, 146-170.

Medvedev, A. P. (2014): "Ellinisticheskie pogrebeniya Vostochnogo nekropolya Fanagorii (raskopki 2005-2007 gg.)", *Rossiyskaya arkheologiya* 3, 123-139.

Melikishvili, G. (1970): *Dvzeli Kolkheti dzv. ts. VI-IV saukuneebshi* [Ancient Colchis in 6th cent. BCE – 4th cent. BCE], in: *Sakartvelos istoriis narkvevebi* [Studies in the History of Georgia], Tbilisi.

Merkelbach, R. (1995): *Isis regina – Zeus Sarapis. Die griechisch-ägyptische Religion nach den Quellen dargestellt*, Stuttgart-Leipzig.

Merkelbach, R., Totti, M., eds. (1990-): *Abrasax. Ausgewählte Papyri religiösen und magischen Inhalts*, 5 vols, Köln.

Merriam, A. C. (1885): "Inscribed Sepulchral Vases from Alexandria", *American Journal of Archaeology and of the History of the Fine Arts* 1 (1), 18-33.

Meyza, H. (2012): "Another Bone Ring from Cyprus with a Portrait of a Ptolemaic Queen", *Études et Travaux* XXV, 262-267.

Michaelides, D., Papantoniou, G. (2018): "The Advent of Hellenistic Cyprus", in: Cannavò & Thély 2018, 267-290.

Mihailescu-Bîrliba, L., Bounegru, O., eds. (2006): *Studia historiae et religionis daco-romanae. In honorem Silviu Sanie*, Bucarest.

Mihailov, G. (1970): *Inscriptiones graecae in Bulgaria repertae. Vol. I. Inscriptiones orae Ponti Euxini, Editio altera emendate*, Sofia.

Minchev, A. (2006): "Odessos aux époques archaïque et classique (VIe – fin du IVe siècle avant J.-C.)", in: Cullin-Mingaud, Doncheva & Landes 2007, 61-65.

Minchev, A. (2007): *Odesos prez Elinisticheskata epoha (kraya na IV v. pr.Hr. – nachaloto na I v. sl.Hr.* [Odesos during the Hellenistic period], Varna.

Mirchev, M. (1967): "Za antichnite hramove na Odesos [Ancient temples in Odesos]", *Izvestia na Narodnia muzey – Varna* III (XVIII), 21-38.

Molev, E. A. (1994): *Bospor v period ellinizma*, Nizhniy Novgorod.

Molok, D. Yu., ed. (1992), *Arkheologiya i iskusstvo Bospora. Soobshcheniya GMII im. A.S. Pushkina* X, Moscow.

Mondello, Cr., Bricault L. (2024-2026): *Isis Moneta. The 'Vota Publica' tokens the IVth century*, 2 vols., London.

Mouton, M., Schmid, St. G., eds. (2013): *Men on the Rocks. The Formation of Nabataean Petra*, Berlin.

Mshvildadze, M. (2002): *Romi da aghmosavluri religiebi ax.ts. I-III saukuneebshi [Rome and Eastern Religions in 1st-3rd cent. CE.]*. Dissertation to obtain doctoral degree. Tbilisi.

Mshvildaze, M., Mamuladze, Sh. (2009): *Serapisi Aghmosavlet Shavizghvispiretshi* [Serapis in Eastern Black Sea Coast], *Istoriani*, 62-72.

Muller, A., Laflı, E., eds. (2015): *Figurines de terre cuite en Méditerranée grecque et romaine* 2. *Iconographie et contextes*, Villeneuve d'Ascq.

Müller, S. (2009): *Das hellenistische Königspaar in der medialen Repräsentation: Ptolemaios II. und Arsinoe II*, Berlin.

Murray, W. M. (2001): "A Trireme Named Isis: The Sgraffito from Nymphaion", *International Journal of Nautical Archaeology* 30.2, 250-256.

Murray, W. M. (2002): "Observations on the 'Isis' Fresco at Nymphaion", in: Tzalas 2002, 539-561.

Müskens, S., Nikoloska, A., eds. (2015): *Romanising oriental gods? Religious transformations in the Balkan provinces in the Roman period. New finds and novel perspectives. Proccedings of the International Symposium Skopje, 18-21 September 2013*, Skopje.

Nagel, Sv. (2019): *Isis im römischen Reich*, *Philippika* 109, 2 vols., Wiesbaden.

Nederveen Pieterse, J. (2015): "Ancient Rome and globalisation: decentring Rome", in: Pitts &Versluys 2015, 225-239.

Nenna, M. D., Seif El-Din, M. (2000): *La vaiselle en faïence d'époque gréco-romaine*, *Études alexandrines* 4, Cairo.

Neverov, O. J. (1974) : "Gruppa ellinisticheskikh bronzovykh perstney v sobranii Ermitazha (k voprosu o vremeni proniknoveniya egipetskikh kul'tov v Severnoe Prichernomor'e)", *VDI* 1, 106-115.

Névérov, O. J. (1976): "Représentations sur les gemmes-cachets, bagues en métal et amulettes des premiers siècles de notre ère", in: Kobilyna 1976, 53-65, 69-70, pl. XLVIII-LII.

Neverov, O. J. (1976a): "Portretnye gemmy i perstni iz Severnogo Prichernomor'ya", *Trudy Gosudarstvennogo Ermitazha* 17, 166-183. (да се оправи в текста на Трейстер + а)

Neverov, O. J. (2010): "Gosudarstvennyy Ermitazh. Gliptika", in: Bongard-Levin & Kuznetsov 2010b, 264-275.

Nikulin, P. A., Sadekova, S. H., Tugusheva, O. V. (2019), *Antichnoe sobranie sem'i Karisalovykh*, Moscow.

Nock, A. D. (1972): *Essays on Religion and the Ancient World*, 1, Oxford.

Olshausen, E., Sauer, V., eds. (2011): *Die Schätze der Erde. Natürliche Ressourcen in der antiken Welt. Stuttgarter Kolloquium zur Historischen Geographie des Altertums 10, 2008,* Stuttgart.

Olszta-Bloch, M. (2011): *Ptolemejski Egipt i Greckie centra Północnego wybrzeża Morza Czarnego. Związki polityczne i gospodarcze*, Toruń.

Ostroverkhov, A. S. (2014): "Yehypets'ki fayansy" v Skifiyi ta yikh mistse v systemi podibnykh starozhytnostey Skhidnoyi Yevropy (dosvid kompleksnoho analizu)", *Arkheolohiya* 1, 41-60.

Orrieux, Cl. (1985): *Zénon de Caunos, parépidèmos, et le destin grec*, *Annales littéraires de l'Université de Besançon* 320, Paris.

Padró i Parcerisa, J. (1980-1985): *Egyptian Type Documents from the Mediterranean Littoral of the Iberian Peninsula before the Roman Conquest*, *ÉPRO* 65, 3 vol., Leiden.

Pagenstecher, R. (1909): "Dated Sepulchral Vases from Alexandria", *AJA* 13 (4), 387-416.

Pailler, J.-M. (1989): "Les religions orientales, troisième époque", *Pallas* 35, 95-113.

Papuci-Władyki, E., ed. (2008): *Pontika 2006. Recent Research in Northern Black Sea Coast Greek Colonies [Новейшие исследования греческих колоний Северного Причерноморья]. Proceedings of the International Conference, Kraków, 18th March, 2006,* Krakow.

Pearson, St. (2021): *The Triumph and Trade of Egyptian Objects in Rome. Collecting Art in the Ancient Mediterranean*, *Image & Context* 20, Berlin-Boston.

Peter, U. (2008): "Mésie et Thrace", in: SNRIS, 201-219.

Petrie, F. (1927): *Objects of Daily Use*, British School of Archaeology in Egypt, London.

Pettazzoni, R. (1937): "Confession of Sins and the Classics", *The Harvard Theological Review* 30, 1, 1-14.

Petzl, G., Malay, H. (1987): "A New Confession-Inscription from the Katakekaumene", *Greek, Roman and Byzantine Studies* 28, 459-472.

Pfrommer, M. (1990): *Untersuchungen zur Chronologie früh- und hochhellenistischen Goldschmucks*, *Istanbuler Forschungen* 37, Tübingen.

Pfrommer, M. (1998): *Untersuchungen zur Chronologie und Komposition des Alexandermosaiks auf antiquarischer Grundlage*, *Aegyptiaca Treverensia* 8, Mainz.

Pfrommer, M. (1999): *Alexandria. Im Schatten der Pyramiden*, Mainz.

Pfrommer, M. (2001): *Greek Gold from Hellenistic Egypt*, Los Angeles.

Pharmakowsky, B. (1909): "Olbia 1901-1908. Fouilles et trouvailles". *Izvestiya imperatorskoj arheologicheskoj komissii* 33, 103-136.

Pharmakowsky, B. (1912): "Archäologische Funde im Jahre 1911, 'Rußland' ", *Arch. Anz.* 27, 323-381.

Phiphia, N. (2014): *Elinuri Eksperimenti dasavlet sakartveloshi – berdznuli akhalshenebi (genesisi, istoria)* [Hellenic Experiment in Western Georgia – Greek Settlements (genesis, history)], Tbilisi.

Picaud, S., Podvin, J.-L. (2011): "Les *isiaca* de Tarse et de sa région", in: Bricault & Veymiers 2011, 211-223.

Picón, C.A., Hemingway, S., eds. (2016): *Pergamon and the Hellenistic Kingdoms of the Ancient World*, New York-New Haven.

Piotrovski, B. B. (1958): "Drevneegipetskie predmetui, naidenui na teritorii Sovetskogo Soyuza [Древнеегипетские предметы, найденные на территории Советского Союза]", *Sovetskaya arheologiya* 1, 20-27.

Pipia, N. (2011): *Beginning of the Migration of Mountaineers in the Western Georgia at the turn of the millennia*, Spekali.

Pisarevskij, N. P. (2020): "Oktera «Izida» (k istoricheskoy interpretatsii ikonograficheskogo pamyatnika III v. do n. e. iz bosporskogo goroda Nimfeya)", *Via in tempore. Istoriya. Politologiya* 47 (3), 455-471.

Pitts, M., Versluys, M. J., eds. (2015): *Globalisation and the Roman world*, Cambridge.

Plantzos, D. (1999): *Hellenistic Engraved Gems*, Oxford.

Podvin, J.-L. (2011): *Luminaire et cultes isiaques*, *Monographies Instrumentum* 38, Montagnac.

Podvin, J.-L. (2012a): "Création et imitation dans le luminaire isiaque", in: Chrzanovski 2012, 295-302.
Podvin, J.-L. (2012b): "Cultes isiaques en Pont et Paphlagonie", in: Tsetskhladze 2012, 207-211.
Podvin, J.-L. (2013): "Les cultes isiaques de la Troade à la Bithynie", in: Tsetskhladze et al. 2013, 167-172.
Podvin, J.-L. (2014): "Médaillons d'applique et moules et de terre cuite à décor isiaque", in: Bricault & Veymiers 2014, 121-137.
Podvin, J.-L. (2014a): "Le tropisme isiaque des Sévères: une acmé reconsidérée?", in: Bricault & Versluys 2014, 300-325.
Podvin, J.-L. (2015a): "Figurines isiaques en terre cuite d'Asie Mineure", in: Muller & Laflı 2015, 209-217.
Podvin, J.-L. (2015b): "Lampes à décor isiaque du littoral égéen d'Asie mineure", in: Kousoulis & Lazaridis 2015, 2071-2082.
Podvin, J.-L. (2016): "Lampes à thèmes isiaques au sud du Danube, de la Germanie supérieure à la Mer Noire", in: Győry 2016, 149-164.
Poole, R.S. (1883): *BMC Greek (Ptolemies) / Catalogue of Greek Coins: the Ptolemies, Kings of Egypt*, London.
Popescu, M., Achim, I., Matei-Popescu, F., eds. (2018), *La Dacie et l'Empire Romain. Mélanges d'épigraphie et d'archéologie offerts à Constantin C. Petolescu*, Bucarest.
Popov, Kh., Tsvetkova, Yu., eds. (2017): *KRATISTOS. Sbornik v chest na profesor Petar Delev*, Sofia.
Potter, D. S. (1999): "Roman religion: Ideas and Actions", in: Potter & Mattingly 1999.
Potter D. S., Mattingly, D. J. eds. (1999), *Life, Death, and Entertainment in the Roman Empire*, Ann Arbor.
Preisendanz, K., Henrichs, A., eds. (1973): *Papyri Graecae Magicae. Die griechischen Zauberpapyri*, Stuttgart.
Preshlenov, H. (2002): "Odessus – a Geostrategic Regional Center in Moesia Inferior. (Geographical and Economic Aspects)", in: Ruseva-Slokoska, Ivanov & Dinchev 2002, 237-244.
Rabadjiev, K. (2017): "Theoi Samothrakes at Pontos Euxeinos", *Archaeologia Bulgarica* XXI, 2, 11-25.
Rakob, F., ed. (1997): *Die deutschen Ausgrabungen in Karthago, Karthago* II, Mainz.
Rasimus, T. (2005): "Ophite Gnosticism, Sethianism and the Nag Hammadi Library", *Vigiliae Christianae* 59 (3), 235-263.
Reeder, E. (1988): *Hellenistic Art in the Walters Art Gallery*, Baltimore.
Reinach, S. (1908): *Répertoire de la statuaire grecque et romaine*, II-1, Paris.
Reitzenstein, R. (1904): *Poimandres. Studien zur griechisch-ägyptischen und frühchristlichen Literatur*, Leipzig.
Rembart, L., Waldner, A., eds. (2022): *Manufacturers and Markets. The Contribution of Hellenistic Pottery to Economies Large and Small*, Wien.
Ricl, M. (1995): *La conscience du péché dans les cultes anatoliens à l'époque romaine. La confession des fautes rituelles et éthiques dans les cultes méoniens et phrygiens*, Belgrade.
Robert, L. (1960): *Hellenica. Recueil d'épigraphie, de numismatique et d'antiquités grecques*, Vol. 11-12, Paris.

Rostovtsev, M. (1904): "Tessères antiques en os du Sud de la Russie", *Bulletin de la Commission Impériale Archéologique* 10, 109-124.
Rostovtsev, M. (1905): "Interprétation des tessères en os avec figures, chiffres et légendes", *Revue archéologique* 1905/1, 110-124.
Rostovtzeff, M., Barbet, A., Schiltz, V., Fraysse, A. (2003): *La peinture décorative antique en Russie méridionale. Saint-Pétersbourg 1913-1914*, MAIBL XXX, Paris.
Roussel, P. (1916): *Les cultes égyptiens à Délos du IIIe au Ier siècle av. J.-C.*, Nancy.
Rubensohn, O. (1907): *Elephantine-papyri.* Ägyptische Urkunden aus den Königlichen Museen zu Berlin, Berlin.
Rüpke, J. (2007): *Religion of the Romans*, Cambridge.
Rüpke, J. (2012): *Religion in the Republican Rome. Rationalization and Ritual Change*, Philadelphia.
Rüpke, J., ed. (2007): *A companion to Roman religion*, Malden-Oxford-Victoria.
Ruseva-Slokoska, L., Ivanov, R., Dinchev, V., eds. (2002): *The Roman and Late Roman City. The International Conference (Veliko Turnovo 26-30 July 2000)*, Sofia.
Rusyaeva, A. S. (2005): *Religiya pontijskih ellinov v antichnuyu epohu: Mify. Svyatilishcha. Kul'ty olimpijskih bogov i geroev*, Kiev.
Sabottka, M. (2008): *Das Serapeum in Alexandria. Untersuchungen zur Architektur und Baugeschichte des Heiligtums von der frühen ptolemäischen Zeit bis zur Zerstörung 391 n. Chr.*, *Études alexandrines* 16, Le Caire.
Savoy, B., Guichard, C., Howald, C., eds. (2018): *Acquiring Cultures. Histories of World Art on Western Markets*, Berlin.
Scherrer, P., Koiner, G., Ulbrich, A., eds. (2013): *Hellenistisches Zypern: Akten der Internationalen Tagung, Institut für Archäologie, Universität Graz, 14. Oktober 2013*, Graz.
Schreiber, T. (2015): "Herrscher ohne Diadem oder ptolemäisches ›Zeitgesicht‹? Zu den sogenannten Ptolemäerringen im Archäologischen Museum der Westfälischen Wilhelms-Universität", *Boreas* 37/38, 227-283.
Schreiber, T. (2018): "Zu den sogenannten Ptolemäerringen – Versuch einer Rekontextualisierung", in: Schreiber 2018a, 59-65.
Schreiber, T., ed. (2018a): *Zugänge zur Kontextualisierung bildlicher Darstellungen in den Altertumswissenschaften*, Münster.
Schubart, W. (1917): "Ägyptische Abteilung (Papyrussammlung). Ptolemaios Philopator und Dionysos", *Amtliche Berichte der königlichen Kunstsammlungen* 38, 189-198.
Schürer, E. (2014): *A History of the Jewish People in the Time of Jesus Christ (175 B.C. – A.D. 135)*, London.
Sfameni Gasparro, G. (2018): "Anubis in the "Isiac Family" in the Hellenistic and Roman World", *Acta Antiqua Academiae Scientiarum Hungaricae* 58, 529-548.
Shevchenko, T. M. (2011): *Relihiinyi svitohliad naselennia antychnoho Khersonesa*, Kyiv.
Shurgaya, I. G. (1965): "Import Aleksandrii v Severnom Prichernomor'e", *VDI* 4, 126-140.
Skeat, T. C. (1974): *Greek Papyri in the British Museum vol. VII: The Zenon Archive*, London.
Smyly, J. G., ed. (1921): *Greek Papyri from Gurob, Royal Irish Academy: Cunningham Memoirs* 12, Dublin-London.
Sokolova, O. Yu. (2004): "Kompleks nakhodok ellinisticheskogo vremeni iz Nimfeya (raskopki 1984 g.)", in: Khodza 2004, 175-185.

Solomonik, E. I. (1984): "O kul'te Afiny v Hersonese v IV—III vv. do n. e.", *Antichnaya i srednevekovaya ideologiya* 21, 7-14.
Spier, J. (1992): *Ancient Gems and Finger Rings. Catalogue of the Collections. The J. Paul Getty Museum,* Malibu.
Spinelli, A., Lapatin, K., Daehner, J. M., eds. (2017): *Artistry in Bronze: The Greeks and Their Legacy XIXth International Congress on Ancient Bronzes*, Los Angeles.
Steimle, Chr. (2008): *Religion im römischen Thessaloniki. Sakraltopographie, Kult und Gesellschaft, 168 v. Chr. - 324 n. Chr.*, Tübingen.
Stern, E. (1910): "K voprosu ob ellinisticheskoj keramike", *Zapiski imperatorskogo Odesskogo obshchestva istorii i drevnostej* XXVIII, 158-190.
Strootman, R. (2019): "The Ptolemaic Sea Empire", in: Strootman et al. 2019, 113-152.
Strootman, R., van den Eijnde, F., van Wijk, R., eds. (2019): *Empires of the Sea: Maritime Power Networks in World History, Cultural Interactions in the Mediterranean* 4, Leiden.
Stroumsa, G. G. (2012): "The Afterlife of Orphism: Jewish, Gnostic and Christian Perspectives", *Historia Religionum. An International Journal* 4, 141-157.
Stoyanov, T., Stoyanova, D. (1997): "The Tholos of Odessos", *Archeologia Bulgarica* I, 3, 22-33.
Sudarev, N. I. (2017): "Pogrebeniya nekropolya Vinogradnyy 7 (Krasnodarskiy kray, Temryukskiy rayon", in: Engovatova 2017, 182-189.
Svoronos, I. N. (1904): *Ta Nomismata tou Kratous ton Ptolemaion*. 1-3, Athens.
Tacheva-Hitova, M. (1983): *Eastern Cults in Moesia Inferior and Thracia (5th Century B.C.-4th Century A.D.), ÉPRO* 95, Leiden.
Takačs, S. A. (1995): *Isis and Sarapis in the Roman World, RGRW* 124, Leiden-New York-Köln.
Tallet, G. (2021): *La splendeur des dieux. Quatre études iconographiques sur l'hellénisme égyptien, RGRW* 193, Leiden-Boston.
Tenekedjiev, V. (2022): "Elinisticheska skulptura i nadpis ot Odesos", in: *Balgarskata arheologia 2021. Katalog kam izlozhba*, Sofia, 2022, 40-41.
Tenekedjiev, V., Mircheva, E. (*in print*): "Otchet za spasitelno arheologichesko prouchvane na ul. "San Stefano" № 36, gr. Varna", *Arheologicheski otkritia i razkopki prez* 2021, Sofia (*in print*).
Tenekedjiev, V., Stefanova, A. (*in print*): "Spasitelno arheologichesko prouchvane na ul. „Tsar Ivan Shishman" №18, Varna", *Arheologicheski otkritia i razkopki prez* 2021, Sofia (*in print*).
Thibault, J. C. (1964): *The mystery of Ovid's exile*, Berkeley-Los Angeles.
Thomassen, E. (2010): "Gnostics and Orphics", in: Dijkstra et al. 2010, 463-474.
Thompson, D. B. (1973): *Ptolemaic Oinochoai and Portraits in Faience. Aspects of the Ruler-Cult*, Oxford.
Tokhtas'ev, S. R. (2006): "K politicheskoy istorii Bospora III v. do n.e.", *Drevnosti Bospora* 10, 416-428.
Tokhtas'ev, S. R. (2011): "Grecheskiy yazyk na Bospore: obshchee i osobennoe", in: Zuev 2011, 673-682.
Tondriau, J. (1946): "Les thiases dionysiaques royaux de la cour ptolémaïque", *Chronique d'Égypte* 41, 149-171.
Toncheva, G. (1967): "Arhaichni materiali ot Odesos", *Izvestia na Arheologicheskia institut* XXX, 157-180.

Toncheva, G. (1969a): "Skulpturata v Odesos ot V – I v. pr. n. e.", *Izvestia na Narodnia muzey-Varna* V (XX), 3-48.

Toncheva, G. (1969b): "Le sanctuaire du Héros Karabasmos d'Odessos", in: *Actes du Premier Congrès international des études balkaniques et Sud-Est européennes, Vol. 2 Archéologie, histoire de l'antiquité, arts*, Sofia, 1969, 353-364.

Tonkova, M. (2017): "Bronzov prsten s portret na ptolemeyska tsaritsa ot kolektsiyata na Natsionalniya arkheologicheski muzey v Sofiya", in: Popov & Cvetkova 2017, 553-561.

Touraieff, B. (1911): "Objets égyptiens et égyptisants trouvés dans la Russie Méridionale", *Revue archéologique* 18, 20-35.

Touraieff, B. (1912): "Terrakotovyj svetil'nik iz Ol'vii (?), izobrazhayushchij chetu Besov". *Izvestiya imperatorskoj arheologicheskoj komissii* 45, 71-75.

Tran tam Tinh, V. (1973): *Isis lactans*, *ÉPRO* 37, Leiden.

Tran tam Tinh, V. (1983): *Sérapis debout: corpus des monuments de Sérapis et étude iconographique*, *ÉPRO* 94, Leiden.

Tran tam Tinh, V. (1990): "Isis", in: *LIMC*, V.1, 761-796 ; V.2, 501-526.

Tran tam Tinh, V., Jaeger, B., Poulin, S. (1988): "Harpocrates", in: *LIMC*, IV.1, 415-445; IV.2, 242-266.

Treister, M. Yu. (1982): "Bronzovye perstni s izobrazheniyami na shchitkakh iz Gorgippii i okrestnostey", *VDI* 3, 67-76.

Treister, M. Yu. (1985): "Bospor i Egipet v III v. do n.e. [The Bosporus and Egypt in the 3rd Century BC]", *VDI* 1, 126-139.

Treister, M. Yu. (1992): "Bronzoliteynoe remeslo Bospora", in: Molok 1999, 66-110.

Treister, M. Yu. (2022a): "Problemy atributsii portretov na perstnyakh «ptolemeevskogo tipa»", in: Zin'ko & Zin'ko 2022, 322-335.

Treister, M. Yu. (2022b): "«Ptolemeevskie» perstni na Bospore i v varvarskom hinterlande (raspredelenie, khronologiya, konteksty nahodok)", in: Zuev 2022, 281-287.

Trofimova, A. A., ed. (2007): *Aleksandr Velikiy. Put' na Vostok. Katalog vystavki. Gosudarstvennyy Ermitazh*, Saint Petersburg.

Trofimova, A. (2010): *The Immortal Alexander the Great. The Myth. The Reality. His Journey. His Legacy*, Amsterdam.

Tsetskhladze, G. R., ed. (2012): *The Black Sea, Paphlagonia, Pontus and Phrygia in Antiquity: Aspects of archaeology and ancient history*, BAR IS 2432, Oxford.

Tsetskhladze, G. R. et al., eds. (2013): *The Bosporus. Gateway between the ancient West and East (1st millennium B.C. - 5th century A.D.)*, BAR IS 2517, Oxford.

Turcan, R. (2000): *The Gods of Ancient Rome*, New York (1re éd. Paris 1989).

Turner, E. G. (1977): *The Typology of the Early Codex*, Philadelphia.

Turner, E. G. (1983): "The Ptolemaic Royal Edict BGU VI 1211 to be Dated Before 215/14 B.C.", in: Loebensstein et al. 1983, 148-152.

Tzalas, H., ed. (2002): *Tropis VII, Proceedings of the 7th International Symposium on Ship Construction in Antiquity, Pylos 1999*, Athens.

Urciuoli, E. R., Rüpke, J. (2018): "Urban Religion in Mediterranean Antiquity: Relocating Religious Change", *Mythos* 12, 117-135.

Urfer, S. (2020): "Une bague en bronze de la palestre Sud d'Érétrie", in: Ackermann, Krapf & Pop 2020, 80-82.

Ustaeva, E. R., Zhuravlev, D. V. (2010): "Tamanskiy muzeynyy kompleks", in: Bongard-Levin & Kuznetsov 2010b, 64-96.

Vaelske, V. (2013): "Isis in Petra. Chronological and topographical aspects", in: Mouton & Schmid 2013, 351-361.

Van Andringa, W. (2007): "Religions and the Integration of Cities in the Empire in the Second Century AD: The Creation of a Common Religious Language", in: Rüpke 2007, 83-95.

Vandorpe, K. (1996): "Seals in and on the papyri of Greco-Roman and Byzantine Egypt", in: Boussac & Invernizzi 1996, 231-291.

Vandorpe, K. (2015): "List of seals on papyri (Greco-Roman Egypt)", in: Depauw & Coussement 141-152.

Van Haeperen, Fr. (2019): Fana, templa, delubra. *Corpus dei luoghi di culto dell'Italia antica*, FTD 6, Paris.

Van Oppen de Ruiter, B. F. (2015): *Berenice II Euergetis. Essays in Early Hellenistic Queenship*, New York.

Von Harnack, A. (1893): *Lehrbuch der Dogmengeschichte,* Leipzig.

Vasil'evič, P. A. (2012): "Le royaume du Bosphore Cimmérien aux époques grecque et romaine : un aperçu", *Études de Lettres* 2012/1-2, 87-110.

Velkov, V. (1969): *Nessebre*, vol I, Sofia.

Versluys, M. J., Bülow Clausen, Kr., Capriotti Vittozzi, G., eds. (2018): *The Iseum Campense from the Roman Empire to the Modern Age: Temple - Monument - Lieu de mémoire, Papers of the Royal Netherlands Institute in Rome* 66, Rome.

Versnel, H. (1998): *Inconsistencies in Greek and Roman Religion*. Volume 1: *Ter Unus. Isis, Dionysos, Hermes. Three Studies in Henotheism*, Leiden.

Veymiers, R. (2009):"Ἵλεως τῷ φοροῦντι. *Sérapis sur les gemmes et les bijoux antiques, Mémoires de la Classe des Lettres de l'Académie royale de Belgique*. Collection in-4°, 3e série, t. I, n° 2061, Bruxelles.

Veymiers, R. (2011): "Ἵλεως τῷ φοροῦντι. Sérapis sur les gemmes et les bijoux antiques, *Supplément* I", *Biblioteca Isiaca*, II, 239-271.

Veymiers, R. (2014): "Le basileion, les reines et Actium", in: Bricault & Versluys 2014, 195-236.

Vidman, L. (1969): *Sylloge Inscriptionis Religionum Isiacae et Sarapiacae (SIRIS), Religionsgeschichtliche Versuche und Vorarbeiten* XXVIII, Berlin.

Villing, A. et al. eds. (2013-2019): *Naukratis: Greeks in Egypt*, London.

Vinogradov, J.G. (1997): The Inscribed Bronze from Vani. Pontische Studien, in: *Kleine Schriften zur Geschichte und Epigraphik des Schwarzmeerraumes*, Mainz.

Vinogradov, Y. G. (1999): "Der Staatsbesuch der 'Isis' im Bosporus", *Ancient Civilizations from Scythia to Siberia,* 5.4, 271-302.

Vinogradov, Y. G., Zolotarev, M. I. (1999): "Worship of the Sacred Egyptian Triad in Chersonesus (Crimea)", *Ancient Civilizations from Scythia to Siberia* 5.4, 357-381.

Vinogradov, Yu. A. (2017): "Ob elite Bospora i ne tol'ko", in: Zin'ko 2017, 3-24.

Vinogradov, Yu. A. (2019): "Traditsii i innovatsii v aristokraticheskoy kul'ture Bospora dorimskoy epokhi", *Bosporskie issledovaniya* XXXVIII, 3-16.

Vollenweider, M.-L. (1958): "Das Bildnis des Scipio Africanus", *Museum Helveticum* 15, 27-45.
Vollenweider, M.-L. (1995): *Camées et intailles, I, Les portraits grecs du Cabinet des Médailles*, Paris.
Waldhauer, O. (1914): *Kaiserliche Ermitage. Die antiken Tonlampen*, Saint-Petersburg.
Walker, S., Higgs, P., eds. (2001): *Cleopatra of Egypt. From History to Myth*, London.
Wallace-Hadrill, A. (2008): *Rome's cultural revolution*, Cambridge.
Walsh, P. G. (2000): *Cicero – On Obligations (De officiis)*, Oxford.
Walter, N. (1964): *Der Thoraausleger Aristobulos: Untersuchungen zu seinen Fragmenten und zu pseudepigraphischen Resten der jüdisch-hellenistischen Literatur*, Berlin.
Walter, N. (1975): *Fragmente jüdisch-hellenistischer Exegeten: Aristobulos, Demetrios, Aristeas*, *JSHRZ* Vol. III.2, Gütersloh.
Walter, N. (1980): *Fragmente jüdisch-hellenistischer Historiker*, *JSHRZ* Vol. I.2, Gütersloh.
Walter, N. (1983): "Pseudo-Orpheus", in : Kümmel 1983, 173-278.
Walter, N. (1983): *Fragmente jüdisch-hellenistischer Epik: Philon, Theodotos.Pseudepigraphisch e jüdischhellenistische Dichtung: Pseudo-Phokylides, Pseudo-Orpheus, Gefälschte Verse auf Namen griechischer Dichter*, *JSHRZ* Vol. IV.3, 135-276.
Wilamowitz-Möllendorff, Ul. von, Ł (1931): *Der Glaube der Hellenen*, vol. 2, Berlin.
Waraksa, E. A. (2018): "The Ptolemaic Oinochoai: A Reassessment", OSF Preprints.
Wells, P. S. (1999): *The Barbarians speak. How the conquered peoples shaped Roman Europe*, Princeton.
Wheeler, A. L. (1988): *Ovid. Tristia. Ex Ponto*, Cambridge-London (1st ed. 1924, 2nd ed. 1939).
Wheeler, Ev. L. (2000): "Legio XV Apollinaris: From Carnuntum to Satala and beyond", in: Le Bohec & Wolff 2000.
Will, E. (1979): *Histoire politique du monde hellénistique (323-30 av. J.-C.)*, I, Nancy.
Willers, D. (2007): "Ptolemäische Fingerringe – Eine Suchanzeige"; *Antike Kunst* 50, 76-92.
Wilkinson, R. H. (2008): *Egyptian Scarabs*, London.
Wobbermin, G. (1896): *Religionsgeschichtliche Studien zur Frage der Beeinflussung des Urchristentums durch das antike Mysterienwesen*, Berlin.
Yashaeva, T. Yu., Mayko, V. V., eds. (2018): *Arkheologiya antichnogo i srednevekovogo goroda. Sbornik statey v chest' Stanislava Grigor'evicha Ryzhova*, Sevastopolo-Kaliningrad.
Zaykova, A.V., Kostromicheva, D.A., Lesnoi, E.S., eds. (2021): *Antichnui Relikvii Hersonesa: Otkritiya, Nahodki, Teorii. Materiali nauchnoy konferencii, Sevastopol, 20-24 sentebrya 2021 goda.*
Zavojkin, A. A. (2010): "Arkhaicheskiy, klassicheskiy i ellinisticheskiy periody (VI–II vv. do n.e.) ", in: Bongand-Levin & Kuznecov 2010a, 12-78.
Zavojkin, A. A. (2017): "Metallicheskie ukrasheniya i drugie predmety iz metalla v svyatilishche Demetry i Kory («Beregovoj 4»)", *Kratkie soobshcheniya Instituta arkheologii*, 249, 231-249.
Zelinskyi, A. (2020): "Persni "ptolemeivskoho typu" i Pivnichne Prychornomoria: vyniatok chy pravylo?", *Skhidnyi svit*, 1, 5-20. doi: https://doi.org/10.15407/orientw2020.01.005.
Zinako, V. N., Zinako A. V.(2021): "Svetilishte Dionisa iz raskopok Tiritaki [Sanctuary of Dyonisus from the excavations of Tiritaki]", Zaykova, Kostromicheva & Lesnoi 2021, 118-121.
Zin'ko, V. N., eds. (2017): *Elita Bospora Kimmerijskogo: traditsii i innovatsii v aristokraticheskoy kul'ture dorimskogo vremeni*, Bosporskie issledovaniya 34, Kerch'.

Zin'ko, V. N., Zin'ko, E. A., eds. (2022): *XXIII Bosporskie chteniya «Bospor Kimmeriyskiy i varvarskiy mir v period antichnosti i srednevekov'ya. Sakral'noe i material'noe»*, Simferopol' & Kerch.

Zuev, V. Yu., ed. (2007): *Bosporskiy fenomen: Sakral'nyy smysl regiona, pamyatnikov, nakhodok: materialy mezhdunarodnoy nauchnoy konferentsii*. Pt. 1, Saint Petersburg.

Zuev, V. Yu., éd. (2011): *Bosporskiy fenomen. Naselenie, yazyki, kontakty*, Saint Petersburg.

Zuev V. Yu. ed. (2022): *"Bol'shie i malye goroda Bosporskogo tsarstva". K 75-letiyu Evgeniya Aleksandrovicha Moleva*, Saint Petersburg.

Zuev, V. Yu., Khrshanovskiy, V. A., eds. (2018): *Bosporskij fenomen. Obshchee i osobennoe v istoriko-kul'turnom prostranstve antichnogo mira*. Pt. 2, Saint Petersburg.

Zunz, G. (1963): "Once More: The So-Called 'Edict of Philopator on the Dionysiac Mysteries'", *Hermes*, Bd. 91, H. 2, 228-239.

Zwierlein-Diehl, E. (1973): *Die Antiken Gemmen des Kunsthistorischen Museums in Wien*. Bd.1, München.

EGYPTIAN CULTS
ON THE BLACK SEA COAST

ЕГИПЕТСКИТЕ КУЛТОВЕ
ПО КРАЙБРЕЖИЕТО
НА ЧЕРНО МОРЕ

Bulgarian / French / English
First Edition

Printed in June 2024
by Paradigma Publishing House (Sofia, Bulgaria)

Legal deposit in France: 4th quarter 2024
Legal deposit in Bulgaria: 4th quarter 2024

Follow us on:

https://editions.efa.gr